PUBLICATIONS
DE L'INSTITUT ET MUSEE VOLTAIRE

SOUS LA DIRECTION DE THEODORE BESTERMAN

STUDIES ON VOLTAIRE
AND THE EIGHTEENTH CENTURY

III

INSTITUT ET MUSEE VOLTAIRE
PUBLICATIONS
VOLTAIRE'S CORRESPONDENCE
EDITED BY THEODORE BESTERMAN

STUDIES ON VOLTAIRE
AND THE EIGHTEENTH CENTURY

EDITED BY THEODORE BESTERMAN

VOLUME III

INSTITUT ET MUSEE VOLTAIRE

LES DELICES

GENEVE

1957

sales agent

LIBRAIRIE E. DROZ
8 rue Verdaine
GENEVE

*the first volume of this periodical was published
under the title of*

TRAVAUX SUR VOLTAIRE
ET LE DIX-HUITIEME SIECLE

TABLE OF CONTENTS

to

OTIS E. FELLOWS

Foreword

As originally conceived, this study was to have dealt with the *Mémoires pour l'histoire des sciences et beaux-arts*, more commonly known as the *Journal de Trévoux*, from its inception in 1701 to the expulsion of the Jesuits from France in 1762. This scope was chosen under the impression that since until 1762 the publication had been under Jesuit direction, careful examination of the periodical would reveal a sustained, well-defined policy throughout its history. Upon further investigation, however, it soon became clear that if the chosen dates were to be retained it would necessitate not one history, but three separate studies dealing with the following periods:

1. 1701-1734, early history of the *Journal de Trévoux*.
2. 1734-1745, new editors, attempt at reform.
3. 1745-1762, the crucial years under Berthier.

The first two periods present the added difficulty of lack of organization and direction owing to the large number of equally important Jesuits on the editorial staff. Indeed, it would even be possible to make separate studies of the more prominent editors, as Donald Schier has done in the case of Castel[1].

During the second period, when father Rouillé was named editor-in-chief, conflicting opinions still frequently appeared in the pages of the publication, thus indicating, at least in some instances, varying points of view among the personnel on the

---

[1] *Louis B. Castel, anti-Newtonian scientist*, Ph.D. dissertation. Professor Schier, however, suggests that Castel's policies were representative of the views held by the Jesuit opponents of the *philosophe* movement. As will be seen, Castel was in reality a thorn in the side of his colleagues, who were often obliged to retract his brash statements, and who frequently disagreed with his too conservative views.

editorial staff. With the assumption of the role of editor-in-chief by Berthier in 1745, the situation changed. Here was at last a man who, upon assuming control, refused additional help, preferring to retain complete responsibility for himself. Henceforth there was to be no opportunity for conflict among members of the staff, and former editors such as Castel, who had been a cause of controversy in the past, were summarily dismissed. Thereafter any editorial statement in the *Journal de Trévoux* was to represent Berthier's own policy; in consequence, a study of this third period in the history of the *Journal* becomes that of its resolute editor-in-chief.

The practical considerations already mentioned, however, did not in themselves constitute sufficient justification for a study of the *Journal de Trévoux*. The publication, because of its reputation and influence as a literary journal of the day, and as an outspoken example of a certain trend in organized thought confronted by the revolutionary movement of ideas in ferment at the time, proved well worth the scrutiny. Under the editorship of Berthier, the *Journal de Trévoux* achieved its greatest influence and highest position as a literary journal, often polemic in nature[2]. It was, moreover, chiefly between 1745 and 1762 that the *philosophe* movement was to crystallize, and the drama of the struggle of ideas to become most evident. During this period, too, praise for or condemnation of the *Journal* and its editor reached their point of greatest significance.

The present study is divided into two parts. Part I considers briefly the history of the *Journal de Trévoux*, and this is followed by a summary of the principal ideas of its editor Berthier; Part II deals specifically with the *Journal* in its relations with the *philosophes*.

[2] although the *Journal de Trévoux* is known today chiefly because of its polemic activity, it must be remembered that this was only one part of the publication. The pages devoted to the *philosophe* movement, for example, are relatively few compared to the volume of articles devoted to scientific and literary subjects.

To date, there has been no such study of the periodical in question. P. C. Sommervogel, and later Gustave Dumas, offered brief external histories of the *Journal de Trévoux* as a publication, but with scant consideration of its intellectual content and still less for the views of its editors. Emmy Allard published a dissertation on the attitude of the *Journal* toward Descartes and Malebranche, but besides dealing with a limited subject, this study is chiefly concerned with the early history of the publication. Similarly, Donald Schier's volume on Castel deals with an editor who, if he represents the principles of the *Journal de Trévoux* at all, does so during the first two periods of its history only[3]. This leaves the most significant period—that dealing with the struggle with the *philosophes*—relatively unexplored.

The published material concerned with Berthier himself is even more sparse, and what has been written about him has almost invariably been from a partisan viewpoint. Indeed, he is best known to us through the attacks made on him, particularly by Voltaire and Diderot. On the other hand there is the equally one-sided *Eloge historique du père Berthier*, by Montjoye, which has been used in the present inquiry merely for biographical data not obtainable elsewhere. The information on Berthier given in de Backer and other Jesuit sources is frequently taken almost verbatim from Montjoye's *Eloge*. It would seem, then, that there is considerable justification for an extensive, impartial study of this controversial figure, so often mentioned in passing and in stereotyped form in scholarly investigations of the currents and cross-currents of eighteenth-century thought. Nor has there been any comprehensive inquiry into the relations between the *Journal de Trévoux* and the *philosophes*. Many studies dealing with the history of ideas in the French enlightenment consider the periodical in passing, but none has presented in sufficient detail the relations between the *Journal* and the chief literary figures of the day. The

---

[3] as this book goes to press, a new study dealing with the first period (1701–1734) has been announced: Alfred R. Desautels, S. J., *Les Mémoires de Trévoux et le mouvement des idées au XVIII ᵉsiècle* (Rome 1956).

present study affords a more ample view of the struggle of ideas and, as a source of reference, obviates constant duplication of effort in the search for information from the numerous volumes of the *Journal de Trévoux*, complete sets of which are very rare.

This lack of readily available information on Berthier has made it necessary to rely heavily on unpublished manuscripts and on sources accessible in Europe alone, notably the Bibliothèque Nationale, the Sainte-Geneviève and Mazarine libraries in Paris; the Bibliothèque municipale at Rouen; the Bibliothèque Calvet at Avignon; Dutch libraries in Leyden, The Hague and Amsterdam; the British Museum in London; the Biblioteca Nacional and the Escorial in Madrid; and the Bibliothèque royale in Brussels.

It is with deep gratitude that I acknowledge here my debt to professor Otis E. Fellows, whose inspiration initiated this study, and whose generous encouragement and invaluable assistance were, in large measure, responsible for its completion. I wish also to thank professors Norman L. Torrey and Lawton P. G. Peckham for their helpful suggestions and criticisms in connection with the reading of the original manuscript. I am especially thankful, too, to mr Theodore Besterman, director of the Institut et Musée Voltaire, for accepting this study for publication by the Institut and for his painstaking and scholarly editing of the final manuscript.

To permit a smoother, more uninterrupted reading, direct quotations in the body of the text have been translated into English, leaving only the longer quotations in the modernized original.

John N. Pappas

The Journal de Trévoux and the philosophes

PART ONE

I

The Journal de Trévoux

In March 1682 Louis Auguste de Bourbon, duc Du Maine, took possession of the principality of Dombes, an independent state which was free from the direct authority of the king. Thirteen years later he caused a new printing establishment to be opened at Trévoux, the capital of Dombes, and in 1701 he asked the Jesuits at the Collège de Louis-le-grand, in Paris, to publish under his auspices, '. . . Memoirs useful to the history of the arts and sciences.'[1] This publication was to have as its chief aim the defense of religion, but the duc Du Maine, anxious also to be known as the protector of letters, wanted his publication to give, 'a faithful report of everything of interest appearing daily in the world no matter in what field it might be.'[2]

The choice of the Jesuits for this enterprise was a wise one for, as Robert R. Palmer says, 'they were men of their time, men of the world skilled in civilized living, and intellectually the most able in the church . . . . More than most unbelievers and most religious apologists, the editors possessed the qualifications for a critical treatment of ideas'.[3] In addition to their intellectual abilities, the Jesuit editors had the advantage of rich resources both in their library at the College, which afforded them references on every

[1] Gustave Dumas, *Histoire du Journal de Trévoux* (Paris 1936), p.20.
[2] *Journal de Trévoux* (March 1701), dedication of the printer to the duc Du Maine.
[3] *Catholics and unbelievers in eighteenth century France* (Princeton 1939), p.18.

subject imaginable, and through their world-wide contacts[4]. Thus we find father Charlevoix writing to sir Hans Sloane, president of the Royal society of London, to ask for information about Japan, or to discuss the differences between American and European plant life. On another occasion he thanks the British scholar for sending his *History of Jamaica* to the Jesuit library in Paris[5]. The men chosen for the task were already well known in the literary world and therefore carried weight with their contemporaries. The list of the first editors includes fathers Catrou, Tournemine, Buffier, Hardouin, Despineul, Souciet, Germon, Marquer and Le Tellier[6].

In March 1701 the first volume of the *Journal* appeared under the official title of *Mémoires pour l'histoire des sciences et des beaux-arts;* it was announced as a bi-monthly publication. After the printer's dedication to their protector the duc Du Maine, the editors promised to report all newsworthy discoveries and scientific advances from every country, explaining that they had established a correspondence in all parts of the world and were ready to publish original articles as well as reviews of published material.

[4] Grosier states: 'Un Jésuite de Paris manquait-il de mémoires, de renseignements sur certains objets dont il s'occupait? Il écrivait au Pérou, aux Philippines, dans l'Inde, à la Chine, sur les côtes de la Californie, et recevait, avec le temps, les instructions qu'il avait demandées.' Quoted by P. C. Sommervogel, *Essai historique sur les Mémoires de Trévoux* (Paris 1864), p.vi.

[5] British museum, Sloane 4059, 4058, 4068.

[6] as confessor to Louis xiv, Le Tellier had unusual power and influence, and was bitterly attacked by the Jansenists. Sommervogel states that Le Tellier had little influence on the *Journal de Trévoux*. His may have been only an honorary position, although he did write several articles for the *Journal*.

Barrière quotes Sénac de Meilhan as writing concerning Le Tellier: 'Le général des Jésuites . . . l'exhortait à la prudence, à la modération; mais comme il jouissait de la confiance entière de Louis xiv en matière de conscience et de religion il fallait que le général le ménageât' (*Bibliothèque des mémoires*, iii.172). Duclos says that he was 'méprisé de ses confrères' (*ibid.*, ii.260). Father Tournemine, who seems to have been the unofficial editor-in-chief during this period, was accused of issuing a memoir attacking Le Tellier, but he denied this saying, 'je ne pense pas comme me fait penser l'imposteur sur le Père Le Tellier, ni sur les autres Jésuites nommés dans ses écrits supposés, il s'en faut beaucoup' (Bibliothèque Sainte-Geneviève, ms.1476, f.376).

The policy of the new journal is then set forth as follows: 'Dans les contestations qui s'élèvent souvent entre les hommes de lettres sur les matières de science, les auteurs des Mémoires ne prendront jamais aucun parti, et ils ne feront alors qu'un simple exposé de ce qui s'écrira de part et d'autre, retranchant cependant ce qu'il pourrait y avoir d'aigre et d'injurieux dans ces écrits. Ils observeront aussi la même neutralité dans tout le reste, excepté quand il s'agira de la religion, des bonnes mœurs, ou de l'état: en quoi il n'est jamais permis d'être neutres'.[7]

This final qualification must be kept in mind if one is to understand the critiques of the *Journal*. While the editors generally attempted to remain true to their purpose of striving for neutrality, in matters of religion they were firm in their determination 'to attack without caution the declared enemies of religion and to unmask its hidden enemies.'[8] Their position, however, did not blind them to the merits of non-Catholic authors, and the editors themselves pointed this out on several occasions by reminding their readers: 'We hate error it is true, but not with a blind hatred which refuses to see in the heretic what is praiseworthy.'[9] And on another occasion: 'We have stated more than once that diversity in religion will not prevent us from giving justice to the intelligence, the erudition and the works of scholars, whose person we love at the same time as we deplore their separation from the Catholic church.'[10] Although the *Journal de Trévoux* was edited by Jesuits, the articles on religion were rather limited and the editors attempted to deal with a wide variety of subjects. This aim was reaffirmed in 1708 when it was editorially stated: 'Il faut

[7] *J. de T.* (Jan.& Feb.1701), 'Préface.' A further indication of the policy of the *Journal* may be obtained from the correspondence of father Thoubeau, who was official correspondent for the publication. In a letter to father Bouhier, a would-be contributor, he states: 'On croit qu'il faut éviter l'air de chagrin contre qui que ce soit et d'acharnement sur certaines personnes:

des airs de modération font plus d'effet; il ne faut aussi prendre fait et cause pour personne; il faut blâmer ce que vous jugez blâmable, dans ceux mêmes que l'on loue d'ailleurs selon la vérité' (Bibliothèque nationale, MS.24420).
[8] *J. de T.* (Feb.1712), p.222.
[9] *J. de T.* (Jan.1708), p.5.
[10] *J. de T.* (Jan.1720), p.5.

enfin que chaque lecteur ait l'équité de ne pas exiger, qu'on n'ait dans les Mémoires égard qu'à une espèce d'auteurs: nous y devons place à tous les livres nouveaux, et nous sommes redevables au théologien, au jurisconsulte, au mathématicien, à l'antiquaire, au philosophe, au médecin; comme au poète, à l'historien, et à l'orateur. Loin d'éviter cette variété, nous sommes déterminés, à la rendre encore plus grande'.[11]

A glance at some of the writers who contributed articles to the *Journal de Trévoux* between 1701 and 1712 (excluding those written by priests), will indicate to what extent this aim was carried out. Among them are: Leibniz (philosophy, Sept.-Oct. 1701, p.263; March 1708, p.488); Jean Bouhier, member of the French Academy (whose seat was later filled by Voltaire; philology, Oct. 1709); Jean Morin of the Academy of Inscriptions (ancient history, Sept. 1709); François Girardon, the famous sculptor (antiquities, Aug. 1703); Antoine Galland, the orientalist (numismatics, Nov.-Dec. 1701; June 1702); the noted Italian archaeologist Luigi Antonio Muratori (library history, June 1713); John Thomas Woolhouse, a celebrated oculist, member of the Royal Societies of London and Berlin (medicine, Feb. 1706; Jan. 1716); Michel Fromont, a noted sinologist (physics, Feb. 1702); and others. Subjects treated in addition to theology include mathematics, anatomy, architecture, sculpture, music, geography, poetry, inscriptions, commerce, meteorology, chemistry, mechanics, astronomy, military art, painting, carving, marine art, and the like.

The new *Mémoires* were well received by the public. By January 1702 the *Journal de Trévoux* had become a monthly publication, and the quality of its articles added to its prestige. However, all was not smooth sailing for the editors. The fact that

[11] *J. de T.* (Jan.1708), p.4. It would seem that the editor sought to avoid articles of a political nature. In thanking father Marchand for 'la continuation de vos nouvelles,' father Tournemine, in an undated letter, states: 'Nous sommes plus curieux des livres [littéraires?] et des livres de religion que des livres de politique.' University of Leyden library, MS. 'Tournemine ad P. Marchand.'

the *Journal* was published a hundred leagues from Paris caused many inconveniences. The editors sent their proofs from their residence at the Collège Louis-le-grand long in advance, but the printer was always late in delivering the copies in time and again the editors had to express their regrets for the printer's errors and delays[12]. In January 1708 they announced that the printer had promised to be more punctual: 'He hopes that the *Mémoires* will be made available in Paris the first day of the following month,' and, by way of further explanation, 'Our press is 100 leagues from Paris and we send the copy for our *Mémoires* two months before they appear.'[13] Four years later they were sending their material three months in advance, and still the printer was late in his deliveries. In 1720 the complaints continued, and in that year the issues from June to December failed to appear. In addition, the printer was careless in his proof-reading, and the names of authors, cities and countries were frequently misspelled. But the printer was not the only one to arouse the ire and complaints of the public. The editors themselves drew the displeasure of their readers upon the publication when they occasionally abandoned the high ideals with which they had started and indulged in a pettiness and sarcasm which soon had them embroiled in a number of controversies[14]. One of the editors, father Hardouin, brought still further embarrassment to the Jesuits when he published his *Opera varia,* wherein he expounded an unorthodox view which considered as atheist anyone, whether Christian or not, outside the Catholic church. This view was immediately attributed to the Jesuits in general, who were being called Hardouinists. In 1708 a

[12] *J. de T.* (Sept.& Oct.1701, p.351; May 1702, p.179).
[13] *J. de T.* (Jan.1708), p.1.
[14] notably with Jean Le Clerc, whose work *Harmonia evangelica* was immoderately criticized by father Despineul (Jan.& Feb.1701, p.71). The quarrel lasted until 1704. Other misunderstandings occurred with Boileau (who wrote an 'épigramme' against the *Journal de Trévoux* in 1704, and another in 1705); and with Jean Baptiste Rousseau, who wrote two epigrams against the editors in defense of his friend de La Fosse. For further examples of controversies involving the *Journal de Trévoux*, see Sommervogel, *Essai historique.*

denunciation of Hardouin's unorthodox writings was officially inserted in the *Journal de Trévoux* with the author concurring in the reprimand. Upon the death of Hardouin in 1733, father Brumoy wrote to the marquis de Caumont that the works of the deceased Jesuit 'are locked up in the college in the superior's quarters for fear they may appear outside.'[15] Despite these precautions, Hardouin's *Opera posthuma* were printed in Holland against the wishes of his superiors, and the editors of the *Journal* were once more obliged to publish an attack on Hardouin's 'système.'[16]

Tired of the numerous complaints he was receiving concerning the publication, the duc Du Maine refused to grant a new 'privilège' in 1731, and the editors had to seek another printing establishment[17]. They chose the printing firm of Claude Perret at Lyons, and the April issue of that year appeared with several modifications. The most apparent was the absence from the titlepage of the coat of arms of the duc Du Maine, and a change from the words 'commanded by the duc Du Maine' to 'begun by the duc Du Maine'.

At about this time another blunder by the editors placed them in a still more difficult position. In 1731 they had questioned the

[15] *Lettres du p. Brumoy* (Paris 1857), p.29.

[16] *J. de T.* (Jan.1734). His unorthodox views were also attacked by fathers Tournemine, Griffet and Berthier. Father Brumoy states that 'on ne sait pas qui a fourni ces ouvrages; on soupçonne l'abbé d'Olivet' (*Lettres*, p.40). It is possible that Hardouin himself had secretly furnished the information to the Dutch printer before his death. In a letter to m. Huguetan, an Amsterdam publisher, the Jesuit writer indicates that he wishes to have a certain 'mémoire' published through him but that 'ce que je vous demande principalement, Monsieur, c'est que vous voulliez bien m'assurer de la même fidelité et du secret pour les choses où je ne mettrai pas mon nom.' Univ. of Leyden Library, MS. *Hardouinus ad Huguetan*.

[17] one factor in bringing about the withdrawal of the duke's support was the controversy with the Academy brought on by an article by Castel, in which the editor takes exception to several points in the society's *Histoire de l'Académie royale des sciences*. The Academy approached the duke and 'demanded a public apology in the next issue and the discharge of the author of the offending review' (Donald Schier, *Louis B. Castel*, p.18).

authenticity of Bossuet's *Elévations à Dieu sur tous les mystères de la religion chrétienne*, published posthumously by his nephew and namesake the bishop of Troyes. The latter caused the parliament to compare the manuscript with other works of Bossuet, and published in 1733 a pastoral instruction on the 'calumnies' advanced by the *Journal*. The Jesuits were obliged to retract their accusations, and promised to maintain a closer supervision over the editors of the *Journal de Trévoux*.

A change in the policies of the *Mémoires* was urgently needed. The editors had apparently abandoned their earlier aspirations and were indulging in unrestrained attacks in which passions rather than rational criticism seemed to be dictating their writings. This change occurred in 1734. The editors, realizing that their attitude was compromising the quality of their articles, and profiting by previous mistakes, published a notice admitting their past errors and promising to avoid them in the future: 'La partialité est un grand danger pour des journalistes et ceux de Trévoux l'ont franchement reconnu. L'esprit de partialité est un écueil dangereux où bien des journalistes ont échoué. Le reproche qu'on fait encore à quelques-uns d'entre eux de juger des ouvrages d'autrui sur le rapport de la passion et des préjugés, n'est que trop bien fondé. On nous saura gré sans doute des précautions que nous sommes résolus de prendre pour ménager la délicatesse des auteurs. Le devoir d'un journaliste se borne à rendre un compte fidèle des livres dont il est chargé de faire l'analyse. S'il lui faut le secours de la critique, la politesse, la probité et la religion lui prescrivent des règles dont il ne doit jamais se départir. Affecter les airs et le ton de censeur ou de juge, c'est usurper un droit qui n'appartient qu'au public, arbitre souverain de la réputation des auteurs et du mérite de leurs ouvrages'.[18]

As a further means of improving their publication, the new editors discontinued printing at Lyons, and engaged a printer in Paris so as to ensure the more prompt delivery of their *Mémoires*

---

[18] *J. de T.* (Jan.1734), p.4.

to the public. The reform introduced by father Rouillé, the new editor-in-chief, with the help of his staff fathers Bougeant, Castel, Charlevoix, La Tour and Brumoy, saved the publication, and the improvement was immediately recognized by its readers. In April 1734 father Brumoy writes that he has little time 'since the renewal of our journal,' and continues: 'It is father Rouillé who has effected it .... The first month has been well received by the public.'[19] The abbé Prévost noted the improvement and informed his readers: 'Notre estime qui s'était fort affaiblie pour cet ouvrage a été réveillé par les promesses des continuateurs, et s'accroît de jour en jour par la manière dont ils les remplissent. L'esprit, le savoir et les agrémens du stile ne suffisent pas pour former des journalistes. Ils l'ont reconnu; et joignant à ces trois qualités l'impartialité et la modération ils ont pris le tempérament qui convient à une entreprise purement littéraire. Le public y gagne un excellent journal'.[20]

The abbé Desfontaines also recognized the change and wrote: 'Je vous ai fait un détail il y a deux ans de differens Journaux littéraires qui impriment en Europe et je me souviens de ne vous avoir pas alors parlé fort avantageusement des *Mémoires pour servir à l'histoire des sciences et des beaux-arts*. Je leur reprochais tantôt de l'affectation, et tantôt de la négligence dans le style et surtout une extrême partialité. Je suis obligé de dire avec la même candeur, qu'il me paraît que ce journal est à présent écrit avec beaucoup plus de soin et de goût, et que ceux qui y travaillent s'étudient à rendre justice aux talens et ne s'écartent plus des règles de la bienséance et de la politesse .... Ils ont donné réellement des preuves sensibles d'impartialité, capables d'effacer entièrement toutes les fâcheuses impressions qu'un recueil d'invectives périodiques avait faites sur le public'.[21]

The abbé Prévost was soon to change his opinion, however, when the *Journal de Trévoux* reviewed unfavourably his 'Remar-

[19] *Lettres du père Brumoy*, p.43.
[20] *Le pour et le contre* (1734), v.49.
[21] *Observations sur les écrits modernes* (1735), i.140.

ques sur la vie de M. de Turenne par M. de Ramsay,'[22] and in 1735 he tells his readers concerning the *Journal*: 'Aussi s'aperçoit-on que ses auteurs commencent à négliger beaucoup les engagements qu'ils avaient pris au commencement de cette année qui se trouvent exécutés très fidèlement dans quelques uns des premiers mois. Ce n'est plus le même air d'équité, de politesse et de désintéressement. C'est une vivacité qui ne se modère plus, et qui s'emporte souvent fort loin au delà des bornes'.[23]

With the death of father Rouillé in 1737, the lack of leadership began to be felt, and the *Journal* tended to go back to its earlier days of contradiction and independent action on the part of the various editors[24]. The tendency of Castel to go to excesses led the *Journal* into a quarrel with Réaumur, whose ire was aroused by Castel's review of his study on insects. The other editors were obliged to arrange the reconciliation which is related by Brumoy. After arranging a meeting with Réaumur 'father Bougeant took charge of writing an extract of the second volume of the *Insectes,* so as to disavow somewhat father Castel.'[25]

In 1745 another change was found necessary if the *Journal de Trévoux* were to retain the moderate spirit which the reform of father Rouillé had attempted to give it. But more important, the Encyclopedist movement was beginning to be noted, and it was becoming clear that an exceptional chief would be necessary to maintain a spirit of moderation and at the same time be penetrating enough to ferret out and expose the irreligious implications in the growing literature from the pens of the 'esprits forts.' The *Mémoires* found such a leader in Guillaume François Berthier.

[22] 'Le P. Rouillé . . . a fait une représaille assez vive à l'abbé Prévost, au sujet de l'extrait de M. de Ramsey' (*Lettres du P. Brumoy,* p.63).
[23] *Le pour et le contre* (1735), vii.6.
[24] J. B. Rousseau is quoted as saying in a letter dated Oct.1737: 'L'amour du paradoxe, dont le P. Hardouin, son confrère vient de donner au monde érudit de si prodigieux exemples [his 'système'], n'est pas le fait du P. Brumoy, et il a même beaucoup de peine à supporter les spirituelles 'excentricités' de son collaborateur le P. Castel' (note by the editor, J. M. Prat, in the *Lettres du p. Brumoy,* p.23).
[25] *Lettres du p. Brumoy,* p.70.

When he assumed the post of editor-in-chief in January 1745—a position he was to hold until the suppression of the Jesuits in 1762—it was not merely as a collaborator. His superiors wanted him to take full charge of the publication. Although the names of fathers Routh, Plesse, Mat, Fleurian, Benoit and d'Orival appear on his editorial staff, 'Quel que pût être ... le talent de ces divers écrivains, il semblait disparaître devant celui du p. Berthier, le lien et l'âme de leur association. Grâce à cette unité d'esprit et d'action, qui à aucune autre époque, ne régna dans les *Mémoires* aussi parfaitement que dans ces dernières années, le p. Berthier devint le centre unique de l'admiration ou de l'estime des uns, et de la haine ou des colères des autres'.[26]

So intent was the new editor on keeping a complete control over the *Journal* that he sought to run the publication with as few collaborators as possible. The manuscript notes of de Quens reveal 'father Berthier, the journalist of Trévoux in a position to do good work, but doing by himself the work of four men.'[27] In the same collection he refers to Berthier's aversion to accepting help on his *Journal* when he remarks that father Plesse has been sent to Paris 'to work on the journal with father Berthier who, nevertheless, did not want any help.'[28] Such an attitude toward his responsibility as editor-in-chief of the *Journal de Trévoux* justifies de Backer's contention concerning the Jesuit editor that 'all the volumes from 1745 to May 1762 could be regarded as his work.'[29]

Having assumed the direction of the *Journal* Berthier published the following statement, announcing his intention to avoid controversies and to follow the path of moderation: 'Ce journal n'a point coutume d'user de représailles contre les satyriques de profession. Pour répondre à ces écrivains, il faudrait prendre le ton des personnalités, des termes de mépris, des accusations hazar-

---

[26] Sommervogel, *Essai historique*, p.lxxx.
[27] quoted by Charma and Mancel, *Le Père André, Jésuite*, (Caën 1844–

1857), ii.130.
[28] *ibid.*, ii.130.
[29] *Bibliothèque des écrivains de la Cie. de Jésus*, i.1378.

dées; manière odieuse d'exercer sa plume, objet d'ennui pour les honnêtes gens.

Nos Mémoires reconnaissent toujours plus volontiers les perfections d'un livre que ses défauts. Cela ne doit pas en exclure une critique saine, modérée, honnête et instructive. S'il arrive qu'on se croie maltraité par quelqu'un de ces jugements littéraires, on sera toujours reçu à produire ses raisons dans une courte apologie, qui pourra trouver sa place dans un journal suivant'.[30] Thereafter we find frequent repetitions of the desire for moderation and impartiality[31]. In 1750, for example, Berthier reiterates his aim of avoiding polemics, declaring: 'Our method is to work in silence; to spare nothing to satisfy a judicious, enlightened and impartial public; to count a little on their indulgence, and should we make mistakes, to avoid all altercation.'[32]

The new editor soon learned that it was impossible to please everyone. It would seem that his attitude had been considered by some readers as over-indulgent, and in October of the same year he repeats his aims and adds: 'Il faut traiter, dans les sciences et dans les arts, avec franchise et gaieté; l'érudition que nous répandons dans nos extraits est la plus indulgente du monde; elle l'est même trop quelquefois, si nous en croyons cent bouches qui s'ouvrent pour parler de nos Mémoires. Que faire toutefois? Il y a longtemps que la fable de *L'Ane, du meunier et de son fils* est l'apologue propre des journalistes'.[33]

Nine years later we find the same theme appearing in an article concerning Voltaire. The editor states: 'On reproche souvent à ce journal sa complaisance pour les auteurs et pour leurs ouvrages; complaisance après tout … qui n'est qu'une attention commandée par la probité et la raison. Il vaut mieux voir partout le bien que le mal; et il est plus de l'intérêt des lettres d'encourager les talents

---

[30] *J. de T.* (Jan.1746), p.187.
[31] 'Ces protestations de modération, ces modestes aveux n'étaient point de simples banalités. Le P. Berthier insistait avec raison sur ce point afin de ramener les esprits prévenus contre ses devanciers' (Sommervogel, *Essai historique*, p.lxxxiv).
[32] *J. de T.* (June 1750), p.1534; cf. also *ibid.* (Apr.1749), p.763.
[33] *J. de T.* (Oct.1750), p.2151.

par des témoignages d'estime, que de les détruire par des critiques insultantes. Il n'y a que les livres contraires à la religion, aux mœurs, à l'honnêteté et à la paix publique, qui ne méritent aucune indulgence. Si le *Journal de Trévoux* s'est acquitté de son devoir à cet égard, quel peut être son crime?'[34] Finally, as if to answer his critics once and for all on this point, Berthier devoted a long article to the problems and pitfalls faced by the journalist, and concluded with a reaffirmation of principles: 'Impartialité, équité, réserve dans les jugements, attention à ne critiquer qu'à propos, à louer plus volontiers, quoique sobrement; fidélité dans les extraits, recherche des nouveautés les plus intéressantes; tels sont les engagements qu'il est rare qu'on ne contracte pas dans le premier moment d'une opération littéraire aussi publique que l'est un journal'.[35]

Why then are such promises so often broken? There are many reasons, continues the editor. 'One cannot reflect upon the thoughts of others without offending their vanity if one does not approve of them completely.' However, if the author's work is accepted without question the critic is considered 'an insipid adulator.' If he merely confines himself to the functions of a reporter, he bores his public. Actually, the public reads to be amused and distracted rather than for information. Therefore 'they are more interested in petty things, particularly if they are malicious.' A journal must build on two supports, he continues, 'the moral,' and the 'literary.' The former consists of probity, wisdom, disinterestedness, zeal for the public good, while the literary 'is a very extensive knowledge, a superior logic, a style free from bombast or baseness, closer to the dissertation than the oratorical style, more proportioned to a conversational than a didactic tone.'[36]

With such an attitude both toward the supervision and the aims

<hr>

[34] *J. de T.* (July 1759), i.1693–94. The *Journal* was originally created to defend religion, and Berthier took this function seriously. As will be seen in the chapters dealing with the *philo-* *sophes*, the Jesuit editor frequently reiterated this primary purpose of the *Journal.*

[35] *J. de T.* (Jan.1760), p.244.

[36] *J. de T.* (Jan.1760), pp.244–247.

of the publication, it is understandable that the new editor-in-chief should wish to drop from his staff such contributors as Castel, who had drawn the *Journal de Trévoux* into quarrels in the past, and whose 'écarts' would be intolerable if the *Journal* were to live up to Berthier's conception of its role. Donald Schier tells us that a quarrel had taken place between Castel and Berthier, and the former had considered attacking the new editor publicly. He then adds: 'It is difficult to imagine the situation between Castel and Berthier,' and suggests that Castel's friendship with Montesquieu may have placed the Jesuit under suspicion[37]. If this were the reason, Berthier would have been under an even heavier cloud, especially as he maintained a friendship with J. J. Rousseau, who was certainly more unorthodox than Montesquieu. The chief reason for the rift probably lies in Castel's temperament which, unlike Berthier's steady, deliberate approach, led him to hastily formed and frequently untenable conclusions. 'He was too impatient of routine, too anxious to settle a question, too unwilling to proceed slowly and methodically and drearily, day after day. What he did not know he imagined, and he all too quickly persuaded himself that he knew what he had assumed'.[38]

This tendency to jump to conclusions and then maintain them dogmatically was precisely why he could not be retained on the *Journal* if its keynote were to be 'moderation.'[39] In his 'Eloge du père Castel,' Berthier points out with obvious disapproval this tendency in Castel: 'Cet esprit naturellement facile, fécond et inventeur, était sans cesse sollicité par l'imagination.... Quand le p. Castel a pû tenir sous les loix de la raison cette puissance d'ima-

---

[37] Schier, p.44.

[38] Schier, p.200.

[39] There had been attempts to remove Castel from the editorial staff of the *Journal* even before Berthier's assumption of his duties as editor-in-chief. As early as 1735 Brumoy had written: 'Que vous dirai-je, par exemple, du *Clavecin oculaire?* . . . Raillerie à part, je fais honneur à l'auteur, que j'estime et qui est un aimable homme, de croire qu'il ne pense pas un mot de ce qu'il dit. Si je suis pourtant cru, il ne mettra plus tant de belles choses dans nos journaux. Que voulez-vous, après tout? nous ne pouvons mais de ces manies poétiques qui saisissent dans un temps de convulsion [*sic*]'(Lettres du p. Brumoy, pp.61–62).

giner qui était en lui au degré le plus éminent, il n'a dit que du vrai.... Mais cette imagination est une infidèle; elle a ses moments de séduction; elle trompe alors les plus sages. Ce philosophe-géo-mètre ... a de temps en temps passé la ligne que lui traçait la Géo-métrie, tant pour le fond des choses que pour la manière de les dire. L'imagination jouait son rôle, elle se décelait par des écarts, par des saillies, par des singularités; et, ce qui doit paraître une sorte de phénomène en ce genre, ces illusions se manifestaient encore sur le retour de l'âge'.[40]

A further reason for the dismissal of Castel might be found in the following statement by m. Bertrand, who says of him: 'He continues to live without realizing the great struggles in prepara-tion and his thoughts on the world outside [of the walls of the Collège] are backward a century and more.'[41] At a time when the *philosophe* movement had finally begun to consolidate, and a struggle to the finish was in preparation, such a blindness to the danger would be intolerable to Berthier who, as we shall see, was quick to sense the inherent danger to church and state in the writ-ings of the *philosophes* and particularly of Diderot, whose plea to Castel in regard to the former's quarrel with Berthier must have convinced the new editor of Castel's naïveté in the matter (see below, p.177).

Still another cause of friction between Castel and his Jesuit col-leagues was probably his obstinate refusal to accept new ideas. 'He opposed the new continually and looked back for inspiration to Descartes, to Kircher, to Grimaldi, and ultimately, in accord-ance with the rule of the Jesuits, to Aristotle.'[42] Berthier decried this subservience to Aristotle, and declared that in actual practice this 'rule of the Jesuits' was all but ignored in their schools. When

[40] *J. de T.* (Apr.1757), ii.1103–05.
[41] *Le P. Castel, un rêve de savant au XVIIIe siècle* (Paris 1868), p.20. Profes-sor Schier makes a similar evaluation of Castel when he states: 'Born in the seventeenth century, and educated ac-cording to its precepts, Castel perso-nifies, in many ways, the opinions of the age of Louis XIV in contact with those of a newer time' (*L. B. Castel*, p.202); or again, 'In a sense, he was outmoded even in his day' (p.200).
[42] Schier, p.202.

the Jesuits were accused of changing their rules to fit the occasion, he replied that on the contrary, they cling too much to their old statutes: 'On peut citer par exemple, les décrets tant de fois répétés en faveur de la philosophie et même de la physique d'Aristote. On n'a jamais pu persuader aux congrégations générales d'abandonner cet article, et de laisser une pleine liberté sur ces matières. L'usage est bien qu'on s'embarrasse peu d'Aristote dans les écoles des Jésuites, surtout en France; mais le langage des congrégations est toujours pour ce philosophe, parce qu'il a été approuvé dans les premiers temps, et lorsqu'on n'avait rien de mieux'.[43]

Berthier's persistent efforts toward moderation gradually won over the readers who had been alienated by his predecessors, and made of the *Journal de Trévoux* one of the best known and most widely read publications of its time. Even such avowed enemies of the *Journal* as the Jansenist Goujet was obliged to respect the new editor[44]. In speaking of the failure of the *Journal* to mention his works, he states: 'Lorsque le p. Berthier eut été appelé à la direction du journal dont il s'agit, il crut qu'il devait suppléer au silence de ses confrères, et il le fit avec cette finesse d'esprit dont on sait qu'il est doué. Par ménagement pour eux il traita leur oubli volontaire "d'espèce d'avanture littéraire dont il ne faut point chercher la raison, parce qu'il n'y en a point." Il donna ensuite dans les *Mémoires* du mois de mai 1746 une esquisse des six premiers volumes de ma *Bibliothèque française,* parla du septième et du huitième, depuis c'est lui seul qui a fait les extraits des volumes suivants, et je ne puis que me louer de la manière dont il en parla.

[43] Berthier, *Recueil de lettres sur la doctrine et l'institut des Jésuites,* pp.33–34.

[44] Goujet had been asked by cardinal Dubois to compose 'un *Journal plus Théologique que Littéraire,* que l'on pût opposer aux *Mémoires de Trévoux*' (Goujet, *Mémoires historiques et littéraires,* p.103). Apparently the feeling was mutual. In the same work Goujet tells of the refusal of the Jesuits to mention his *Bibliothèque française*: 'Ce silence était affecté: un de mes amis qui était aussi des leurs, et qui a continué de les favoriser, en fit quelques reproches au Père de Charlevoix: "Que voulez-vous," répondit le Père? "Nous ne pouvons dire du mal de l'ouvrage; et à cause de l'Auteur il ne nous convient pas d'en dire du bien"' (*ibid.,* p.113).

L'abbé des Fontaines et quelques autres critiques n'ont pas toujours été si judicieux ni si modérés'.[45] As he reminisces over the many disputes he had had with the former editors of the *Journal de Trévoux* Goujet speaks of one 'which father Berthier would probably not have aroused if he had then been in charge of the *Mémoires de Trévoux*.'[46]

Similarly, Berthier managed to satisfy Charles de Quens, a partisan of Malebranche, whose teacher père André had been attacked by the Jesuits for his 'Malebranchisme.'[47] Whereas André's *Essai sur le beau* had not been mentioned in the *Journal de Trévoux* when it appeared in 1741, with the printing of a second edition in 1758 'the Trévoux journal although its director, Father Berthier, did not like the *Essai sur le beau*, devoted to it somewhat later, in 1760, a rather kindly article.'[48] Bachaumont attests to Berthier's reputation when he indicates that the Jesuit was named as editor of the *Journal* 'which he directed for 17 years with a critical tone which was always wise, impartial and firm.'[49] Similarly, Barbier

[45] *Mémoires historiques et littéraires*, pp.113–114.

[46] *ibid.*, p.116. It would seem that the Jesuit editor encouraged the Jansenist abbé in his literary endeavours, first suggesting that Goujet publish his translation of Meerman's *Plan du traité des origines typographiques*, and finally obtaining from him a contribution to the May 1750 issue of the *Journal de Trévoux* in the form of a 'Lettre sur la famille de Boyslève de la Maurouzière.' Cf. *Mémoires historiques et littéraires*, p.143.

[47] as early as 1712, André had been warned by Hardouin, an editor of the *Journal*, to abandon his adherence to Descartes and Malebranche or 'vous allez vous attirer de très fâcheuses affaires' (Charma and Mancel, *Le P. André*, p.265). Emmy Allard states: 'Die jesuitische Streitschrift gegen den

Cartesianismus datiert vom Jahre 1712, sie wurde André unterbreitet als das Formular eines mündlichen und schriftlichen Widerrufs seiner Lehre' (*Die angriffe gegen Descartes & Malebranche im Journal de Trévoux* [Halle 1914], p.2).

[48] Charma and Mancel, *Le Père André*, i.129. In another note de Quens makes the following evaluation of the editor of the *Journal de Trévoux*: 'Savant; a beaucoup lu et beaucoup retenu. Hardi, comme ses prédécesseurs. Juge assez bien d'un fait historique . . . .' However, Berthier's attitude toward Malebranche earns him a demerit and de Quens goes on to say: 'superficiel en philosophie, n'entend point la métaphysique de Descartes, ni de Malebranche, dont il parle sans être au fait' (*ibid.*, ii.130).

[49] *Mémoires secrets*, xxii.6.

declares: 'Les *Mémoires de Trévoux* n'ont jamais été plus intéressants ni plus utiles que quand le père Berthier y a travaillé. Il a su
répandre dans ses différents extraits une sagesse de critique, une
pureté de goût une sûreté d'érudition qu'il serait à souhaiter de
voir dans tous les journaux'.[50]

No amount of moderation could have avoided the eventual
coming to grips of the Jesuit editor with the *philosophes*. Indeed,
the very impartiality and firmness of Berthier's critiques, by winning him more readers made him all the more dangerous an adversary. But this phase of the story belongs to another chapter. Suffice
it to say at this point that the concerted efforts of both the *philosophes* and the Jansenists to rid France of the Jesuit order succeeded in a manner unexpected by both sides. The Jesuit fathers
La Valette and Sarcy had contracted a debt in connection with
shipments of supplies to their mission in Martinique. When the
cargo ship was seized by the British, the Jesuits refused payment
on the grounds that debts contracted by individual Jesuits were
not binding on the whole Society. The creditors, Lioncy &
Jouffres of Marseilles, appealed to the courts of that city and the
Jesuits were ordered to pay the debt. They appealed to a higher
court, and the case was referred to the grand council in Paris.
Since one could accept or reject this privilege, the Jesuits refused
on the insistence of father Frey at the 'maison professe' in Paris.
(He was considered 'one of the best political minds of the order').
They decided to submit the affair to the parliament and to decline
the jurisdiction of the grand council. Frey believed that many of
those who would review the case 'are our pupils; the parliament
knows our rights and will be responsive to the confidence we are
showing it by submitting ourselves to their jurisdiction.'[51] This
proved to be a blunder because whereas the court would merely

[50] *Nouvelle bibliothèque d'un homme
de goût*, v.177. Cf. also Hatin, *Histoire
politique et littéraire de la presse*, ii.260;
and Montjoye, *Eloge*, p.69. Sommervogel attests to the reputation of the
Journal when discussing translations
of the *Mémoires* in Italy and Holland.
[51] Barrière, *Bibliothèque des mémoires*, iii.166–169.

have ruled on the question of the solidarity of the Society in connection with the contracting of debts, the parliament, 'examina en entier leur constitution; et le 8 mai 1761, un arrêt du parlement condamna les Jésuites à payer les sommes dues.... Pendant qu'on plaidait cette cause, les ennemis des Jésuites excitaient contre eux des clameurs dans les lieux publics et dans les sociétés.... Les Jansénistes fortifièrent de tous les moyens de l'esprit de parti les dispositions défavorables du parlement et l'aveuglement des Jésuites à ne pas avoir recours au grand conseil acheva ce que depuis longtemps leurs ennemis avaient si ardemment souhaité'.[52]

Despite the intervention of the dauphin and the king in the matter, the Jesuits were ordered to close their schools on 1 April 1762, and on 6 August of the same year, they were forbidden to wear the habit of their order, live under obedience to their general or other superiors, or engage in assembly, communication or correspondence among themselves. They were further forbidden to hold any employ unless they swore an oath abjuring their institution[53].

With the closing of the Collège Louis-le-grand in April 1762, the April issue of the *Journal de Trévoux* appeared, 'but father Berthier has declared that it was the last one he would present.'[54] It would seem that he stayed on long enough to prepare the May issue, for on 16 May Bachaumont announces that 'despite the protestations of mr Berthier, *Trévoux* appeared again this month: his paternal tenderness could not stand to see a favoured child strangled

---

[52] *ibid.*, iii.170. An incident which hastened the destruction of the Jesuits was the uncovering by Camille Falconet, Diderot's friend, of a letter in Le Tellier's handwriting, admitting a plot against the Jansenist cardinal de Noailles. The letter was sent to 'l'abbé Chauvelin, rapporteur du procès contre les jésuites, convenant lui-même qu'il allait faire arrêter le Cardinal ... exiler le procureur général du parlement [d'Aguesseau]; et combien il lui fut facile d'enflammer les esprits contre un ordre aussi dangereux' (*ibid.*, iii.172). The letter reads in part: '. . . les lettres de cachet sont toutes prêtes pour arrêter le Cardinal de Noailles . . . . Lorsque nous aurons abbatu cette figure, nous n'aurons plus rien à craindre.' Bibliothèque Mazarine, MS.2459, p.263.

[53] on 22 February 1764 the oath was made a requirement for residence in France.

[54] *Mémoires secrets*, i.69.

in this manner.[55] There is evidence indicating that the *Journal*, far from being an 'enfant chéri' for Berthier had actually been an undesired burden to him. When, after the suppression of the Jesuits, the chancellor de Lamoignon offered the ex-editor an annuity of 1500 francs in addition to a residence at the Bibliothèque du roi provided he continue the *Journal de Trévoux*, Bachaumont states that 'he still refuses, however, the very kind offers of the chancellor. This chief magistrate wants to retain its privilege for him, his heirs, male or female, his inheritors or those having claims, etc.'[56] Referring to Berthier's refusal, Montjoye says: 'He had no desire to do for gain what he had done only as a duty.'[57] Berthier himself, when accused by Voltaire of editing the *Journal* for financial gain, had pointed out that, while other journals had raised their prices, that of *Trévoux* was the only one whose price had not risen within the last four years, and as to the ambition of the 'journalist of Trévoux,' he added that some of his superiors 'savent que le Journaliste... n'a point choisi cette profession: qu'il s'y est trouvé engagé comme le Vultejus d'Horace fut, sans y penser, investi d'affaires très-éloignées de son goût; et qu'enfin, excédé de soins et de fatigues, il répète aussi à son "Patron" cette prière qui n'est le cri ni de l'ambition ni de l'intrigue.

> Pol! me miserum, patrone, vocares,
> Si velles, inquit, verum mihi dicere nomen.
> Quod te, per genium, dextramque,
> Obsecro & obtestor, vitae me reddi priori'.[58]

---

[55] *ibid.*, i.83. Berthier sent one further contribution to the *Journal* in answer to an attack made against him in the *Nouvelles ecclésiastiques* accusing him of hypocrisy in his earlier articles condemning father Hardouin's 'système.' In a letter to the new editor Berthier emphasizes the sincerity of his censure of his Jesuit predecessor (*J. de T.*, June 1762).

[56] *Mémoires secrets*, i.83.

[57] *Eloge historique*, p.81.

[58] *J. de T.* (July 1759), i.1694. The editor answers in this article the attacks contained in Voltaire's *Ode* on the death of Wilhelmina of Bayreuth. If one recalls that the year 1759 marks the publication of Voltaire's severest attack against the editor, the *Relation de la maladie, de la confession, de la mort et de l'apparition du Jésuite Berthier*, the editor's desire to 'get away from it all' is understandable.

With the suppression of the Jesuits, a new editor was sought for the *Journal de Trévoux*, and when the abbé de La Porte refused the responsibility[59], the lot fell to Jean Louis Jolivet, a doctor of medicine from the faculty of Rheims. It was not necessary to announce that a change in command had taken place—the harsh tone of the new editor was so strikingly different from the carefully phrased criticisms of his predecessor that it reminded Bachaumont of the early days of the *Journal*: 'Ce triste médecin avait jeté dans cet ouvrage une sécheresse, une insipidité, qui leur avaient donné beaucoup de discrédit. Aussi grave, aussi raide que les premiers auteurs, il n'avait pas su y joindre une aménité de style, dont le p. Berthier parait son pédantisme'.[60] It was obvious that the man was inferior to the task, but when returning to the subject of the *Journal de Trévoux*, Bachaumont recognized the advantages enjoyed by the Jesuits when the publication had been theirs: 'On s'aperçoit facilement que ce ne sont plus les mêmes coopérateurs qui travaillent au *Journal de Trévoux*; il n'est plus ni aussi bien écrit ni aussi savamment discuté. On conçoit en général, qu'il est impossible à des particuliers d'exécuter cet ouvrage périodiquement dans la même perfection que le faisaient les Jésuites, et le Père Berthier en dernier lieu. Une bibliothèque immense, où vérifier à chaque instant les citations, et des élèves sans nombre et pleins de talents qui travaillaient en sous-œuvre; comment rencontrer les mêmes secours?'[61] Realizing the disadvantage of the new editor, Bachaumont does not see much chance for improvement, and he concludes: 'We shall miss for a long time to come this journal, which is degenerating and which will degenerate more and more.'[62] Several months later an *Ode* in the new *Journal* evokes another comment from Bachaumont, who exclaims in what seems to be a tone of exasperation: 'This time it is apparent

---

[59] 'On a tâté l'abbé de la Porte: les libraires lui ont proposé de remplacer ce journaliste [Berthier]. Le modeste abbé a refusé, sentant combien il était inférieur pour ce rôle' (*Mémoires secrets*, i.83).

[60] *Mémoires secrets*, ii.68. For examples of Jolivet's criticisms, see below, the chapter on J. J. Rousseau.

[61] *Mémoires secrets*, i.109.

[62] *Mémoires secrets*, i.109.

that Father Berthier, now an abbé, is no longer at the head of the *Journal de Trévoux*: its dullness cannot be imitated; they make use of anything. Among other things, they have printed an ode on electricity. It is the height of ridiculousness.'[63]

Upon the death of Jolivet on 18 June 1764, there was talk of discontinuing the *Journal* entirely[64]. However, the publication escaped extinction and Bachaumont recorded its fate as follows: 'Quoique m. de Sartine et le vice-chancelier paraissent avoir le projet de supprimer tout à fait le *Journal de Trévoux*, depuis la mort du continuateur, m. Jolivet, ces magistrats se sont laissés aller aux sollicitations de mm. de Sainte-Geneviève, et il paraît que cet ordre s'est emparé de la continuation: il est actuellement entre les mains de m. Mercier, bibliothécaire de Sainte-Geneviève et de m. le duc de la Valière. C'est un littérateur de beaucoup d'érudition, et qui a un génie caustique, propre à répandre le sel nécessaire à un pareil ouvrage. On commence à en être plus content depuis qu'il est entre ses mains'.[65] Mercier received little help from his colleagues, and Sommervogel suggests that this lack of cooperation may have been the cause of his abandonment of the *Journal* only two years after his assumption of duties as editor[66]. Whatever the reason, the July 1766 number appeared with several slight modifications and the names of abbé Aubert and father Didot le jeune as the new editors. 'Abbé Aubert,' relates Sommervogel, 'a rather ordinary literary man aspired only to a peaceful existence; he said as much in his dedication .... The wishes of the

[63] *Mémoires secrets* (5 Sept.1762), p.123.

[64] 'M. le vice-chancelier n'a pas jugé à propos de continuer cet ouvrage; on doit le terminer à la demi-année; après quoi il reste supprimé' (*Mémoires secrets*, xvi.197).

[65] *Mémoires secrets*, ii.52. Hatin gives substantially the same account in his *Histoire politique & littéraire de la presse française*, when he says of the *J. de T.*, 'M. de Sartine et le chancelier . . . en

confièrent la rédaction au P. Mercier, si connu depuis sous le nom d'abbé de Saint-Léger' (p.277). The same author writes that the *Journal de Trévoux* 'prolongea cependant son existence quelques années encore, grâce surtout à l'abbé de Saint-Léger, qui était parvenu à lui donner quelque vie' (ii.260).

[66] *Essai historique*, p.97. The last issue under Mercier's direction was that of June 1766.

editor were granted, his *Journal des Beaux-Arts et des Sciences* flowed on in tranquil days.'[67]

When the abbé was given the chair in literature at the Collège royal in November 1773, the publication was taken over by the former editors of the *Journal encyclopédique*, messrs Castilhon[68]. Sommervogel indicates that the new editors 'attracted attention by the equity of their judgments; the supplements which they issued also give testimony to their zeal.'[69] After again changing the format of the publication in 1776, the new editors relinquished their post two years later to a new editor, the ex-Jesuit abbé Grosier. This most recent change evokes another comment by Bachaumont: 'On sait que le *Journal de Trévoux* depuis la déstruction des Jésuites, a passé dans différentes mains et n'a fait que se détériorer. Il semble qu'il était réservé à un ex-Jésuite de le réparer et de lui rendre son lustre; ce que vient de faire m. l'abbé Grosier, qui, brouillé avec Fréron, a pris la direction de ce journal sous le titre de *Journal de Littérature, Sciences et Arts*. Pour lui donner plus de véhicule par plus de fraicheur, il a imaginé de le distribuer par cahiers, comme le *Mercure*, de dix jours en dix jours'.[70]

The abbé soon ran into difficulties when he tried to include political as well as literary news through letters to himself or sent to him by friends to be inserted in his *Journal*. 'But mr Panckoucke was not fooled by this trick; he complained to the *garde des sceaux* and the [*Journal*] was condemned to pay him a substantial sum if it discussed political matters.'[71] Barbier states that Jean Baptiste Dubois helped Grosier as co-editor 'since February 1780,' but these editors in turn apparently abandoned the publication entirely, possibly because of the difficulties encountered with the

[67] *ibid.*, p.98.
[68] Sommervogel gives January 1774 as the date. He bases his assumption on the remark of Bachaumont dated January 1774, 'Le journal subit une nouvelle métamorphose.' However, a printed circular by the editors Castilhon announcing their new *Mémoires* shows November 1773 to be the correct date. B.N.Fr.22085.
[69] *Essai historique*, p.99.
[70] *Mémoires secrets*, xiv.54.
[71] *Mémoires secrets*, xiv.54.

authorities. Barbier adds that 'it ceased completely to appear about the year 1782.'[72]

As has been seen, the history of the *Journal de Trévoux* after the suppression of the Jesuits in 1762 is one of confusion, rumours of discontinuation, constantly changing hands and form. It never recovered fully from the blow it received in 1762, and its shaky career thereafter seems an anticlimax after the high place it had achieved under Berthier. The coverage of these declining years has taken the form, in this study, of a brief outline of the successive changes in the *Journal de Trévoux* until its discontinuation. The same ground is covered more amply first in Sommervogel's *Essai historique*, and then in Dumas's *Histoire du Journal de Trévoux*, which benefits greatly from Sommervogel's spade work, as does the present outline.

Before going on to a study of the relations of the *Journal de Trévoux* with the *philosophes*, it will be well first to stop and consider the life and ideas of its most notable editor, Guillaume François Berthier, in order to have a basis for understanding his attitudes toward the movement in which he took such an active part.

[72] *Nouvelle bibliothèque*, v.179.

Guillaume François Berthier

Guillaume François Berthier was born at Issoudun, in the province of Berry, on 7 April 1704. His father, Guillaume Berthier, a
lawyer of that city, and his mother, the former Catherine de
l'Estang, sent him to the Jesuit Collège at Bourges when he was
twelve years old, and there he distinguished himself as an out-
standing pupil. Upon completion of his studies five years later, he
indicated his desire to become a Jesuit but was refused permission by his parents for a year. When he was eighteen, he was sent
to Paris to begin his novitiate. Young Berthier seems to have been
an indefatigable worker, sleeping only four or five hours a night
and reading voluminously. After a year his superiors were sufficiently impressed with him to send him to the Collège de Blois to
teach the humanities. There he met Le Forestier, a 'préfet des
études' who was to guide and influence him, and who remained
his close friend throughout his life. After seven years at Blois,
Berthier was required to undergo another year of novitiate in
Paris, and then he was sent to Rennes as professor of philosophy,
and thence to Rouen[1]. A later assignment as professor of theology brought him back to Paris, where, in addition to his profes-
sorial duties, he was charged with the task of continuing, upon
the death of father Brumoy in 1742, the *Histoire de l'église gallicane* begun by Longueval. The assiduity and application with
which he accomplished this latest task, as well as the quality of
his work, brought him to the attention of his superiors, who were

[1] 'Notice historique sur le P. B., par un directeur de séminaire [de Baudry]' in Berthier, *Les Psaumes* (Lyon 1831). R. Boileau, in the preface to Berthier's *La présence de Dieu*, as well as de Bau- dry's 'Notice historique,' state that Berthier taught philosophy at Rouen, but Montjoye in his *Eloge* makes no mention of this assignment.

then seeking a man capable of organizing their *Journal de Tré-voux*[2]. The publication, as we have seen, had fallen into its earlier errors of disputes and contradictions. In addition, its editors were not sufficiently conscientious in the preparation of the *Journal*. Montjoye tells us that Berthier's predecessor 'had all the talents, all the qualities one might wish in a scholar, but he was not sufficiently industrious.'[3] The Jesuits found their man in Berthier, and in January 1745 he was named editor-in-chief of the *Journal de Trévoux*.

Berthier's serious attitude toward his duties has already been seen in Chapter i, and his aim of moderation and conciliation has similarly been mentioned. A few words, however, will be useful to illustrate how he sometimes went about avoiding a quarrel. One such means was to notify a contributor to the *Journal* in advance of publication as to how his article would be criticized in the *Mémoires*, thus ironing out any disagreement privately. An example of this may be seen in a letter to Grosley concerning an article he had submitted on Hannibal. The editor wrote: 'I am very disposed to use your critique on Hannibal's age; and if you judge it appropriate, I shall insert it as soon as possible in our Journal: but I cannot avoid adding a few notes to it — and here is approximately what I shall observe.'[4] Berthier then continues with four and a half pages of comments which he intends to insert in the Journal.

A further example of Berthier's attempts to avoid disputes is visible in a letter written by the Jesuit editor to an editor of the *Journal des savants*. The *Journal de Trévoux* had reviewed a history of Germany wherein the author was shown to have borrowed much of his material almost verbatim from other modern writers. The *Journal des savants* later published a review of the

---

[2] Boileau states of Berthier: 'Sa réputation d'écrivain sérieux lui vint de son *Histoire de l'Eglise gallicane*, ouvrage commencé par Longueval, mais qu'il continua et où il éclaircit divers points de discipline de l'Eglise de France avec une grande érudition' (Berthier, *La présence de Dieu* [Montreal 1952], p.3).

[3] *Eloge historique*, p.32.

[4] Bibliothèque Nationale, Nouv.acq. franç.803, p.88.

same history stating that the author 'took great care to examine things himself and in their sources.' Berthier begins his letter: 'I have the honour of addressing you with that confidence which your kindness towards me permits.' After summing up the purpose of his letter, he goes on to say that in view of the fact that some people have considered the article written by the addressee to be a criticism of that written in the *Journal de Trévoux*, he thinks it best to write to the *Journal des savants* privately rather than make a public issue of the matter, and he suggests that the latter publication take it upon itself to correct the false impression because, 'the public, persuaded by the reputation of the *Journal des savants*, could think that the author had in fact always consulted "the sources".' This would be preferable to having the *Journal de Trévoux* contradict their article, continues Berthier, because, 'as we have in hand enough material to prove all the literary adoptions made by P. B., the historian of Germany, it would be difficult for the public not to see the justice of our cause.' He wishes to avoid the necessity of contradicting a fellow journalist because of the consideration due to the *Journal des savants* and those who work on it. Therefore, concludes Berthier: 'Je m'adresse à vous parce qu'il me semble que vous avez fait quelques extraits de l'histoire d'Allemagne et parce que vous pouvez mieux que personne écarter toute occasion de mécontentements réciproques. Permettez que je compte sur votre bonté et sur votre amitié'.[5]

Apparently, Berthier had a likeable personality and was endowed with a considerable amount of tact. He seems also to have had a quiet and unassuming manner. Bachaumont says of him: 'He was a simple man with very mild ways.'[6] La Harpe refers to him as 'that man universally admired by scholars for his vast knowledge, and by all Europe for his modest virtues.'[7] De Baudry, author of the 'Notice historique' in the 1831 edition of Berthier's

[5] Bibliothèque Municipale de Rouen, MS. Duputel 7, dated 7 June 1749.
[6] *Mémoires secrets*, xxii.6.
[7] 'Discours préliminaire,' *Pseautier*, i, p.vii.

Psaumes, remarks: 'Sa vertu n'avait rien de rebutant ou de farouche; austère pour lui-même, il était plein d'égards, d'attentions, de complaisances pour les autres; retiré par goût et par attrait, il ne manquait point cependant aux devoirs de la bienséance, il les rendait avec exactitude, se montrait quand il le fallait ou qu'on l'exigeait, mais ne portait dans la conversation aucun air de prétention, ne faisait jamais d'étalage de son savoir, ne parlait d'érudition que malgré lui, et toujours avec beaucoup de réserve et de modestie'.[8]

It would seem that Berthier did not discourage visitors. According to his biographer, Henrion, 'His small cell, where there was never any fire in the most rigorously cold weather, was always open to anyone wishing to consult him.'[9] Berthier himself attests to his availability when he apologizes to the marquis de Cambie-Velleron for his delay in writing: 'Vous savez bien, Monsieur, ce que c'est qu'un champ sans haie, une maison sans porte, un pays sans places fortes. Tout le monde entre, pille, dévaste; et c'est la figure toute naturelle d'un journaliste; plus il a d'ancienneté dans le métier, plus on ravage son temps, ses forces, sa bonne volonté'.[10] Nor could the criticism leveled by Montjoye at Berthier's predecessor that 'he lacked industry' be applied to the new editor. According to that writer: 'On lui écrivait de tous les côtés; on le consultait; on voulait entrer en correspondance avec lui....Il avait donc journellement une foule de lettres à lire, une foule de réponses à faire: il avait à surveiller le travail de ses coopérateurs, à s'occuper de sa propre rédaction, à lire un nombre considérable d'ouvrages écrits en toutes langues, sur toutes sortes de matières....

---

[8] Berthier, *Psaumes*, i, p.xxii. The 'Notice historique' of the Paris 1829 edition was written by Henrion, but that in the Lyon 1831 edition quoted above is by de Baudry.

[9] 'Notice historique' in Berthier's *Psaumes*, i, p.xiv. In connection with the lack of heat in Berthier's room, a postscript in a letter from the Jesuit editor to Grosley reads: 'Je vous prie d'excuser le mauvais caractère de ma lettre. Il fait un froid extrême qui empêche de transcrire quelqu'un qui est dans une petite chambre pleine de livres et sans feu'. Bibliothèque nationale, MS.803.

[10] Bibliothèque Calvet, Avignon, MS.3467.

Ajoutez à cela les visites qu'il recevait, les exercices de piété qui lui étaient commandés par son état et par sa propre dévotion, et vous aurez sans doute peine à concevoir qu'un seul homme pût suffire à porter un fardeau dont tout autre eût été écrasé'.[11]

In addition to his regular duties, Berthier found time to continue working on the *Histoire de l'église gallicane* to which he had added six more volumes by 1749.

Since it has been stated that Berthier strove towards impartiality in all matters except those dealing with church and state, it might be well first to clarify this statement, particularly as regards his views on the monarchy. As will be seen more clearly in the chapters dealing with Diderot and the *Encyclopédie*, the Jesuit editor, according to his own lights and sympathies, was intransigent when it came to religious questions. His defense of the monarchy, however, since it was not a doctrinal question, was not motivated so much by his religious fervour as it was by practical considerations. It is true that Berthier was convinced that a monarchy wherein the king was as a father to his people was the ideal form of government because as he stated in 1762, 'paternal authority, model of all government is the work of nature, or rather, of the one who is its author.'[12] This, however, did not preclude any other form of government: 'From this it does not follow that all governments must be a paternal monarchy; it follows only that the monarchical form is the first and the most natural.'[13] His defense of the monarchy for France was similar to that of Montaigne. After discussing the merits of various forms of government, Berthier concludes: 'Au reste toutes ces théories de gouvernement sont inutiles, puisqu'elles se réduisent à désirer que chaque gouvernement soit bien réglé, qu'il n'abuse point de son pouvoir, et qu'il rende les sujets heureux. Quand ces avantages se trouvent, il importe peu de disputer sur les caractères particuliers de chaque gouvernement. Tous sont bons, et il ne s'agit plus que

[11] *Eloge historique*, p.71.
[12] Berthier, *Observations sur le Con-* trat social (Paris 1789), p.44.
[13] ibid., p.45.

de se tranquilliser dans la possession de celui sous lequel on est né'.[14]

The vices which are found in a monarchy are indicative of poor administration and do not reflect on monarchy as a form of government, since the same vices could be found in any poorly administrated government, argues Berthier: 'Ce qui dépeuple les états, ce sont les guerres, le défaut de travail, les tributs trop onéreux, le luxe répandu dans toutes les conditions, etc. Or ces choses peuvent se trouver dans les républiques qui entreprennent trop ou qui sont mal gouvernées'.[15] When Rousseau identifies tyranny with monarchical power, Berthier calls this false and excessive because 'there have been tyrants in republics, and indeed the tyranny of several is the most unbearable of all tyrannies.'[16] Nor is Rousseau right in stating that democracy is above monarchy because only petty intriguing men succeed in the latter form of government. Intrigue is not indigenous to the monarchical form of government, retorts the Jesuit critic: 'Faction, impetuosity, and enthusiasm very often prevail in popular elections over prudence, moderation and wisdom.'[17] There are disadvantages in all forms of government, and the political theorist should not set out to demolish one form in particular, and, he continues: 'Il ne faut presser contre aucune forme de gouvernement, ce qui n'est que le vice de ceux qui gouvernent. L'essentiel est d'exposer, sans partialité, les avantages et les désavantages de chaque gouvernement, de convenir qu'il se trouvera des inconvénients partout, et d'apprendre aux hommes à tirer parti de toutes les positions où ils se trouvent'.[18]

[14] *ibid.*, p.147. This would not apply to a despotism, of which Berthier states: 'Ce n'est point un gouvernement mais l'abus de tout gouvernement, quel qu'il soit' (*ibid.*, p.197).
[15] *ibid.*, p.196.
[16] Berthier, *Observations*, p.193. A similar idea is expressed by Berthier in an article in the *Journal de Trévoux* wherein he states that despotism, which he calls 'l'excès ou l'abus de tout gouvernement quelconque,' is not confined to monarchy but 'le despotisme peut avoir lieu même dans la démocratie, comme on l'a vu quelquefois à Rome et à Athènes' (Jan.1761, p.320).
[17] *Observations*, p.160.
[18] *Observations*, pp.148–49.

Since we have a monarchy, Berthier adds, let us strive for a good one. After all, the monarchy has the advantage of being not only the most natural form of government but the most stable as well. Should we try to change it, 'the resistence which the people would show toward the princes would bring on seditions, civil wars, and perhaps the ruin of the state.'[19] This would be self-destruction because 'in general, civil war is the greatest misfortune which can come to a state.'[20] Since, in the words of Rousseau, 'there is no government so subject to civil wars and internal agitations as the democratic or popular because there is none which tends so strongly and continuously to change form,' this leads Berthier to conclude that 'this reason would prove that democracy is the least natural of all governments and the least capable of bringing about man's happiness.'[21] Thus democracy is looked upon with suspicion by the Jesuit editor chiefly because it appears to him to be too unstable, and prone to bring about civil strife and unrest, whereas 'there remains in the monarchical government, tempered by laws, a spirit which is approximately even; there even remain invariable principles whereas republics often change their maxims, even those which are fundamental....I am speaking especially of democracy.' In view of this, even if the monarch happens to be a bad one, 'I ask whether it would be better to suggest, as does m. Rousseau, principles of dissension and even revolt, than to teach men to live tranquilly under whatever administration may be in existence?'[22] This does not mean that the abuses of a régime were to be condoned or ignored. The rulers have specific duties toward their subjects. They must not occupy the throne without having any regard for the welfare of their people. 'Their policy must not consist in being whatever passions or caprice make of them; they must take to heart the interests of their people.'[23]

That Berthier was aware of and condemned the abuses of his age is manifest in his solicitude for the plight of the peasants and

[19] *Observations*, p.153.
[20] *Observations*, p.202.
[21] *Observations*, p.143.

[22] *Observations*, pp.169–72.
[23] *Observations*, p.173.

workers who to him were the real wealth of the nation. It was his
opinion that 'for the man who thinks about it, the humble labourer
who works for the good of society is more respectable than the
proud rich man who dazzles him . . . by the external brilliance
which surrounds him, and who obtains so many advantages from
society without being useful to it.'[24] In the same vein, Berthier
pictures the abuses of the court which result from 'the most shame-
ful prostitution of power' when a king is weak in the government
of his household. He writes: 'De là, en effet, les profusions de do-
mestiques, des charges entassées sur la tête de l'autorité, des hon-
neurs jetés dans le sein de l'infamie, le trésor de l'état livré au
pillage de l'importunité, et une troupe d'illustres oisifs abreuvés
du sang d'un peuple laborieux'.[25] With such a view of the court,
it is no wonder that, when it was rumoured that Berthier might
be attached to the court as tutor to the king's children, Bachaumont
remarked: 'This scholar, of simple and mild manner, will be very
much out of place in that world.'[26] Similarly, the abbé de Baudry,
relating in his 'Notice historique' the Jesuit editor's repugnance
to his assignment at the court notes: 'Il vivait donc très . . . retiré,
très appliqué à la prière et à l'étude, voyait fort peu de monde, ne
se mêlait que de ce qu'il regardait comme ses devoirs, et montrait
partout une discretion, une prudence et une modestie qu'on ne
pouvait s'empêcher d'admirer'.[27]

The revulsion which Berthier felt against the arrogance, luxury
and hypocrisy of courtly life, as well as the corresponding solicitude for the 'peuple laborieux,' stemmed from his deeply religious outlook stressing as it did the brotherhood of man under
God. This is illustrated in Berthier's review of an 'Essai de l'éducation' wherein the author develops his thesis that noblemen
should not be educated with the bourgeois children but should

[24] *J. de T.* (Dec.1746), p.2606. In the same article the 'riche désœuvré' is pictured as one who 'nous importune et dévore la substance du vrai pauvre' (p.2607).
[25] Bibliothèque nationale, Nouv.acq. franç.6280, 'Discours sur la fermeté,' p.17.
[26] *Mémoires secrets*, i.117.
[27] 'Notice historique' in Berthier's *Psaumes*, p.xviii.

rather have private tutors since, having been born to command, they should not have to undergo the same education as those born to obey. The editor disagrees, declaring: 'Les jeunes gens ne prennent que trop tôt un certain air de hauteur, qui n'est bon qu'à les faire oublier, ce qu'ils ne doivent jamais ignorer, qu'ils sont hommes comme les autres et qu'en quelque situation qu'ils puissent se trouver, la modestie, l'humanité, la subordination, la dépendance sont des vertus qui leur sont nécessaires, et qui bien loin de les avilir, relèvent beaucoup l'éclat que leur donne la naissance'.[28]

The insistence on Christian virtues, particularly humility and charity, permeates most of Berthier's writings. He had a bleak, Rousseauistic outlook on the evils of his day, principally because, in his view, such virtues were becoming rare. The doctrines being preached by the 'esprits-forts,' he felt, by striking against Christianity, were destroying the curbs to man's selfish instincts and were giving free rein to his passions. 'They have prided themselves as philosophers,' he declared, 'and they have attacked the foundations of behaviour, laws and reason. They have spoken of humanity and they have become attentive solely to self-interest, which is so often hard, inhuman, despotic and unjust.'[29] When Trublet prescribes rules for social behaviour, Berthier replies, 'Of these rules we prefer those which recommend kindness, charity and benevolence to those which teach the art of pleasing.'[30] To the remark by Trublet that 'a man is indeed fortunate who looks first at the good in things and in people,' Berthier replies pessimistically: 'A coup sûr un tel homme, s'il converse ou s'il écrit, doit être insipide et ennuyeux à la longue; car le siècle est plus méchant que bon, plus critique qu'admirateur: mais qu'importe? Cet homme, après tout, sera droit, honnête, vertueux. Le siècle a-t-il quelque chose de meilleur à lui donner?'[31]

The remedy for the evils in the existing monarchy was to be found in the proper education of the future king. The ideal being

[28] *J. de T.* (Nov.1747), p.2240.
[29] *J. de T.* (Feb.1760), p.473.
[30] *J. de T.*, p.483.
[31] *J. de T.* (Feb.1760), p.483.

a paternal monarchy wherein the ruler's first concern would be the welfare and happiness of his people, heirs to the throne were to be educated in 'all the principles of equity, humanity, goodness, and beneficence.' In addition, it would be necessary 'to give them lessons in all virtues,' and forewarn them against all vices, 'especially against the poison of flattery and against voluptuousness.'[32] However, 'The purest virtue in a soul incapable of firmness is a precious treasure entrusted to the most fragile vase.'[33] The task of the prince's tutor was to strengthen his character by impressing upon him the need for firmness. This Berthier tried to do when he was named assistant in the education of the young dauphin, and even during his exile (after 1764), by means of various 'discours' written at the request of the king. In the only one that has come down to us, the 'Discours sur la fermeté,' Berthier, after suggesting 'Recte et fortiter, justice et fermeté,' as the motto for the future Louis XVI, goes on to show, almost prophetically, what will happen to his kingdom if he is too weak: 'Il est pour un ministre un art d'enchaîner un roi faible. C'est de l'affaiblir de jour en jour encore davantage, de le transporter pour toujours du trône des affaires au berceau des plaisirs; de l'endormir profondément et au point que la clameur publique ne puisse le réveiller; de ne lui offrir dans de courts intervalles de veille que des objets d'ennui, de dégoût et de terreur . . . d'environner son sceptre d'épines, et lui rendre suspects ses plus fidèles sujets pour les lui rendre odieux, de forcer ceux qu'on ne peut lui rendre odieux à devenir rebelles, . . . de mettre sans cesse entre son Peuple et lui, pour empêcher leur communication réciproque, le fantôme de la gloire, ou l'épouvantail des soupçons, de se rendre nécessaire ou formidable à ses yeux, de faire de l'état une espèce de labyrinthe où il craigne de s'égarer sans Dédale, ou une espèce d'enfer où il ne puisse rester sans Hercule; de prévenir son inconstance par sa lâcheté, de lier sa faiblesse par sa sottise, de l'abrutir pour

---

[32] *Observations sur le Contrat social,* pp.166–67.

[33] Bibliothèque nationale, Nouv.acq. franç.6280, 'Discours sur la fermeté.'

45

le fixer. C'est ainsi que Richelieu conduisit jusqu'à sa mort la France et Louis XIII, malgré la résistance de l'une et l'inconstance de l'autre, montrant à l'univers que le grand secret d'asservir les peuples est de les étonner, et que le grand secret d'asservir les rois est de les intimider'.[34]

The danger of this condition, continues Berthier, is that the ministers who succeed one another are more interested in strengthening their own position than in carrying out the duties of their post, and the state, in consequence, crumbles into ruin. The welfare and happiness of a society consists 'in the certain and tranquil possession of all natural rights, and that possession is always uncertain without a protective authority which maintains liberty against license and property against usurpation.'[35] This sustaining authority is lacking when the ruler is weak, and the nation becomes divided against itself. Then 'force, which is always useful when it is guided by law . . . always necessary when it comes to its aid to prevent great evils, ceases to be the shield which defends the people, and is nothing more than the club which crushes them.'[36] Under these conditions, he continues, even anarchy would be preferable to the weakness of a king who, while retaining the title of power, 'has allowed its exercise to pass into the hands of a multitude of tyrants. When there is no longer a sovereign, everyone has an interest in reestablishing the government and everyone has a right to do it.'[37]

These are harsh words when we consider that only a few years earlier, when writing his *Observations sur le Contrat social*, Berthier had rejected the view that in a monarchy the sovereignty remains with the people who have a right to reassert that sovereignty if the king fails in his duties to the kingdom. At that time Berthier had replied to Rousseau by saying that such a doctrine would lead to sedition and revolt. To say that even in a monarchy the community remains sovereign, he had stated, 'is in effect to recognize neither monarchy nor aristocracy.' This the Jesuit editor had

[34] 'Discours', p.9.
[35] 'Discours', p.11.
[36] 'Discours', p.11.
[37] 'Discours', p.11.

rejected saying, 'The people or the community are not the only sovereigns we should recognize among men; in the monarchy, the king is also sovereign'.[38] He had even gone so far as to say: 'The authority of the sovereign continues independently of the sentiments and the affections the subjects might have.' It is easier to defend a good king than a bad one, he had conceded, 'but that bad one will still have the right to command.'[39] Perhaps Berthier is writing here for the benefit of his pupil who is to be the future Louis XVI, and his seeming acceptance of the principle of the people's right to revolt may be only an attempt to impress the lesson on his charge. However, in view of the fact that Berthier is writing his 'Discours' while in exile and after having seen the Jesuits suppressed in France partially because of the weakness of Louis XV in asserting his objections to the move, it is not inconceivable that he is beginning to look more sympathetically on Rousseau's theory.

To underline his idea that the monarch's first concern should be the welfare of his people, Berthier proceeds to show the prince the effects on the masses when this condition of tyranny has come upon a nation due to the weakness of the king. When he abdicates his power by not using it, begins Berthier: 'L'autorité est déplacée mais elle existe encore dans tous les Agents intermédiaires qui la prostituent; elle est la honte du Monarque; mais elle est en même temps le désespoir de ses Peuples. Ils sont enchaînés par le respect dans le temps qu'ils sont écrasés par la violence. Ce triste esclavage n'a plus de bornes que la durée du règne léthargique qui le vit naître; car le brigandage public imite l'action et parle le langage des Lois; toutes se taisent à l'exception de celles qui condamnent le Peuple à l'obéissance et dont on abuse même pour imposer silence à ses plaintes'.[40] He concludes by declaring: 'Let the happiness of your people be the first, most intense, most active of your desires: it will be the principle of that courage without which there is no firmness.'[41]

[38] *Observations*, p.105.
[39] *Observations*, p.151.
[40] MS.6280.
[41] *ibid.*,p.34. The emphasis through-

It has already been stated that Berthier was uncompromising in questions of religion. To him, the church should be intolerant 'as regards dogma and morality.' It would be inconsistent, he asserted, to maintain the Catholic religion to be the true religion established by Christ 'and that nevertheless it permit error to be taught.' However, stated Berthier, 'It would be wrong to confound Catholic intolerance with the zeal for persecution.' Christian virtues preclude the use of violence. The church 'combats violence as much as it does error; it recommends charity as much as the integrity of faith.'[42] Nor did he see any conflict between religious and scientific truths. Since religious truths as known through revelation are beyond the scope of human reason, he argued, 'a true philosopher limits his search where he cannot reasonably penetrate.' The 'incrédules' are those who 'did not know sufficiently the difference between the method for believing the mysteries of religion, and the method for fathoming the sciences.'[43] The unbelievers have attempted to place faith in opposition to reason to avoid believing in revealed truths, argued the Jesuit editor. 'They have alleged . . . the impossibility of reconciling mysteries with the first principles of truth: that is only an illusion; the procedure of false philosophy.' There is no conflict

out the 'Discours' on the need for firmness and the evils of weakness in a king shows the accuracy of Montjoye's remark: 'Il paraît, au reste, que le Père Berthier avait acquis une connaissance parfaite du caractère du prince destiné à régner après Louis xv' (*Eloge*, p.99).

[42] *J. de T.* (March 1762), pp.726-27.

[43] *J. de T.* (Nov.1747), pp.2257-58. An illustration of this may be seen in Berthier's reaction to Diderot's statement in his *Pensées philosophiques*: 'Si la religion que tu m'annonces est vraie, la vérité peut être mise en évidence et se démontrer par des raisons invincibles. Trouves-les ces raisons. Pourquoi me harceler par des prodiges?'

The journalist remarks: 'C'est confondre les méthodes; demander de la géométrie, où il ne faut qu'un rapport de témoins, et vouloir procéder par des axiomes d'évidence, où l'on ne doit discuter que des faits. Quelle manière de raisonner est-ce là? . . . Il est question de savoir si Dieu s'est révélé, s'il a fait des prodiges en témoignage de cette révélation: voilà des questions de fait. Je puis et je dois raisonner pour les résoudre: mais comment? de la même façon qu'on développe des points historiques . . . méthode de fait, méthode de rapport, de témoignage.' *J. de T.* (May 1748), pp.1050-51.

between faith and reason, he affirmed. 'Human reason is sufficient to assure that the mysteries do not contradict natural intelligence; but it is insufficient to penetrate the mysteries themselves.' He then accuses the unbelievers of refusing even to consider the evidence for revelation, and adds: 'This resistence is an insult to reason.'[44] Because of this outlook, scientific discoveries will not be attacked by Berthier but he will, of course, attack anyone attempting to utilize those discoveries to discredit religion. As regards those churchmen who attacked valid scientific theories simply because they did not hold the same views, they would, the editor felt, be proven wrong.

We find this attitude reflected in Berthier's answer to Voltaire's charge that the church retards scientific progress. He replies, in what could be an allusion to the Jansenists and the Sorbonne, that if the spirit of Christianity 'recommande aux sociétés savantes de respecter et de conserver le dépôt de la foi, il ne gêne ni l'établissement ni les travaux utiles de ces sociétés, etc. Mais arrive-t-il quelquefois que dans le sein même de la religion, des particuliers traitent avec trop de rigueur leurs semblables, pour des systèmes indifférents ou pour de simples opinions? Ce sont des inconvénients tantôt légers en eux-mêmes; tantôt punis par le ridicule de ceux qui les ont fait naître; tantôt désavoués par la société entière des sages'.[45]

To Berthier, new scientific discoveries, far from endangering religion, inspired one to a greater admiration for the creator, and he encouraged clerics to engage in scientific inquiry. When the abbé Sigorgne publishes his *Institutions Newtoniennes*, Berthier tells his readers that, in this author 'on continuera de trouver un physicien profond qui ne s'est pas borné à l'intelligence des questions nécessaires aux séminaristes, et qui a compris heureusement pour l'avancement de la philosophie, qu'il n'est pas indécent aux ecclésiastiques d'étudier à fond le merveilleux mécanisme de l'univers: objet bien capable de nous inspirer de la vénération et de la reconnaissance pour le créateur'.[46]

[44] *J. de T.* (March 1762), p.717–23.   [46] *J. de T.* (Dec.1747), p.2448–49.
[45] *J. de T.* (July 1759), i.1702.

In such matters as scientific investigation, since they were not involved with religious doctrine, the Jesuit editor urged complete liberty and a scientific attitude. He decried the extreme partisanship with which the exponents of various theories defended their 'système' to the exclusion of all others, thus becoming blind to the good in other theories. The scientist should certainly adopt a hypothesis, he felt, but should be ready to abandon it when something better developed. This is discussed in a review of Nollet's *Essai sur l'électricité*. Before considering the essay itself, Berthier asks his readers what is the best method for the scientist to follow in investigating natural phenomena: 'Must he, after a great number of observations, not even try a physical explanation?' or is it better to 'establish first of all principles based on these new phenomena, publish boldly and in an affirmative tone what its cause, its secret mechanism might be?' Both are 'ridiculous extremes; two effects of too little and too much confidence,' and both are prejudicial to the progress of science. Nollet is then praised for having used the proper approach: 'M. l'abbé Nollet . . . sait éviter ces deux écueils. Il a fait beaucoup de tentatives, il a réfléchi sur mille effets du tube, du globe, des corps électrisés, soit immédiatement soit par communication, et il se croit autorisé par là, non à prononcer encore sur le principe de tant de merveilles, mais à donner des ouvertures, à insinuer des probabilités, à commencer une théorie, qui pourra s'avancer dans la suite. Il fait comme tous les sages observateurs de la nature, qui tâchent de la surprendre dans ses opérations délicates; qui déclarent ce qu'ils ont eu l'avantage de découvrir; qui soupçonnent ce qu'ils n'ont pu pénétrer encore, et qui forment de leurs découvertes, de leurs conjectures, un tout qu'on appelle système; prêts de l'abandonner quand on trouvera quelque chose de mieux, mais déterminés à le suivre, à le perfectionner, tant qu'ils ne verront rien de plus plausible'.[47]

Of the two extremes, Berthier probably felt that the dogmatic 'esprit de système' was the most harmful; throughout his writings

[47] *J. de T.* (Feb.1747), pp.324–25.

on science we find the same desire to avoid partisanship in scientific questions, and an attempt to weigh the merits of all theories. In reviewing a translation of Needham by Trembley, for example, the journalist shows again his aversion for dogmatic theories when he declares of observers of natural phenomena: 'La candeur et la bonne foi leur sont encore plus nécessaires que la patience et la sagacité. Il est si naturel de se laisser séduire par l'esprit de système! et alors on oblige les observations de se plier au système qu'on a adopté. D'ailleurs les observateurs sont comme des voyageurs; ils aiment à décorer leurs découvertes de circonstances singulières et merveilleuses dans le dessein de plaire ou d'appuyer une hypothèse chérie. On ne doit rien craindre de semblable de m. Trembley et de m. Needham'.[48]

One reason for his admiration for Needham was founded in part on the scientist's cautious approach in stating his findings. When noting that Needham has not yet decided whether the bladders found on shrimps and which give birth to soles are sole embryos or shrimp embryos, the editor approves of this caution saying: 'One sometimes gains much with intelligent readers by not taking a decisive or dogmatic tone. The wise doubts of an author who knows how to evaluate the strength of proofs, persuade more than the assertions of the dogmatizers.'[49]

In approaching the controversy over Cartesian versus Newtonian physics, the Jesuit editor decried the extreme partisanship of both sides. Speaking of Descartes and Newton he stated: 'These two chiefs, each at the head of a large army, have chosen a battlefield where all their troops and war machines can be deployed; on either side, no one must join the enemy, but one must do his utmost to crush him.'[50] While it is visible from his writings on the subject that Berthier prefers Newton to the 'rash partisans of the horror of the vacuum,'[51] his was not a blind adherence to

[48] *J. de T.* (April 1750), p.858.
[49] *J. de T.* (April 1750), p.868.
[50] *J. de T.* (Dec.1747), p.2468. In the same article he had remarked of their disciples that 'chacun se croit bien fon- dé à défendre sa doctrine, et à détruire toute doctrine nouvelle dont il est incommodé' (p.2199).
[51] *J. de T.* (Feb.1747), p.324.

all of Newton's 'système'. As in the case of Needham, he admired Newton's approach and his experimental method. 'The English philosopher,' he tells his readers, 'grants nothing to hypotheses.... Experimentation alone shows him the path he must tread.' Continuing his review of Newtonian physics, Berthier declares: 'Dès le commencement des *Institutions Newtoniennes*, on voit claire-ment une opposition irréconciliable entre Descartes et Newton.... Le premier, raisonnant sur des notions métaphysiques, admit le plein et se déclara même pour l'impossibilité du vide. Le second s'appuyant plus sur les faits, ... décida non-seulement que le vide n'était pas impossible, mais qu'il existait'.[52]

In reviewing a textbook on experimental physics which considers 'the principle of the vortices' as 'incontestable,' Berthier declares: 'Oserait-on croire au contraire, que tandis qu'on s'obstinera à expliquer par-là la pesanteur, cette question sera irrésoluble, et qu'il faut recourir à un principe qui rayonne du centre à la circonférence pour ramener les corps de la circonférence au centre? Le tourbillonnement ... ne peut avoir rien de commun avec le mouvement de la pesanteur.'[53] The Jesuit journalist did not think that the Cartesians would ever accept the principle of gravitation because 'it would be the total destruction of those vortices.'[54] He considered gravity to be 'the weak point of Newtonianism,' unless it was viewed as a result of the sustaining hand of God. 'What is more incomprehensible than this mutual tendency, if one does not see it as a continuous impulsion by the creator!' If we view it in this way, then many mysteries of nature can be explained, he continues, and he proceeds to apply the theory to the solar system.[55]

---

[52] *J. de T.* (Nov.1747), pp.2204–05. In a similar vein, Diderot, seven years later, was to contrast rationalist philosophy with experimental philosophy, saying of the former, 'Elle dit hardiement: "on ne peut décomposer la lumière": la philosophie expérimentale l'écoute, et se tait devant elle pendant des siècles entiers; puis tout à coup elle montre le prisme, et dit: "la lumière se décompose"' (*Œuvres*, ii.20–21).

[53] *J. de T.* (Jan.1745), p.62.

[54] *J. de T.* (Nov.1747), p.2208.

[55] *J. de T.* (Nov.1747), p.2209.

The following month, Berthier continued his review of the *Institutions Newtoniennes*, and after having explained the effect of the moon on the tides according to Newton's theory, he indicated that the author, the abbé Sigorgne, had not said much about Newton's *Optica*. 'The little he says about it, nevertheless, gives a high idea of Newton. Where can one find more sagacity, more dexterity, penetration, application, geometry, and everything which makes up an extraordinary man?'[56] Newton's chronology fared less well with the Jesuit editor who, while favouring the views in Frèret's *Défense de la chronologie fondée sur les monuments de l'histoire ancienne contre le système chronologique de m. Newton*, offered a few words of conciliation for the partisans of Newton by adding to his criticism: 'Qu'on n'imagine pas, dans l'illustre Anglais, cette qualité inférieure au titre de géomètre. Il y a moins de vérités dans la chronologie de Newton, que dans sa géométrie: doit-on s'en étonner? Les objets sont différents; la chronologie porte toujours en tout ou en partie sur des faits; la géométrie est toute fondée sur des rapports et sur des calculs. Mais on retrouve ici le même génie'.[57]

In dealing with the Descartes versus Newton controversy, Berthier adopted a conciliatory attitude toward both sides. Even when he favoured the views of Newton, he gave credit to Descartes for his genius. In reviewing Newton's theory of light, for example, the editor turns to that of Descartes and says: 'What he had invented on this subject is not the least ingenious part of Descartes's system, and even if it were completely demonstrated that he was in error, it would still be indeed glorious to have been mistaken in this manner.'[58] In this regard, Berthier held the view that we should not wonder that Newton made greater advances than his predecessors in explaining the universe. Scientific knowledge was cumulative and the pioneers should not be condemned for being wrong but rather praised for having opened the way for new advances. We have already seen his views concerning Aristotle,

[56] *J. de T.* (Dec.1747), p.2471.
[57] *J. de T.* (Oct.1758), pp.2335–6.
[58] *J. de T.* (Dec.1747), p.2468.

who was useful 'when we had nothing better.' On another occasion, the journalist had stated: 'Aristote a excellé dans les belles-lettres, dans la politique, dans la dialectique, dans la morale: il a connu de la physique et de l'histoire naturelle plus de choses que la plupart de ses devanciers n'en avaient même aperçu ou soupçonné. L'expérience et le progrès des arts ont ajouté depuis à ses découvertes: cela est-il fort surprenant?'[59] Similarly, in the case of Newton and Descartes: 'Le journaliste n'entreprend pas de poser dans la balance deux philosophes d'un aussi grand poids que Descartes et Newton. Quel bras serait assez fort pour les tenir en équilibre ou pour les abaisser l'un au préjudice de l'autre? ... Ce que désirerait le journaliste, c'est qu'on considérât que Descartes et Newton n'ont pas vécu ensemble. Descartes a précédé, et a ouvert le chemin de la véritable physique. Quelle gloire pour son nom!'[60]

As we have seen in the preceding chapter, the *Journal de Trévoux* was to Berthier a burden assumed out of obedience to his superiors. His primary interest had always been in theological and devotional writings. With the suppression of the Jesuits in 1762 the way seemed clear for him at last to devote himself completely to religious pursuits. When the order had been dissolved, he wrote to a fellow Jesuit, father Wastelain: 'I wish to see the end of this struggle, after which I shall leave Paris and go to some solitary place to meditate on eternity.'[61] And in fact, refusing to continue the *Journal de Trévoux*, Berthier went to a Trappist monastery for a retreat, and then asked to be admitted to that order. The general of the Jesuits, however, believing that the

[59] *J. de T.* (Jan.1761), ii.310.
[60] *J. de T.* (Dec.1747), p.2472. Elsewhere Berthier had said: 'C'est à Descartes que nous devons l'art de méditer, de raisonner, de réfléchir, de découvrir: et quiconque aime la raison et les sciences du raisonnement, doit la plus profonde admiration à ce vaste génie' (*ibid.* [Dec.1746], p.2777). In 1734 Voltaire reflected a similar view-

point in his *Lettres philosophiques* when he stated that 'celui qui nous a mis sur la voie de la vérité vaut peut-être celui qui a été depuis au bout de cette carrière. Descartes donna un œil aux aveugles; ils virent les fautes de l'antiquité et les siennes. La route qu'il ouvrait est, depuis lui, devenue immense' (M.xxii.132).
[61] *Mémorial catholique*, p.237.

storm which had disbanded their own order was only temporary, and recognizing Berthier's value to the society, refused to grant him permission.

The controversy over the suppression of the Jesuits had aroused many violent accusations against them, and Berthier had not been spared. Some well-meaning friends of the ex-editor had apparently attempted to defend him by showing him as a sincere, good-hearted man who had been duped and who had not realized the perfidy of the order to which he had belonged. Bachaumont recounts this view as follows: 'Ce jésuite [Berthier] convient qu'il ouvre enfin les yeux; qu'il n'avait jamais lu les *Constitutions* que depuis qu'elles ont été épluchées si sévèrement, et qu'il s'aperçoit qu'il était, sans s'en douter, l'espion du général, à l'égard de tous les savants dont il parlait dans ses ouvrages; qu'il recevoir [*sic*] fréquemment des lettres de ce supérieur, qui l'interrogeait successivement sur leur compte; qu'il lui répondait dans la sincérité de son cœur; en sorte que ce chef pouvait connaître leurs écrits dans son journal, et leurs mœurs et leur caractère par ses réponses'.[62]

The inaccuracy of this version became clear when the ex-editor was singled out by his superiors to take up the pen in defense of his society. In a *Recueil des lettres sur la doctrine et l'institut des Jésuites*, Berthier begins by expressing his surprise at the recent course of events. He continues by stating: 'Cependant, monsieur, au milieu de tant d'orages les personnes qui se flattaient de connaître le monde et la position des affaires, n'imaginaient pas qu'on fût si près d'en venir aux dernières extrêmités, ils croyaient que des discours injurieux, des libelles insultants, des procédés pleins d'animosité, se borneraient à l'humiliation de cette société, et que le système de leur anéantissement était un projet chimérique; mais ce qui se passe aujourd'hui fait voir toute la grandeur du mal'.[63]

Berthier then goes on to answer the numerous accusations which were being levelled against the Jesuits, beginning with the charge

---

[62] *Mémoires secrets*, i.69–70.   [63] *Recueil des lettres*, p.3.

that because the *Journal de Trévoux* had announced a new edition of a book by the German Jesuit Busenbaum, the *Journal*'s editors shared his casuistic doctrine which Berthier calls 'very false.' The ex-Jesuit replies: 'There is nothing more simple than the whole procedure for the announcement of publications. Yet today it is the source of a terrible cry against the journal and against the journalists.' Actually, he goes on, the *Mémoires* merely transcribed the résumé sent by the publisher, who naturally would praise the book he was trying to sell. 'But should this praise written in a corner of a journal when no one yet was inculpating Busenbaum or his commentator, be a reason for reproaching the journalists today?' Are they to be held responsible for a book which they only pointed out, and could they have forseen that thirty years later 'a violent storm would be raised against this book printed more than fifty times under the eyes of pastors and magistrates?'[64] He then considers other writers who have been quoted in condemning the Jesuits and points out that Bossuet in 1691 had named Tolet and Azor's books as 'works fitting for the instruction of ecclesiastics in the diocese of Meaux.' Similarly, 'saint Francis de Sales judged the works of Lessuis as very useful,' as did many other pious men. But in condemning the Jesuits of France, he continues, 'why bring up these doctrines so generally proscribed? Has any school been formed recently determined to uphold them? Have they been seen in the modern writings of Jesuits?' He then names such French Jesuit writers as Petau, Antoine, Bourdaloue, Cheminais and Colombière, and concludes: 'It is by these that one must judge the teaching going on in the schools of the Jesuits of France, and not by ancient books written in foreign countries.'[65]

[64] *Recueil des lettres*, pp.12–13. A few years later Diderot reiterated the charge when he wrote in the *Encyclopédie* under 'Scandaleux': 'L'éloge de l'ouvrage de Busenbaum, qu'on lit dans les *Mémoires de Trévoux* est scandaleux' (*Œuvres*, xv.84). While still editor of the *Journal* Berthier had strongly censured 'les casuistes catholiques dont le saint siège a si justement condamné un grand nombre de propositions' (*J. de T.* [May 1754], p.827).
[65] *Recueil des lettres*, pp.15–18.

After a detailed analysis of the constitutions of the Jesuits, with explanations of their various provisions, Berthier answers the accusation that the general of the Jesuits has unlimited power and must be obeyed blindly. He shows how the constitutions have rules providing for the deposition of the general, and even for his exclusion from the order if there is sufficient cause. Nor has the general any power 'to require a submission which would violate principles and which would contradict the rule of faith and morals.'

The accusation that really hurts the ex-Jesuit is the suggestion of disloyalty to France. He returns to the point that the loyalty of a French Jesuit should not be impugned by quoting foreign authors, and referring to the declaration of allegiance made by the Jesuits of France, he exclaims: 'Mais si les Jésuites qui sont taxés d'avoir tenu ces sentiments répréhensibles n'ont point été Français, si ce sont des particuliers qui ont écrit en Italie, en Espagne, en Allemagne, etc., en quoi ces ouvrages mêmes répétés et multipliés peuvent-ils rendre suspecte la sincérité des déclarations données par les Jésuites en France?'[66] Such a foreign author was Molina, of whom Berthier notes: 'Molina is but an individual doctor whom we are not obliged to believe, and Molinism . . . has no more authority than other theological opinions. Indeed, Molina's book . . . is a rare work which the Jesuits hardly read and which a number of them have never seen.'[67]

After a discussion of alleged privileges obtained by the Jesuits, Berthier concludes his defense by stating: 'Tel est, monsieur, le compte exact que j'ai cru devoir vous rendre, et de la doctrine des Jésuites, et de leur institut. Attaqués dans ces deux points, ils ont la ressource d'une conscience qui ne se reproche rien; mais le public ne perce point les replis du cœur, et en attendant que le souverain juge dévoile toutes les vérités, il était très nécessaire de prendre la défense d'une société longtemps utile, et que ses malheurs avertissent encore d'être plus attentive à bien remplir les devoirs de sa vocation'.[68]

[66] *Recueil des lettres*, p.115.
[67] *Recueil des lettres*, p.115.
[68] *Recueil des lettres*, p.153. It would seem that Berthier's defense of the

For a time the ex-editor's future seemed uncertain. He may have been offered a position in a Paris church, for we find the refusal of an offer in a letter to the 'chanoine' of the church of Paris, dated 2 July 1762, in which Berthier states: 'Il me serait impossible de déterminer mon état futur: les circonstances et le cours d'événements seront probablement le cri de la providence auquel il se faudra rendre. Je ne disputerai plus par des arguments contre votre ingénieuse bienfaisance; mais je prévois toujours qu'il ne me sera pas possible d'accepter vos offres'.[69] A month later, it seemed that the ex-Jesuit would again be obliged to resume his journalistic career. On 17 August 1762 Bachaumont records the rumour that 'they are still saying that the former father Berthier is going to Rome, where his general is calling him to preside over a journal.'[70] In the meantime, however, king Louis xv had indicated to the minister of Paris, comte de Saint-Florentin, that he wanted the governor of his children, the duc de La Vauguyon, to obtain Berthier as 'associate in the education of the children of France and keeper of his library.' When de La Vauguyon notified Berthier of the king's decision, the ex-editor was torn between his own desires and a sense of duty to the king. Montjoye quotes him as saying: 'I was quite embarrassed at first; but what could I do? I ended by resigning myself to it. After all, I had to obey the king.'[71] Bachaumont records the event as follows: 'The abbé

Jesuits was intended to be a final appeal to the king for his intervention on their behalf. The Jansenist historian Guettée says of the ex-Jesuit's *Recueil des lettres*: 'Ces religieux élevèrent la voix, comme s'ils avaient été de tendres et innocents agneaux sacrifiés par les ennemis de la religion et du bien . . . . Leurs plaintes, adressées au roi sous forme de lettres, ne produisirent-elles aucun effet, malgré l'éloquence avec laquelle le p. Berthier s'appliqua à les rédiger' (*Histoire de l'église de France* [Paris 1856], xii. 97). The fact that Berthier was chosen to be the spokesman for the Jesuits of France speaks well for their confidence in their colleague, and seems to nullify Bachaumont's previously quoted view that the ex-editor was an unwitting dupe of his order.

[69] quoted by Henrion in his 'Avertissement' in the posthumous publication of Berthier's *Psaumes*, i, p.xix.

[70] *Mémoires secrets*, i.116.

[71] *Eloge historique*, p.90. Similarly, de Baudry, in the 'Notice historique' in Berthier's *Psaumes*, after pointing out that the Jesuit editor 'roulait toujours dans son esprit des projets d'une vie pauvre, obscure et retirée,' indi-

Berthier is no longer to go to Rome; they are attaching him to the court, where he is named as instructor of the children of France.'[72]

We have already seen Berthier's aversion to the life at court. He seems to have lived a rather secluded and retired life while at Versailles, shunning society and turning toward the religious pursuits to which he had always aspired. It was at this time that he began writing his *Réflexions spirituelles*, and the editor of the posthumous publication of that work, the abbé Du Pinet, describes the ex-Jesuit's activity as follows: 'Des notes jetées à la marge du manuscrit apprennent non-seulement les jours qu'il se mettait à ce travail, mais encore l'heure où il prenait la plume. C'était souvent au milieu de la nuit, dans le temps que le reste des hommes donne au repos.... C'est à Versailles qu'il commença son "Commentaire" [on the first epistle to the Corinthians], le premier de l'année 1763, à trois heures du matin. Il le continua le 29 du même mois; il le poursuivit la nuit du vendredi saint, le reprit, à Compiègne, le six août même année; il s'y mit de nouveau le premier janvier 1764 à trois heures du matin'.[73]

Berthier was not to remain long as instructor to the children of the king. On the promulgation in 1764 of more rigid regulations concerning the Jesuits, he left Paris and began his exile at Baden. Bachaumont notes the event by stating, not too accurately: 'The life of the court did not agree with him and, unable to renounce a society of which he was always a member in his heart, to escape the persecutions in 1764, he had retired to Bourges where he died.'[74] Berthier remained a short time at Baden and later accompanied father de La Noue to Offenburg, where he remained until 1776. After his expulsion from France he decided never to have anything

---

cates that when called to Versailles, Berthier 'surmonta la répugnance qu'il avait à se montrer dans une région si étrangère, si inconnue pour lui; il obéit donc et se rendit à la cour' (p.xvi).

[72] *Mémoires secrets*, i.117.

[73] 'Discours préliminaire' of Ber-

thier's *Réflexions spirituelles*, i, pp.v–vi.

[74] *Mémoires secrets*, xxii.5–6. Bachaumont wrote this in 1783 upon the death of Berthier. Actually, he did not go to Bourges until his return from exile in 1776.

more printed nor to accept any honours. Montjoye quotes him as saying: 'I have made a vow to renounce all dignities, both ecclesiastic and secular.'[75] His years of exile were not without literary activity for him, however, but they were devoted almost exclusively to religious writings. True to his vow, he refused an invitation from the empress Marie-Thérèse to come to Vienna, as well as a request from the duke of Milan that he accept the post of librarian at his capital. Other than several manuscripts written at the request of the duc de La Vauguyon for the education of the dauphin[76], the only additional secular production from the pen of the ex-Jesuit was a memoir concerning the coronation of Louis XVI. The archbishop of Rheims being ill, Berthier had been asked who should perform the coronation ceremony. He decided in favor of the 'coadjutor of Rheims,' but he later learned that his 'mémoire' had been published against his wishes. In this connection he wrote: 'They have caused me to be unfaithful to the resolution I had made never to have anything more printed.'[77]

Another secular pursuit engaged in by the ex-editor at this time was his study of oriental languages, but the major part of his energies was devoted to a series of religious works including an ascetic work in five volumes, begun at Versailles and entitled, *Réflexions spirituelles; Isaïe traduit en français avec des notes et des réflexions;* and *Les Psaumes traduites en français avec des notes et des réflexions,* in eight volumes[78]. Concerning the translations of the psalms, La Harpe, after discussing the difficulties of translation, states in the 'Discours préliminaire' of his own *Pseautier:* 'Il me fallut donc avoir recours au travail des savants; et le travail

[75] *Eloge historique*, p.129.

[76] Montjoye states that the duc de Berry, through the duc de La Vauguyon, wrote Berthier in Offenbourg thanking him for his manuscript for the education of the prince and asking for more on various subjects (*Eloge*, p.151). Montjoye also mentions that the manuscript has been lost, but the *Essai sur la fermeté*, uncovered and exposed to the light of day for the first time in the present study, although it is undated, is probably the manuscript in question.

[77] Quoted by Montjoye, *Eloge*, p.118.

[78] Henrion tells us that Berthier knew Hebrew, Greek, Latin, English, German and French ('avertissement' of Berthier's *Psaumes*).

le plus parfait en ce genre, sans nulle comparaison, celui sans lequel je n'aurais pas même entrepris le mien, celui qui m'a fourni des secours dont je n'aurais pu me passer, est le pseautier en huit volumes du père Berthier'.[79]

When Louis XVI mounted the throne of France, the seventy-two year old ex-Jesuit asked his permission for père de La Noue and himself to return to France. They arrived in Paris in June 1776, and almost immediately de La Noue proceeded to Orleans, while Berthier went to Bourges to live with his brother and nephew. On 9 December 1782 the 'assemblée du clergé' granted him a pension of 1000 francs, but he did not live to enjoy it. Two days later he fell down a flight of stairs, and he died on the thirteenth of December at the age of seventy-eight[80]. Bachaumont records his death by saying: 'Le chapitre de la métropole a rendu un hommage public à ses vertus et à ses talents, en lui donnant une sépulture distinguée dans son église [Saint-Etienne de Bourges]. La dernière assemblée du clergé venait de le gratifier à son insu d'une pension'.[81]

His epitaph, written in Latin by father Brothier, reads, as translated by the abbé de Baudry:

Au Dieu Immortel, Gloire

Guillaume-François Berthier, Prêtre, né à Issoudun, entra chez les Jésuites l'année 1722. Il s'y distingua par la simplicité de ses mœurs, par l'éclat de ses vertus, par son zèle pour la défense de la religion, par ses connaissances en littérature, et par l'étendue et la profondeur de son érudition. En 1762, nommé garde de la bibliothèque du Roi, et adjoint à l'éducation de Louis XVI, Roi très-Chrétien, il édifia la cour par sa modestie et par sa piété. Les derniers temps de sa vie ont été tous consacrés à Dieu, à des œuvres

[79] *Pseautier* (Paris 1797), i, p.vi. La Harpe goes on to say: 'L'auteur était un des plus savants philologues et des plus judicieux critiques de l'Europe' (*ibid.*, p.vii).

[80] 'Notice historique' in Berthier's *Psaumes*, i, p.xxiv. Henrion, in the 'Avertissement' to the Paris 1829 edition of the *Psaumes* erroneously sets the date at the fifteenth (p.xxi).

[81] *Mémoires secrets*, xxii.6.

de piété et de charité, et à la méditation continuelle des années
éternelles. Il mourut le 13 Décembre 1782, âgé de plus de 78 ans,
et pleuré de toute la ville. Par une délibération du chapitre, cet
excellent citoyen a été inhumé dans ce Temple pour y servir toujours de modèle et d'encouragement à la vertu. Heureux les morts
qui meurent dans le Seigneur. Apocal. xiv, 13.[82]

After his death, Berthier's library and papers were inherited by
a widow in Issoudun who had no idea of their value. As a result,
his books and manuscripts were sold to anyone who wanted
them, including the local grocer. His books containing marginal
notes were sold by the pound or at bargain prices. Fortunately,
friends were able to obtain some of his manuscripts, including the
Réflexions sur le Contrat social, and the major religious works
already mentioned, and these were published posthumously.

Such was the man who was one of the chief foes of the *philosophes*. While unquestionably their opponent, he was a man of
his century, and as such, held many ideas in common with them.
His criticisms of the abuses in the monarchy, for example, bear a
strong resemblance to Fénelon's *Lettre à Louis XIV*, his concern
over the peasant's plight parallels that of La Bruyère, while his
views on education reflect many ideas presented by Diderot in
his *Education d'un prince*. Similarly, his views on tolerance, science
and other issues of his day show, as we have seen, a considerable
degree of enlightenment. Had he been born a century earlier,
Berthier probably would have reacted to the French eighteenth-
century enlightenment in much the same way as did Castel or
some of his other predecessors. Being of a later generation, Berthier reflects, in no small measure, the drive toward social, economic, political and moral reform which preoccupied advanced
thinkers of the age. On the other hand, if Berthier found himself
at odds with many of the leaders of the enlightenment, it was
because of his profound religious sentiment which made silence

[82] 'Notice historique' of Berthier's
Psaumes, i, p.xxvii.

impossible when his religion was attacked. It is from this point that their chief differences stem, and the relations between Berthier and the *philosophes* depend to a large extent on their attitude toward Christianity. How the Jesuit editor, then, approached the problem of dealing with the *philosophes*, who, despite certain common interests, were among his most formidable adversaries, is a primary concern of our inquiry.

I

Montesquieu

The friendship between Montesquieu and father Castel, who was on the editorial staff of the *Journal de Trévoux* before 1745, had a great influence on the relations between the celebrated political philosopher and the *Journal*. Castel went to great lengths to build up his friend in the eyes of his fellow-Jesuits, even witholding information from them when such information might jeopardize Montesquieu's reputation with the society. Wishing also to afford his friend more publicity, as well as to enhance the *Journal de Trévoux* with the writings of such a noted author, Castel sought to persuade his friend to submit articles for publication in the *Mémoires*. When, for example, he learned that Montesquieu was preparing to write his *Considérations*, he wrote asking him to send a chapter to the *Journal de Trévoux* 'as an essay to sound out the public,' and suggesting that he include a short letter developing his plan[1]. In another letter written the same year (1725) Castel again pleaded with him to send something for publication in the *Journal* saying: 'Everything is good, I say: everything from your pen is good ... even a fleeting idea is worth presenting.' Castel then concludes with the reminder that it was by filling journals with such 'random ideas' that Leibnitz gained a reputation[2]. Montesquieu refused these advances, however, perhaps fearing to be too closely connected with the Jesuits. In 1726 he wrote to J. J. Bell that the reason he did not contribute to the *Journal* was that 'I had received word from Paris that the journal

[1] Montesquieu, *Correspondance* (Paris 1914), i.109.   [2] *ibid.*, i.112ff.

in question had displeased the minister; I thought it useless to appear in a work which would not be read and in which, besides, it was more prudent not to appear.'[3]

Whatever Montesquieu thought of the Jesuits, his friendship for Castel did not seem to suffer. While in the process of writing his *Considérations* he submitted the manuscript to Castel with the request that he point out any passages the Jesuit editor might consider unorthodox. When such passages were indicated with suggested changes, the author went to great lengths to comply —so much so that the journalist wrote to him saying: 'I should not have asked for so many corrections and circumspections in your work.' But he shows his pleasure by adding: 'Still, I can only applaud the generous decision you have made to tone down everything.'[4] When the *Considérations* were completed Castel sent the author a copy of the extract which he intended to insert in the June 1734 issue of the *Journal de Trévoux*, stating that he had obtained permission to make it longer than usual. He then suggests that Montesquieu see the chief censor before publishing his book to make sure that it be not suppressed, and he adds: 'Je sais bien que si le reviseur de notre journal ... allait soupçonner seulement que le livre souffrît la moindre difficulté aux sceaux, qu'il est même fait par l'auteur des *L. P.* [*Lettres persanes*], il n'en laisserait pas passer l'extrait sans consulter ses maîtres. C'est pourquoi même je vous prie que ce que j'ai l'honneur de vous dire ne soit dit qu'entre vous et moi, sans aucun ami confident: nous réveillerions le chat qui dort. Je ne le dirais pas ici à l'ombre d'un seul jésuite! Encore ne croirai-je cet extrait imprimé que lorsqu'il sera lâché au public. Chut!'[5]

---

[3] *ibid.*, i.176. Another factor influencing his decision may have been his dislike for the then editor-in-chief, Tournemine. In a letter to Guasco explaining why he stopped frequenting the abbé Oliva's salon, Montesquieu states: 'Il ne fallut pas moins que le despotisme et les tracasseries d'un père Tournemine pour me faire quitter une société dont j'aurais voulu profiter' (*ibid.*, i.326).

[4] *ibid.*, i.302–03. Further details concerning corrections made by Castel may be found in Schier, *L. B. Castel*.

[5] *ibid.*, i.311ff. Donald Schier states of the review of the *Considérations*:

The secretive and somewhat melodramatic manner in which Castel handled the *Journal*'s review of the *Considérations* seems rather exaggerated when one considers that the policy of the Jesuits toward the *philosophes*, particularly before 1751, was one of conciliation, in an effort to win them back to the church. Robert R. Palmer tells us: 'If apologists for the Church were relatively liberal in countenancing the new system of thought, it was in the hope . . . that the authority of the Church might be better preserved. Such was especially the policy of the Jesuits....To keep the Philosophes Catholic, they turned to philosophy themselves'.[6]

Berthier's review in 1748 of the second edition of the *Considérations* seems to bear this out. Whereas Castel's review refrained from praising the author or from naming him, Berthier's praise is liberal, and renders Castel's early fears somewhat unnecessary. The new editor-in-chief begins by saying: 'Ce livre, déjà bien connu, méritera, pour chacune des éditions, l'accueil qu'on fait toujours aux bons ouvrages. L'auteur trouve le moyen d'y réunir le ton philosophique avec les richesses de l'histoire, les profondeurs de la politique, et les agréments du style'.[7] After comparing Montesquieu's attitude toward the Romans with that of Saint-Evremond in his *Sur les divers génies du peuple romain*, Berthier concludes that Montesquieu is 'more studied, more profound, and borders more on the paradoxical,' and that he has 'the charm of novelty.' The review then terminates with the reflection: 'Everywhere there is to be noted a depth of learning devoid of any pedantry; an ease in reflection, inspired by a good mind fashioned by good breeding.'[8]

The *Esprit des lois* was another matter, however. Montesquieu

'Even here Castel was compelled to be careful, for the "reviseur" of the *Journal* (probably Berthier is meant) was not to know that the *Considérations*, which had been published anonymously, were by the author of the scandalous *Persian Letters*' (*L. B. Castel*, p.32). The 'reviseur' was more probably Rouillé, since Berthier, who at this time was teaching philosophy at Rennes, did not assume direction of the *Journal de Trévoux* until 1745.

[6] *Catholics and unbelievers*, p.22.
[7] *J. de T.* (Sept.1748), p.1876.
[8] *J. de T.* (Sept.1748), pp.1878ff.

did not submit this manuscript to Castel for review, but later admitted to him 'that he had purposely hidden it from him, looking upon this work as being exclusively his own.'[9] When the book appeared, Castel wrote to Montesquieu complaining that he had not been able to obtain a copy, and that Berthier was going to review it in the *Journal de Trévoux* 'without having my zeal for you . . . . Someone is needed who can give the right tone, a certain tone . . . . I know very well that I can do it.'[10] The review, in the form of a 'Lettre au P. B. J. sur le livre intitulé, *L'Esprit des loix*,'[11] begins in the same laudatory tone as that of the *Considérations*, but adds a 'mais.' The editor states: 'En général, je puis vous assurer que *L'Esprit des loix* part d'une plume très légère, et très exercée à écrire; que l'érudition y est répandue sans affectation et sans pédanterie; que l'auteur a une connaissance singulière de l'histoire ancienne et moderne; de la jurisprudence des Grecs et des Romains, des Asiatiques et des Européens. Mais je ne vous dissimulerai pas non plus qu'il est souvent aussi faible de preuves que fertile en conjectures et en paradoxes'.[12]

Berthier goes on to state that the author 'does not show enough consideration toward religion,' and reveals his main preoccupation with the book by announcing that his aim is 'to point out to you whatever injures religion in this work, whether directly or indirectly.' Such passages include Montesquieu's excusing of suicide in England, 'for to look upon it as a malady caused by the nature of the climate is to excuse it.' If suicide were caused by climate, 'the climate and the physical constitution of men were the same in England three or four hundred years ago: was the

---

[9] Sommervogel, *Notice historique*, p.xlviii.

[10] Montesquieu, *Correspondance*, i.83. At this time Castel had already been removed from the editorial staff of the *Journal*.

[11] Berthier, in common with nearly all eighteenth-century journalists, often presented his critiques in the form of letters to himself from anonymous writers. When Diderot, in a letter, chided him for this, Berthier answered: 'Nous croyons savoir quand il convient de nous en écrire, et quand il convient de parler à découvert: tout se fait avec une droiture et un zèle qui n'ont en vue que le bien des Lettres et la satisfaction du public' (*J. de T.* [Feb.1751], pp.569ff).

[12] *J. de T.* (April 1749), p.719.

practice of suicide at that time more noticeable there than elsewhere?' But it is clear, the editor continues, that suicide in England
is not caused by climate but is rather 'a sort of fashion which has
become established there, either through vanity . . . or more probably through irreligious principles.' Similarly, he attacks Montesquieu's statement that 'the law of polygamy is a matter of
arithmetic.' Population or climatic factors did not cause polygamy, Berthier answers, the responsibility lies with false religions
and loose morals. Other passages challenged include one on the
divorce laws in Mexico and among the Maldives, the calling of
'a good policy' the Roman practice of killing their deformed or
ugly children, and an uncomplimentary remark on the celibacy of
the clergy. The *Journal* refutes these and then goes on to the
principle for political laws regarding religion which Montesquieu
offers, that is, 'It would be a very good civil law, when the state
is satisfied with the religion already established, not to allow the
establishment of another.' The editor reminds the author that
had this principle been followed, Christianity would never have
been established in the world, nor would missionary work be
justified in countries where pagan religions are established[13].
After considerably detailed refutations of various points in the
Esprit des Lois, the article concludes as follows: 'Je finis ici ma
très longue lettre, qui n'attaque pas l'auteur de l'*Esprit des loix*
par animosité ou par jalousie, puisque je ne le connais pas. Je
puis vous assurer au contraire, que j'applaudis de grand cœur aux
talents de cet écrivain et que je ne refuserais pas d'entendre ses
raisons, s'il en avait de bonnes à produire pour sa défense'.[14]

Two months later, Barbot sent Montesquieu a copy of Berthier's
article stating, 'I do not wish to influence your judgment on this
letter but I am persuaded that the author of the *Esprit des lois* will
not answer this critique.'[15] That was in fact Montesquieu's decision. However, in January 1750, when it was rumoured that the
Esprit des lois might be placed on the index, the author wrote to

---

[13] *J. de T.* (April 1749), p.737.
[14] *J. de T.* (April 1749), pp.740–741.
[15] Montesquieu, *Correspondance*, ii. 168–169.

the duc de Nivernais to explain his silence. He writes: 'Il parut, il y a environs un an, une lettre dans le *Journal de Trévoux*, par laquelle on prétendait prouver qu'il y avait dans le livre de l'*Esprit des loix* des choses qui intéressaient la religion; comme les objections ne me paraissaient pas fondées, je crus qu'il était plus sage de ne pas répondre. Depuis ce temps, les *Nouvelles ecclésiastiques* ont fait, sur le même livre, une terrible sortie; j'ai fait une réponse qui paraîtra dans quatre jours d'ici; j'y détruis si bien toutes les objections qu'on m'a faites, qu'il ne reste pas pierre sur pierre et, comme les deux ouvrages critiqués ne contiennent que les mêmes objections, la réponse qui fait tomber l'un fait tomber tous les deux'.[16] Montesquieu then promises a new edition in which he will remove the objectionable passages from his book and he concludes with the question: 'Now, is it not better that I myself remove all pretexts for condemning me, than if I were to be condemned?'[17]

The promised *Défense de l'Esprit des lois* appeared shortly thereafter and, except for an answer on a purely literary question, Montesquieu ignored the *Journal de Trévoux* article, confining himself to the criticisms of the *Nouvelles ecclésiastiques*. Castel immediately wrote the author to tell him that he was urging all his Jesuit colleagues to read the *Défense*, and explaining to them that the author refrained from answering the *Journal* 'through consideration, esteem, and love for all of us.'[18] Castel tried to convince the Jesuits that the *Défense* was in fact proof of Montesquieu's high regard for their society. While most of his colleagues went along with Castel's view, the letter continues, Berthier, who was convinced that the book contained irreligious principles in disguise, immediately inserted an answer, which was to appear in the next issue of the *Journal*, to the literary question touched on by Montesquieu[19]. In his letter, Castel tells his friend

[16] Montesquieu, *Correspondance*, ii. 248.

[17] *ibid.*, ii.250.

[18] *ibid.*, ii.258.

[19] *ibid.*, ii.255. In reviewing the *Défense*, Berthier, in a letter to the editor, begins by saying: 'Ce mot n'est pas une réponse à toute ma lettre dont les

that he must not ignore Berthier but must clear himself of the theological charges because that is what is being held against him. He writes: 'Voilà mon raisonnement sur tout cela: ou vous êtes un ennemi théologique ou vous ne l'êtes pas. Si vous ne l'êtes pas, il faut la défense complète; si vous l'êtes — quod Deus advertat! — mon amitié, très vive, très pure assurément, ne peut ni ne veut vous absoudre. Amitié de toutes parts, ou pour que vous ne soyez pas, ou pour que vous ne paraissiez pas ennemi théologique. Je vous dis que vous ne serez jamais absous si notre journal, si mon amitié effective ne vous absout'.[20] Castel concludes his letter by telling his friend that he has succeeded in convincing his colleagues of the author's good will toward religion but the only one not amenable to his persuasions is Berthier: 'Now, you have only this enemy; he is not really an enemy, but, but .... '[21]

The willingness of most of Castel's Jesuit colleagues to accept the *Esprit des lois* as inoffensive to religion illustrates to an extent the intellectual climate of opinion at the time. A spirit of worldliness, with its emphasis on civilized living and sociability, and a naturalistic outlook were not characteristic only of the *philosophes* but were shared by everyone including the clergy. The Jesuits as well as many other Catholics stressed rational living and the cultivation of human nature, rather than an ascetic or saintly ideal. The arguments of some of the *philosophes* for a natural standard of morality apart from revelation were to be found in Jesuit writings as well, but whereas the *philosophes* tried to separate moral truth from revealed religion in order to show that the church was unnecessary, the Jesuits desired to strengthen the

objections subsistent, mais à une critique purement littéraire que je faisais d'une citation de Diodore de Sicile. L'objet est de la plus légère conséquence et dans ce point particulier je donnerais volontiers gain de cause à l'auteur de l'*Esprit des loix* et à son apologiste.' He then goes on to discuss Montesquieu's answer to the *Journal,* and then

pointedly remarks: 'Je ne m'imaginais pas que dans une lettre qui contient vingt-trois pages de vos mémoires, ce fût là le seul endroit qui pût attirer l'attention d'un apologiste de l'*Esprit des loix*' (*J. de T.* [Feb.1750], pp.533ff.).

[20] *ibid.*, ii.257.
[21] *ibid.*, ii.258.

church by showing that reason not only imposed moral duties but also showed men that natural religion necessitated and supported revelation. Even the Sorbonne was assimilating worldly ideas, and dissertations on politics and history were more frequent than those on theology[22]. In general, the atmosphere was one of varying and ill-defined views. The clergy itself was divided on many issues and the Jansenist movement was still very strong. 'Everywhere one could see only confusion, incoherence, anarchy in religious as well as financial, political and literary matters.'[23]

Berthier, while a man of his century, was not quite so optimistic about progress as were many of his colleagues. The trend toward irreligion could only lead society to its ruin, and he felt that something must be done 'to halt us on the edge of the abyss into which irreligion, lack of probity, disorder in morals, blindness and hatred toward truth are precipitating us.'[24] Many of his fellow-churchmen seemed unaware of how far they were going into the abyss envisioned by Berthier, and it was not until the scandal engendered by the Prades affair that they realized there was a line beyond which no Christian could go[25].

On 18 November 1751, a young abbé, de Prades, presented at the Sorbonne a thesis bearing the title, 'Quel est celui sur la face duquel Dieu a répandu le souffle de la vie?' The thesis was actually an exaltation of natural religion, and presented an exposition of philosophical principles taken from Locke and from d'Alembert's 'Discours préliminaire' to the *Encyclopédie*[26]. In spite of the unorthodoxy of the thesis, the Sorbonne accepted it, thus making it part of the official doctrine of the university. As soon as the

[22] cf. Palmer, *Catholics and unbelievers*, pp.12–15.

[23] Belin, *Le mouvement philosophique au 18ème siècle*, p.21.

[24] *J. de T.* (Aug.1758), p.2085.

[25] Palmer states: 'The Prades affair was for many people the first revelation that the *Encyclopédie* was in the hands of religious unbelievers' (*Catholics and unbelievers*, p.118).

[26] the theory is sometimes suggested that the thesis was written by Diderot. Belin states: 'Non seulement la personnalité de de Prades, mais encore la conduite des Encyclopédistes dans l'affaire nous fait penser qu'il n'a été qu'un instrument entre les mains de ces derniers.' *Le mouvement philosophique*, p.203.

thesis appeared in public it was attacked by the Jesuits, who were quick to see the danger of its principles to religion. The Jansenists, who had been suppressed by the official arm of the church, seized the opportunity for revenge against the Sorbonne and accused it of having passed during the preceding years a whole series of doubtful opinions on miracles. The *parlement*, which represented the Jansenist point of view, insisted that the Sorbonne retract its decision. To condemn the thesis after having passed it meant a condemnation of the Sorbonne itself, but there was no alternative. Paris was alarmed, a plot against the faith was suspected, and even the Sorbonne, the pillar of orthodoxy, seemed tainted with forbidden ideas. De Prades was condemned in January 1752, his thesis was expunged from the record of the university, and he himself deprived of his academic standing and degrees. The Encyclopedists were suspected as the perpetrators of the incident and, as Palmer has pointed out, 'it soon became clear that the Encyclopedists were not simply gifted writers of whom educated Catholics might approve, though with reservations, but were determined and implacable enemies of the Church who must be tirelessly combatted.'[27] Even before the Prades affair Berthier had begun to realize this, particularly after his quarrel with Diderot in February 1751[28]. This apprehension felt at the increasing volume of *philosophe* publications caused the Jesuit editor to be particularly alert for the irreligious implications in the works he reviewed in the *Journal*. In the case of the *Esprit des lois* matters were complicated by Castel's earnest desire to protect his friend whether he was guilty of the accusations or not, but Berthier remained firm in his intention of exposing what he considered to be an attack on Christian principles, and in addition to his articles in the *Journal de Trévoux*, he assisted Claude Dupin in preparing a three volume *Observations sur un livre intitulé l'Esprit des loix*[29].

[27] *Catholics and unbelievers*, p.20.
[28] see below the chapter dealing with Diderot and the *Encyclopédie*. The Prades affair did not occur until November of the same year.
[29] de Backer, in his *Bibliothèque des*

When he heard of Dupin's refutation, Montesquieu wrote to the abbé Venuti: 'There is going to appear in Paris an ample criticism, written by m. Dupin, the farmer-general; thus, here I am cited at the tribunal of the tax office, as I was cited by the *Journal de Trévoux*.'[30] While taking Dupin's work lightly, Montesquieu was probably more concerned with the attack in the *Journal*. Possibly with the desire to avoid any difficulties with the authorities, which could be brought on by further attacks from the Jesuits, the author arranged a meeting with Berthier[31]. Whether as a result of this meeting, or whether out of consideration for Castel, Berthier refrained from further mentioning the *Esprit des lois* within the lifetime of either Castel or the author[32].

In view of Castel's loyal defense of Montesquieu, it is not surprising that the noted philosopher should call for him when on the point of dying. The controversy concerning the sincerity of Montesquieu's reception of the sacraments before his death may never be fully resolved—determining a man's true motivation necessarily leads one into the realm of conjecture—but it does not seem unreasonable to suppose, in view of their lifelong friendship, that Montesquieu did in fact wish to see Castel. This assumption is particularly plausible inasmuch as it is reported in one of the eye-witness accounts of Montesquieu's last days, that by mme Dupré, who was strongly anti-clerical[33]. In a letter to Suard, she recounts

écrivains de la Compagnie de Jésus, says that Berthier helped Dupin, 'en ce qui concerne le commerce et les finances' (i.1378). Chaudon states that Dupin's refutation of the *Esprit des lois* is 'extrêmement rare, car il n'en existe que 12 exemplaires' (*Dictionnaire universel*, ii.513).

[30] Montesquieu, *Correspondance*, ii.215.

[31] Castel writes to his friend: 'Il me revient dans le moment que vous devez dîner avec P. B. chez l'évêque de Sen [lis], et que vous l'avez demandé' (*ibid.*, ii.256).

[32] Castel, however, did write an unpublished defense of his friend in connection with Berthier's criticism concerning Diodorus of Sicily, in the form of a 'Lettre au R. P. Berthier sur un passage de Diodore.' It is not known whether the letter was ever sent to Berthier; cf. Schier, *L. B. Castel*, p.47.

[33] mme d'Aiguillon wrote to Guasco a week after Montesquieu's death: 'Je ne l'ai pas quitté jusqu'au moment qu'il a perdu toute connaissance, dix-huit heures avant la mort; mme Dupré lui a rendu les mêmes soins . . .' (Montesquieu, *Correspondance*, ii.577).

that Montesquieu, when seeing the name of the *curé* on the list of visitors, asked why he had not been admitted, and added that should the prelate return, he wished to see him. Upon his return, the *curé* was ushered into the sick room and he asked Montesquieu whom he wanted as a confessor. The patient replied that if he had a choice 'there was someone in Paris in whom he had great confidence, that he would send for him, and he would ask for the blessed sacrament after confessing himself.' She concludes her letter with the following description: 'Le curé s'est retiré et le Président a envoyé chercher, qui croiriez-vous? Le P. Castel Jésuite, qui est arrivé avec son second: "Père Castel, lui a dit le président en l'embrassant, je m'en vais devant." Après quoi le p. Castel a laissé le près. seul avec le Jésuite. Il s'est confessé et m. le curé de Saint-Sulpice lui a porté le bon Dieu vers les trois heures.... Après quoi, le bon Dieu, le curé et les Jésuites sont revenus très contents, chacun chez eux [*sic*]. Quant au p. Castel, il ne se sent pas de joie. Il croit avoir plus fait que François-Xavier, qui prétendait avoir converti douze mille hommes dans une île déserte'.[34]

After Montesquieu's death, Castel's Jesuit colleague Routh, whom he had brought along as confessor to the dying author, wrote his account of the event in a letter to 'Monseigneur Gualterio, nonce de sa sainteté à Paris,' wherein he first attempts to show that Montesquieu had always shown concern for religion, as for example his request that Castel educate his son in the truths of Christianity. Even after the appearance of the *Esprit des lois*, continues Routh, its author had persuaded a dying relative, m. de Marnes, to become reconciled with the church and had personally gone out to call a confessor for him; and finally, when he himself was on the point of death, 'he sent his secretary with his coach to the Jesuit college to ask father Castel, who had always been his friend, to come to see him and to bring him a confessor.' Montesquieu, observes Routh, seemed satisfied with Castel's choice and, 'since he has permitted me to publish all the information

[34] *ibid.*, ii.572–573.

necessary to justify his faith, I shall not withhold any of it.' When
he questioned the author on his beliefs, he continues, 'I can say
with the most exact truth that he satisfied me on all these matters
with a simplicity and candour which both edified and touched
me.' In reply to the question whether he had ever ceased to believe,
Montesquieu admitted 'that certain clouds, certain doubts had
come to him, as could happen to all men, but he had never had in
his mind anything irrevocable or fixed against the articles of faith.'
When asked why he had written propositions which placed his
belief under suspicion, he answered that it was due to the taste
for novelty, the desire to pass as a genius superior to common
prejudices and maxims, and the desire to 'earn the applause of
those who set the tone for public esteem.' The Jesuit confessor
then goes on to describe Montesquieu's illness, stating that during
their talk, 'he had begun to give of his own accord certain details
on the corrections which he had planned to make in his writings.
I felt it necessary to stop him in this exposition, seeing that he
lacked the strength.'[35] Routh then made Montesquieu promise
that if he regained his health he would make a public declaration
of faith, and that he would permit him to make public their interview. Routh then describes the ceremony wherein Montesquieu
received the last sacraments, and concludes by stating that besides
himself and Castel, those present were the curé de Saint-Sulpice
with two of his ecclesiastics, m. le comte d'Estillac and his wife, a
doctor, Montesquieu's secretary, and several persons unknown
to Routh, as well as many servants.[36]

This letter was printed shortly after Montesquieu's death in the
Gazette d'Utrecht and in Chaudon's *Dictionnaire anti-philoso-*

[35] according to mme d'Aiguillon,
another eye-witness, 'les Jésuites qui
étaient auprès de lui, le pressèrent de
leur remettre les corrections qu'il avait
faites aux *Lettres persanes*. Il me remit
et à mme Dupré son manuscrit, en
nous disant: "Je veux tout sacrifier à la
raison et à la religion, mais rien à la
Société [the Jesuits]; consultez avec
mes amis et décidez si ceci doit paraître"'
(*ibid.*, ii.575).

[36] Biblioteca Nacional, Madrid, *Noticias de la muerte de Monteschieu*. This
document is not the original manuscript but is labeled, 'Copie d'une lettre
écrite par le R. P. Routh, Jésuite.'

phique. Voltaire, who was later to call for a priest himself, although perhaps for a different reason, reacted to Routh's statement as follows: 'Ce fut une chose comique, dans une triste occasion, que l'empressement de ce jésuite anglais nommé Routh, à venir s'emparer de la dernière heure du célèbre Montesquieu. Il vint, dit-il, rendre cette âme vertueuse à la religion, comme si Montesquieu n'avait pas mieux connu la religion qu'un Routh, comme si Dieu eût voulu que Montesquieu pensât comme un Routh. On le chassa de la chambre et il alla crier dans tout Paris: "J'ai converti cet homme illustre".'[37]

After the death of Montesquieu, Berthier continued to maintain his silence on the *Esprit des lois* until the death of Castel in 1757, at which time he began a series of articles dealing with Montesquieu's works. In the first review of Gauchat's *Lettres critiques, ou analyse et réfutation de divers écrits modernes contre la religion*, Berthier turns to the *Lettres persanes* saying: 'Il y a encore plus d'artifice que d'esprit dans la manière dont l'auteur des *Lettres persanes* attaque notre religion. Usbeck, Français, ne serait qu'un impie, qu'un incrédule de l'ordre le plus commun.... Mais Usbeck persan est un étranger parmi nous, un voyageur Musulman: ses observations, comme ses regards, ne se promènent que sur la surface de notre culte, il n'en saisit que l'écorce, il y cherche des rapports au culte qu'il professe; il en imagine qui mettent notre religion au niveau et quelquefois audessous de sa superstition'.[38] In examining Christian doctrines and morality, continues Berthier, the Persian visitor 'confuses Christian dogmas with the scholastic systems, approved definitions with tolerated opinions, essential duties with arbitrary practices.' All these critical observations,

---

[37] M.xix.503. Elsewhere Voltaire shows his suspicion of deathbed conversions when he states: 'Les derniers moments sont accompagnés, dans une partie de l'Europe, de circonstances si dégoûtantes et si ridicules qu'il est fort difficile de savoir ce que pensent les mourants. Ils passent tous par les mêmes cérémonies. Il y a eu des jésuites assez impudents pour dire que m. de Montesquieu était mort en imbécile, et ils s'en faisaient un droit pour engager les autres à mourir de même' (M.xliii.310).

[38] *J. de T.* (Jan.1757), p.80.

notes the editor, although couched in an oriental style, are emblematic, allegorical allusions. Usbeck writes his 'impieties' quite innocently, not realizing the 'horrors' which flow from his pen; 'the oriental style is a veil which covers over the indecency of the boldest satire.'[39] Once Usbeck's reflexions are divested of their Persian garb, they become merely 'trivial impieties,' and the author of the work under review should not have bothered to try to refute them, he continues.

Turning to Usbeck's plea for tolerance, the Jesuit editor reiterates his assertion that 'in the Catholic church, intolerance flows necessarily from the infallible authority of which that church is the depositary.' Would one wish the ecclesiastical authorities to treat error and truth with 'an equality marked by indifference and impartiality'? However, the editor goes on, 'intolerance animated by a real zeal for truth is neither harsh nor cruel, but mild and charitable.' To embrace tolerance in doctrinal questions 'would be to arm oneself against God, against truth, in favour of error,' he affirms, adding: 'Depuis qu'on la prêche, cette tolérance, ne voit-on pas l'esprit républicain fermenter dans le sein des monarchies? Si l'on ne se hâte d'étouffer ce levain, on doit craindre qu'il ne cause de révolutions funestes. Quand les hommes ne sont pas retenus par le frein de la religion, ils ne sont pas si éloignés qu'on le pense, des excès où le fanatisme entraîne'.[40] Berthier concludes his article by remarking that the *Lettres persanes* advance false principles and ingenious sophisms on the prescience of God, the eternity of the world and on suicide. They cannot be examined deeply because 'these dreams of a fine wit vanish at the least effort of reason to recognize and examine them.'[41]

It would seem that after having refrained for seven years from mentioning the *Esprit des lois*, Berthier could hardly wait to give free expression to his objections after the death of Castel. The latter having died in April 1757, a lengthy article appeared two months later in the *Journal de Trévoux* wherein Berthier reiter-

[39] *J. de T.* (Jan.1757), p.82.
[41] *J. de T.* (Jan.1757), p.87.
[40] *J. de T.* (Jan.1757), p.87.

ates the criticisms he had made of the book when it had first
appeared, namely, that laws should be based on God-given universal principles rather than on expediency or relativity: 'Or, dans
le livre qu'on nous donne pour l'esprit des lois, loin de comparer
la nature et le but de toute législation humaine avec cette législation divine, loin d'approuver les lois nationales selon leur liaison,
ou leur répugnance, avec ces principes éternels et universels qui,
parmi les hommes doivent être toujours inviolables, . . . m. de
Montesquieu s'attache uniquement aux climats, aux mœurs, aux
coutumes, aux intentions des peuples particuliers'.[42]

The result, pursues Berthier, is that in Montesquieu's work the
rules of justice and injustice are arbitrary and flexible, bending to
the character and customs of each nation, and, since these customs
are only a matter of climate, the influence of the land must be the
legislator's inspiration. Turning to other matters, the editor pre-
faces his consideration of the author's attacks on religion with the
following remark: 'L'*Esprit des Lois* est un vaste labyrinthe, où
l'érudition la plus vaste, sans être la plus exacte, s'élance dans une
immense carrière; où sa trace lumineuse s'obscurcit souvent et
s'éteint dans des ténèbres ménagées avec art; où le génie également heureux et subtil s'égare et se retrouve avec aisance; où sa
main légère rompt et renoue avec adresse le fil de sa marche quelquefois tortueuse, et toujours agréable'.[43] Then follows a detailed
list of irreligious principles found in the work, such as the placing
of all religions on the same basis so that 'their truth or falseness
becomes indifferent'; the use of a deterministic standard with the
result that man's liberty and the spirituality of his soul count for
nothing; the making of vices and virtues contingent on latitude;
the placing of religions among popular customs, thus making
their acceptance dependent on the influence of climate—contentions, exclaims the critic, 'highly belied by the establishment and
the progress of Christianity in every nation in the world.' Berthier
follows with the enumeration of 'other shafts equally odious and

[42] *J. de T.* (June 1757), p.1488.   [43] *J. de T.* (June 1757), p.1490.

unjust against the Catholic religion,' after which he notes that in spite of all these attacks, some readers have seen in this book proof that the author believes and loves the Christian religion[44]. Such a mistaken view is understandable, he concludes, when one considers the manner in which the book is written: 'Ce qu'il y a de plus séduisant dans ce livre, c'est un certain air d'humanité, qui, dans toutes les pages, se mêlant à des critiques plus fines que justes, dégénère insensiblement dans un doux et dangereux relâchement: à moins qu'on n'ait le zèle comme la notion des bons principes, à peine est-on tenté de s'en défendre ou de s'en défier'.[45]

The following year, a book by Pecquet entitled *Analyse raisonnée de l'Esprit des Loix* furnishes Berthier another occasion to voice his opinions on Montesquieu's work. Before reviewing Pecquet's *Analyse*, the journalist—perhaps thinking back to the days when Castel and his Jesuit colleagues received the *Esprit des Lois* so favourably—remarks: 'The *Esprit des lois* is a work in which genius shines forth in so many ways that while reading it one has the impression of being both enlightened and dazzled.' In order to distinguish between truth and the appearance of truth, strength of character and extensive knowledge are necessary. It is easy to see that 'few people indeed have been able accurately to evaluate this famous book.'[46] When the work first appeared, Berthier continues, 'a large public incensed it so freely that individuals scarcely dared to censure it.' Later on, some censors dared criticize it but only with the greatest praise for the author. Thus some of the enthusiasm which the *Esprit des lois* had evoked at the beginning continues today. Why is this so? A glance at the work itself will give the answer, he states, and he proceeds to analyse the source of this enthusiasm: 'Dans son livre, comme nous l'avons observé ailleurs, m. le président de Montesquieu paraît le plus doux des législateurs: sensible aux maux publics, il ne vise qu'à les adoucir: indulgent pour la faiblesse humaine, il ne s'irrite que contre les excès monstrueux où elle se porte, et même

---

[44] *J. de T.* (June 1757), p.1506.   [46] *J. de T.* (July 1758), pp.1693-94.
[45] *J. de T.* (June 1757), p.1508.

l'aversion qu'il en inspire, est toujours plus philosophique que véhémente: son zèle moins éloquent qu'ingénieux n'a ni chaleur, ni mouvement fort sensibles: il n'est fertile qu'en réflexions fines. Il ne commande presque aucune vertu austère; il ne proscrit que des vices odieux. En se promenant chez tous les peuples de l'univers, s'il rencontre quelque part des habitudes ou des coutumes vicieuses, il aime mieux s'en prendre à la nature du climat qu'à la corruption de ses habitants. Il penche toujours plus pour tolérer tout, que pour rien réformer'.[47]

Montesquieu is most outspoken against intolerance, continues Berthier, which is in fact a natural prerogative of truth. The essence of truth is repugnant to an alliance with falsehood—it has a right to be intolerant of untruth. The editor then returns to his analysis of why readers are won over by Montesquieu by concluding: 'A ce fond d'idées et de sentiments si commodes, ajoutons la forme la plus séduisante, le charme d'une érudition variée, l'agrément des pensées neuves, la hardiesse des réflexions saillantes, la singularité des contrastes agréables, la magie d'un style enchanteur, où l'expression, sans être toujours pure, est toujours piquante; où les tours même les plus irréguliers, choquent moins qu'ils n'imposent; et où le sens, quoique souvent tronqué n'en paraît que plus profond'.[48] After apologizing for this long preamble, Berthier turns his attention briefly to Pecquet's book, which, he says, falls into the same error of not being always in agreement with itself, of which Pecquet accused Montesquieu, and he ends his article by saying of the *Analyse*: 'We wish that the resemblance between the style of this *Analyse* . . . and that of the *Esprit des lois*, which is its model, might be more perfect.'[49]

The October 1758 issue of the *Journal* returns to Gauchat's *Lettres critiques*, in which the critic compares Montesquieu's *Esprit des lois* with Mirabaud's *Traité de la population, ou l'ami des hommes*. 'This contrast alone,' affirms Berthier, 'makes the most just and most sensible criticism yet made of the *Esprit des*

---

[47] *J. de T.* (July 1758), p.1696.
[48] *J. de T.* (July 1758), p.1697.
[49] *J. de T.* (July 1758), p.1705.

Lois.' He points out that in the *Traité*, the author does not rely on principles of expediency for government but rather has recourse to God-given principles of justice, and Berthier adds: 'Dans l'*Esprit des Lois*, pour gouverner les hommes, on n'a que des rènes qui se plient au gré des caprices, des passions, des goûts de nations et de climat: ce sont des liens qui n'ont aucun terme immobile d'union et de force, non plus qu'aucun terme fixe et solide de tendances et de direction'.[50] In such a system, he continues, the government is merely 'an arbitrary policy, which refines upon national prejudices and local customs, and which humours them along for its own profit, for fear of opposing them to its own ruin.' The other writer, on the contrary, tries to 'purge humanity of its weaknesses and correct its disorders in order to enrich it in virtues which bring about its happiness.' He concludes by stating that the *Esprit des lois* 'does not offer any means of curing our errors and uprooting our vices.'[51]

Having thus expressed his long-withheld views on the *Esprit des lois*, Berthier no longer returned to the subject in the *Journal de Trévoux*, but when writing his *Observations sur un livre intitulé le Contrat social* (which he never published), he had occasion to refer briefly to Montesquieu in order to contrast some of his political ideas with those of Rousseau. One detail of Berthier's criticism of the *Esprit des lois* had been Montesquieu's statement that virtue was not necessary in a monarchy. The journalist had retorted that virtue should be the basis of all good governments. When Rousseau makes the same criticism, Berthier remarks: 'M. Rousseau himself has sensed this truth while reading the *Esprit des lois.*' The *Contrat social* points out that virtue is not only the basic principle of a republic, as Montesquieu asserts, but it should be the basic principle of every well-ordered state, remarks the editor. But the Jesuit critic disagrees with Rousseau when the author insists that in a monarchy sovereignty always remains with the people, and he cites Montesquieu as being also in disagreement

---

[50] *J. de T.* (Oct.1758), p.2532.   [51] *J. de T.* (Oct.1758), p.2533.

with this view, pointing out that the noted political theorist would deny that legislative authority rests always with the people. 'He did not deprive the monarch of that authority, he recognized that authority in the principal citizens when an aristocracy was the accepted government.'[52]

When in the *Contrat social* Berthier comes to Chapter VIII, entitled, 'That every form of government is not suitable for all countries,' he exclaims: 'The doctrine of Montesquieu on climates seemed to be buried with its author. Its weakness had been felt, its falseness had been demonstrated'; and he reaffirms his objections to such a view as follows: 'La liberté personnelle, et dont jouit chaque individu de la nature humaine, ne dépend point du climat: c'est la puissance de se déterminer, de choisir le bien ou le mal, de s'attacher à un bien plutôt qu'à un autre. Tout cela est dans la nature de l'homme, et non dans les qualités du climat. La liberté civile, qui consiste à vivre sous un gouvernement conforme à la raison et aux lois, n'est point non plus un fruit du climat. Il y a partout, indépendamment des degrés de la sphère, des gouvernements bons et mauvais, c'est-à-dire, des administrations dures ou modérées, sages ou passionnées, injustes ou équitables; et ces choses ne sont pas commandées par le plus ou le moins de chaleur qui règne dans les divers pays du monde habitable'.[53]

Finally, Berthier contrasts the views of Montesquieu and Rousseau concerning the latter's 'false principle of the separation of the sovereign and the government,' and decides in favour of the author of the *Esprit des lois*, pointing out that Montesquieu, unlike Jean Jacques, places the legislative power with the government whether it be monarchical, aristocratic or democratic, and the government cannot be changed unless it becomes a despotism or an anarchy. In this matter Berthier favors Montesquieu's view by pointing out that although he was not always exact in his observations on the causes and effects of the corruption of each form of government—and the editor gives examples of such

[52] *Observations*, p.142.   [53] *Observations*, p.176.

errors in a footnote—'his doctrine, after all, is more acceptable than that of m. Rousseau.'[54]

The fact that Berthier, in spite of his friendship for Rousseau, did not hesitate to point out his errors and even compare him unfavourably with Montesquieu illustrates not only a sense of equity, but especially the editor's fidelity to his main purpose, that of combatting ideas running counter to Christian principles. As will be seen, Berthier's general policy was that of remaining on good terms with a writer, even when he proved guilty of unorthodoxy in his thinking, until the journalist was convinced that he had definitely allied himself against religion. Such a policy is illustrated somewhat by his early attitude toward Montesquieu when reviewing the *Considérations*, with a change occurring upon the appearance of the *Esprit des lois*. Montesquieu, however, never made the complete and open break with Christianity which characterizes some of the other writers of the time, and so averted an open clash with his critic. Preferring to live at peace with the traditional customs and beliefs of his day, he sought to reassure Berthier of his good intentions, even arranging for a meeting with the Jesuit journalist. Such was not always the reaction of those *philosophes* who were exposed to Berthier's criticisms.

[54] *Observations*, p.205.

II

Voltaire

When Voltaire left the Jesuit Collège Louis-le-grand in 1711, it was with a regard and attachment for his former teachers which were to make his early relations with the *Journal de Trévoux* most cordial and friendly. While an occasional statement such as that made against pagan priests in *Oedipe* (1718)[1] might have been construed to suggest an anti-clerical attitude, the author's correspondence with his former teachers must have been reassuring. Thus in 1730 we find him submitting his *Henriade* to Father Porée with the following request: 'Surtout, mon révérend père, je vous supplie instamment de vouloir m'instruire si j'ai parlé de la religion comme je le dois: car s'il y a sur cet article quelques expressions qui vous déplaisent, ne doutez pas que je ne les corrige à la première édition que l'on pourra faire encore de mon poème. J'ambitionne votre estime non seulement comme auteur, mais comme chrétien'.[2]

Even while undergoing the influence of English writers, Voltaire discussed their ideas freely with Tournemine, who had been the second editor-in-chief of the *Journal de Trévoux*. Their correspondence deals with many of the problems which the *philosophe* was to develop in his later writings; such questions, for example, as the immortality of the soul, conjectures as to whether God could impart to matter the ability to think, discussions of Locke, Newton, and the like. One such letter written to Tournemine in 1735 attests to the writer's regard for the Jesuits when he states: 'L'inaltérable amitié dont vous m'honorez, est bien digne d'un cœur comme le vôtre; elle me sera chère toute ma vie. Je vous

---

[1] the lines read: 'Nos prêtres ne sont point ce qu'un vain peuple pense / Notre crédulité fait toute leur science' (M.ii.93).
[2] Best.369.

supplie de recevoir les nouvelles assurances de la mienne, & d'assurer aussi le père Porée de la reconnaissance que je conserverai toujours pour lui. Vous m'avez appris l'un & l'autre à aimer la vertu, la vérité, & les lettres. Ayez aussi la bonté d'assurer de ma sincère estime le révérend père Brumoy. Je ne connais point le père Moloni, ni le père Rouillé dont vous me parlez; mais s'ils sont vos amis, ce sont des hommes de mérite'.[3]

Similarly, in his *Temple du goût* published in 1733, the author voiced his opinion of the Jesuits by remarking that, although the Jansenists accuse them of intruding everywhere, 'the truth is that of all the religious orders the Jesuits are those who best understand literature, and who have always succeeded in oratory and poetry.'[4] While Tournemine strove to guide the young writer in his philosophical speculations, Voltaire in turn attempted to influence the Jesuits into accepting Newtonian principles. In one of his letters to his ex-teacher, Voltaire, after discussing Newton at length, concludes: 'Je souhaiterais que les jésuites, qui ont les premiers fait entrer les mathématiques dans l'éducation des jeunes gens, fussent aussi les premiers à enseigner des vérités si sublimes, qu'il faudra bien qu'ils enseignent un jour, quand il n'y aura plus d'honneur à les connaître, mais seulement de la honte à les ignorer'.[5] Three years later he contributed an article to the July 1738 issue of the *Journal de Trévoux* entitled, 'Eclaircissements nécessaires donnés le 20 mai 1738 sur les Eléments de la philosophie de Newton.'

These cordial relations were not without their ominous forebodings, however. The Jesuits may not have been too alarmed by the possibly anti-clerical bent reflected in *Oedipe*, but with the appearance in 1734 of the *Lettres philosophiques*, there could be little doubt that its author was straying from the religion he had learned at the Jesuit College. While privately deploring many of the ideas in the *Lettres*[6], the editors of the *Journal* sought to foster

[3] Best.871 (iv.103).
[4] M.viii.593.
[5] Best.871 (iv.105).

[6] in a letter dated 1734, Brumoy, an editor of the *Journal de Trévoux*, speaks of the *Lettres philosophiques*, which are

the friendly relations enjoyed with Voltaire and, ignoring his irreligious writings, praised his literary productions liberally in the hope that the errant philosopher would not drift further away from his religion. A glance at the statements concerning Voltaire in the various issues of the *Journal de Trévoux* will illustrate this attitude. In July 1724 the editors state: 'We shall speak of m. de Voltaire's *Poème de la Ligue* only when he gives it to the public himself. We owe that respect to authors we hold in esteem.'[7] Voltaire's *Histoire de Charles XII* evokes the comment that 'its style is lively, ingenious, but pure and natural. We can say that the work is well written and that the author seems to succeed in this style of writing as much as in any other.'[8] When they refer to his epic, the *Henriade*, it is with high praise: 'Ce poème n'est-il point trop célèbre et trop répandu dans l'Europe pour en donner un extrait? Véritablement, il serait difficile de le faire, sans intéresser ce qui en fait le principal mérite; à savoir la justesse du plan, la beauté singulière de la versification, et surtout l'enthousiasme et le génie qui en font l'âme'.[9] Returning to the subject of the *Histoire de Charles XII* in the following year, the editors state: 'The author sustains himself perfectly; it is his usual fire, style, and rapidity.'[10]

In January 1735 an anonymous *Lettre servant de réponse aux Lettres philosophiques de M. de V.* caused the *Journal de Trévoux* to break its silence on Voltaire's *Lettres*, chiefly because the unknown author had chosen to refute the work through insults against its author. Such a method will make people think that these are the only arguments possible against unorthodox ideas, affirms the editors, and they explain their reversal of their policy of silence on the matter as follows: 'De telles attaques, dira-t-on, méritent de telles réponses. Nous conviendrions bien plutôt qu'elles n'en méritent point. Aussi avions-nous pris le parti de laisser tomber

'against religion and the French nation,' and remarks: 'C'est dommage qu'un homme de beaucoup d'esprit ait donné dans le travers, pour se venger des coups de bâton qu'un Français lui a donnés' (*Lettres du p. Brumoy*, p.44).

[7] *J. de T.* (July 1724), p.1341.
[8] *J. de T.* (March 1731), p.389.
[9] *J. de T.* (April 1731), p.649.
[10] *J. de T.* (Sept.1732), p.1554.

les *Lettres philosophiques*, sans en faire mention dans nos *Mémoires*. Mais puisqu'on les relève, et qu'on annonce une réponse, il ne sera pas dit qu'il n'y ait que des invectives à repliquer à un livre qui attaque la religion, les mœurs, le gouvernement, et tous les bons principes'.[11]

It was a mistake for Voltaire to leave the brilliant sphere in which he had made his reputation, to dogmatize on theology, laws, and gravitation, pursue the editors. These subjects require a serious, mature, reasoning mind rather than a 'keen and salient wit which shines and sparkles.' The article then deals with the work itself, accusing Voltaire of embellishing the situation in England for his own purposes and pointing to his praise of liberty as an example: 'Who does not know that in all those bloody catastrophies of England, the people and liberty were only obvious pretexts and were really the victims of the ambition of princes or individual lords.'[12] The following month, the review of the *Lettres philosophiques* continues with a strong attack on Voltaire's statement: 'I am a body, and I think; I know nothing more about it.' The editors exclaim: 'Quel excès! c'est Dieu même qui le permet, qu'un des plus beaux esprits de notre siècle s'avilisse ainsi à dire lui-même, en parlant de lui-même; "je suis corps, etc." Nous osons sans impolitesse l'assurer, qu'il n'a pas assez d'esprit pour nous persuader qu'il n'en a pas infiniment et sans doute trop'.[13] The remainder of the article defends Pascal against some of Voltaire's statements and upholds Cartesian versus Newtonian physics[14].

The *Journal de Trévoux* did not return to the *Lettres* again but continued to give their author favourable reviews. His *Philosophie de Newton* is reviewed in numerous articles, the first of which declares: 'There is only praiseworthiness in m. de Voltaire's project of becoming a philosopher, and of rendering, if possible, the whole universe Newtonian.' The editors then show their chief

---

[11] *J. de T.* (Jan.1735), p.96.
[12] *J. de T.* (Jan.1735), pp.96ff.
[13] *J. de T.* (Feb.1735), p.320.
[14] *J. de T.* (Feb.1735), pp.320ff.

Castel was science editor at this time. See Schier, for the editor's anti-Newtonian stand.

preoccupation with the author by noting that he has spoken with decency of God and of his attributes, and stressing that he recognized, published and even avenged the rights of the creator, his power, his wisdom, even his liberty and his providence[15].

While the *Journal de Trévoux* was thus encouraging Voltaire to continue respecting religious principles, Tournemine had not ceased to correspond with the *philosophe* nor had he given up the hope of winning him back to his former religious beliefs. In August 1738 he writes his erstwhile pupil: 'Vous voilà donc poète, historien, philosophe, architecte, politique, etc., car j'ai été charmé de l'amour du bien public que vous faites paraître dans une lettre très sensée. J'ai été encore plus charmé d'apprendre plusieurs traits de votre générosité. Quand me donnerez-vous le plus sensible de tous les plaisirs? Quand étudierez-vous la religion sans prévention, sans préjugés? Elle vous plairait sans doute. Ma tendresse paternelle pour vous me le fait souhaiter ardemment et le demander tous les jours au maître des cœurs, au père des lumières; sa miséricorde et votre excellent esprit me le font espérer'.[16]

Despite Tournemine's expressions of good-will and affection, Voltaire must have felt some uneasiness at the obvious stress on the religious aspects of his *Philosophie de Newton* in the August 1738 issue of the *Journal de Trévoux*. In a letter dated 17 November 1738 to Porée, the *philosophe* reveals this preoccupation when he reaffirms his attachment for the Jesuits and adds: 'Je vous supplie si vous êtes ami de ceux qui travaillent à votre journal de leur dire que je suis votre disciple et que vous m'aimez, dic eis quia discipulus tuus sum ut mihi bene sit propter te'.[17]

The review of a new edition of Voltaire's *Elements* in the *Journal* for June 1744 probably convinced the author that the Jesuits bore him no ill-will because of his earlier irreligious writings. The editors reminded their readers of their earlier articles in August and September 1738 when the first edition had appeared, and pointed out that in those articles 'this esteem which we had for m. de V.

---

[15] *J. de T.* (Aug.1738), p.1669.   [17] Best.1586 (vii.454).
[16] Best.1530 (vii.344).

as a poet caused us to regard him when he became a Newtonian as a sort of phenomenon of which everyone wished to be a witness, we spoke of his *Eléments* only with admiration, and as of a metamorphosis.'[18] While this change from poet to philosopher came as a surprise, continues the article, philosophers were grateful to him for his writings: 'Il honorait la philosophie; il se faisait honneur à lui-même, il marchait à la suite de Newton, du grand Newton. Car il ne fallait rien moins qu'une philosophie aussi brillante par la célébrité de son auteur pour balancer tous les attraits d'une poésie heureuse. Elle avait quelque chose de plus relativement au génie de m. de Voltaire. Toute géométrique dans ses principes et ses résultats systématiques, elle devait naturellement amorcer un esprit comme le sien capable de raisonnements abstraits, et même de calculs compliqués de l'analyse'.[19]

When Berthier assumed the direction of the *Journal de Trévoux* the following year, he continued the policy towards Voltaire initiated by his predecessors, and in the first article concerning the noted writer appearing in the *Journal* under its new chief, we find the same laudatory tone. In reviewing the *Poème de Fontenoi*, the new editor begins by stating: 'Only a great master could set the proper tone; a muse well versed and frequently applauded was to be the first to celebrate so beautiful a victory.' Turning to Voltaire's answer to his critics in the 'Discours préliminaire,' Berthier upholds the author and compliments him for his moderation, saying: 'The tone of modesty which pervades the answers is a merit upon which authors rarely pride themselves. M. de Voltaire does not boast about the superiority of his intelligence.'[20] After quoting from the poem, the editor exclaims: 'Is there a man of good taste who has not given himself the pleasure of reading them [the verses] several times?' and turning to the description of the warriors in the battle, which Voltaire had added to his poem, Berthier remarks: 'These portraits, which are not in the other editions, here give an admirable effect. They are from the hand of

[18] *J. de T.* (June 1744), p.1006.
[19] *J. de T.* (June 1744), p.1006.
[20] *J. de T.* (Sept.1745), p.1531.

a master.'[21] Following the quotation of further passages of the
poem with the comment, 'Is it possible not to recognize in these
verses the genius and the elevation of m. de Voltaire?' the article
concludes: 'Il en est de cet ouvrage comme de tous ceux du même
genre dont m. de Voltaire a enrichi la république des Lettres. On
y admire le bel esprit, on y reconnaît le grand poète. Nous nous
estimerions heureux, si dans le compte que nous venons d'en rendre, on pouvait remarquer quelqu'une de ces grâces dont il est ordinairement si prodigue, et qui charmeront toujours ses lecteurs'.[22]

The tone of praise assumed by Berthier in dealing with Voltaire
is understandable when we consider that at this time the *philosophe* had been particularly conciliatory toward the church. He
had dedicated his play *Mahomet* (1742) to pope Benedict XIV and
had received a complimentary letter in reply. When the Jansenist
Nouvelles ecclésiastiques had decried this deference of the pope
toward the 'irreligious' author of the *Lettres philosophiques*[23], Voltaire wrote a letter to father de la Tour, principal of the Jesuit
Collège Louis-le-grand, declaring his affection for the Jesuits and
his fidelity to the Catholic cause, denying at the same time the
authorship of the *Lettres philosophiques*[24]. Father de la Tour's
answer, accepting Voltaire's letter as a mark of conversion, evoked another attack on its author as well as on the Jesuits in the
Nouvelles ecclésiastiques, whose editor saw in de La Tour's reply
a naïve credulity in thus accepting the *philosophe*'s declarations[25].
The Jesuits no doubt knew only too well that their former student
was drifting away from orthodoxy, but probably thought it more

[21] *J. de T.* (Sept.1745), p.1540.
[22] *J. de T.* (Sept.1745), p.1546. In
April 1745 the *Journal* had reviewed
briefly a *Lettre d'un Quaker nommé
Josias Martin à M. de Voltaire*. The
article is written in a light vein, and is
more concerned with describing some
of the curious customs of the Quakers
than it is with Voltaire's views.
[23] *Nouvelles ecclésiastiques* (Jan.
1746), p.3.

[24] Best.3044; in a footnote (xv.41)
mr Besterman discusses Condorcet's
statement that Voltaire wrote this letter in order to facilitate his entry into
the Academy; La Tour's reply is
Best.3045.
[25] *Nouvelles ecclésiastiques* (1 May
1746), p.69. The issue for 17 April 1746
had attacked Voltaire's letter as a hy-
pocritical subterfuge (p.61).

prudent to avoid alienating him from the church altogether through attacks similar to those made by the Jansenist periodical. Rather, they praised him freely and encouraged him in his literary activities.

Thus, when Voltaire published in Italian his *Essai sur les changements arrivés au globe de la terre* a year later, the *Journal de Trévoux* gave it a glowing review, and its editor refrained from disagreeing with those views he did not share. Berthier begins his review by assuring his readers that the *Essai* comes from the pen of a Frenchman who is 'consummate in the French language, whether in prose or in verse; indeed, one of the forty arbiters of the language, capable, in addition, of excelling in all languages and in all categories of science and erudition.' The essay, he continues, was written by Voltaire to thank the Academy of Bologna for admitting him as a member, and he adds: 'Un homme à talents ordinaires n'aurait pas tenté deux essais à la fois, et celui d'une langue nouvelle pour lui, l'aurait assez occupé: un génie naturellement profond et étendu, en s'essayant même sur les "mots" ne perd jamais de vue les "choses," et son entrée dans une Académie, lui ouvre naturellement la porte de toutes les autres. Nous osons d'avance en faire le compliment à m. de Voltaire'.[26] An extract of the *Essai* is then begun, and when Berthier presents Voltaire's arguments against the view that fossils indicate that the land was once inundated, the author is called 'ingenious in all his conjectures.'[27] The concept of a well-ordered universe, and Voltaire's

[26] *J. de T.* (July 1746), p.1503. The previous month, the *Journal* had already announced Voltaire's entry into the French Academy, at which time the editor had announced: 'M. de Voltaire se présente à l'Académie Française, et m. l'abbé d'Olivet est son introducteur. Cela doit faire une époque dans l'histoire de cette compagnie, et les discours de l'un et de l'autre seront des monuments' (*J. de T.* [June 1746], p.1339).

[27] *J. de T.* (July 1746), p.1506. Although the editor refrains from commenting further on this point, he was not in agreement with Voltaire's position, but rather maintained that fossils were evidence for the deluge. In commenting on fossilized cuttlefish on another occasion, Berthier states that 'les bélemnites sont des pierres pointues, restes du déluge apparemment; mais qu'on rapporte tantôt au règne végétal, tantôt au minéral, et tantôt à l'animal: en sorte que la nature de ce fossile est presque inconnue' (*J. de T.* [Oct.1754], p.2586).

contention that fossils do not attest to earlier violent upheavals in nature are even more warmly received by the Jesuit editor, who agrees that merely on the evidence of a few fossils one need not think 'that it is necessary to convulse the whole of nature, or to believe that the earth was turned upside down.' His reason for a more enthusiastic acceptance of this portion of the *Essai* is suggested by Berthier's explanation: 'Car, qu'on ne s'y trompe pas, m. de Voltaire est *philosophe*, est bel esprit, m. de Voltaire est tout ce qu'il veut, et un fonds de génie comme le sien a bien des ressources pour le vrai, pour le bien. L'opinion qu'il combat ici, et qu'il a toujours combattu dès son Newton, est une branche d'athéisme'.[28]

Continuing his extract of the *Essai*, the editor turns to an idea which he calls 'new and salient,' wherein Voltaire upholds the utility of mountains in nature. Berthier concurs, adding: 'There is a narrowness of spirit and an infinite want of physics, with an excessive ill-will toward nature or toward God in treating mountains as deformities, as irregularities on the globe.'[29] After presenting the remaining portions of the *Essai*, the editor concludes by agreeing once more with Voltaire that the Atlantic ocean is not the result of the sinking of a continent. The author is right, he states, 'in not believing in the generation of the Atlantic ocean through the swallowing up of a continent that was once there, and which is probably nothing more than the ancient loss of the new world which we have recovered, or rather refound.'[30]

When a work appeared anonymously in 1748 with the title of *Panégyrique de Louis XV*, the *Journal de Trévoux* began its review

[28] *J. de T.* (July 1746), p.1507. Berthier is probably agreeing here with Voltaire in deference to the author so as to encourage him to continue attacking atheism. Elsewhere he takes the view that the earth has changed considerably with the passage of time, declaring: 'Il paraît certain que ce monde a souffert quelque bouleversement, et qu'il n'est qu'une copie faible et défigurée du monde original. La physique se joint à l'histoire pour établir cette vérité. On ne voit que des ruines, des débris, des décombres, des montagnes escarpées, des rochers entassés les uns sur les autres, des précipices, des crevasses, des cavernes, des monceaux de sable et des coquillages' (*J. de T.* [April 1749], pp.461–462).

[29] *J. de T.* (July 1746), p.1513.

[30] *J. de T.* (July 1746), p.1516.

of this most recent production by Voltaire with words of praise for the unknown author, but then declared the *Panégyrique* to be full of antitheses, adding that there was 'something desultory in the style...something arid, poorly sustained,' and concluding with the remark: 'In short this whole discourse is more deserving than eloquent, more ingenious than sublime. Still, happy is the genius who can produce one like it!'[31] While Voltaire was preparing a new edition of his *Panégyrique*, including an answer to Berthier's review of the work, the Jesuit editor turned to another unsigned publication, *Zadig*, and while noting that its anonymous author must have 'a great deal of intelligence, a wide experience in writing, and much knowledge,' and that 'he narrates with lightness and depicts with grace,' the editor condemns a number of its unorthodox ideas, such as Zadig's belief that all religious cults are equally good; the angel's picture of the passions as essential to man, and his statement that 'everything is dangerous here below and everything is necessary.' To say that everything which exists had to be absolutely, asserts the editor, would authorize the 'very false idea, that in the production and arrangement of this universe, God would not have been perfectly free, etc.'[32]

When the true authorship of the *Panégyrique* became known, Berthier, obviously embarrassed, inserted a second article on Voltaire's work, in which he attempted to explain his criticisms in a manner more favourable to the author. After stating that the panegyrist has revealed his identity, the editor recalls the words of praise from his previous article by noting: 'We applauded his glory and we here willingly confirm the praises which we gave him without knowing him, in our extract of October.' In that article, the editor admits, 'we criticized modestly several sections,' and he adds rather uneasily: 'Or nous venons d'apprendre que m. de V. a orné son édition nouvelle d'une réponse dans les formes à nos observations. Nous n'avons pu acquérir encore un exemplaire de ce livre si récent, mais nous supposons que la réponse de

[31] *J. de T.* (Oct.1748), pp.2220–21.   [32] *J. de T.* (Nov.1748), pp.2449ff.

cet académicien sera, comme il convient à l'apologie d'un homme de lettres, honnête, modérée, sans personnalités, sans épisodes malins ou inutiles; et qu'on y aura tenu compte du bien que nous avons dit de l'ouvrage en question'.[33] Judging from the apologetic and apprehensive tone of the article, it is probable that Berthier had really not known Voltaire to be the author of the *Panégyrique*, and that he now feared that he had antagonized unnecessarily an author he had always made it a point to praise.

Voltaire's awaited reply in the second edition betrayed the justifiable resentment which Berthier's critique had aroused in the author. Describing the Jesuit editor's criticisms as unjust and ill-considered, he refutes them point by point and, while he refrains from engaging in personalities, he is visibly angered. When, for example, the critic had questioned the term of 'a rare triumph' in designating the love of the people for Louis xv, Voltaire replies: 'A quoi pense-t-il quand il dit que rien n'est plus naturel, plus général, qu'une telle tendresse? où a-t-il trouvé qu'en France on ait marqué un tel amour pour ses rois, avant que Louis xiv et Louis xv aient gouverné par eux-mêmes? Est-ce dans le temps de la Fronde? est-ce sous Louis xiii, quand la cour était déchirée par des factions, et l'état par des guerres civiles? quand le sang ruisselait sur les échafauds? est-ce lorsque le couteau de Ravaillac, instrument du fanatisme de tout un parti, acheva le parricide que Jean Châtel avait commencé, et que Pierre Barrière et tant d'autres avaient médité? est-ce quand le moine Jacques Clément, animé de l'esprit de la ligue, assassina Henri iii? est-ce après ou avant le massacre de la Saint-Barthélemi? est-ce quand les Guises régnaient sous le nom de François ii? Est-il possible qu'on ose dire que les Français pensent aujourd'hui comme ils pensaient dans ces temps abominables?'[34]

Berthier chose to remain silent on the matter, and continued to speak well of Voltaire, perhaps desiring to undo the damage he had caused in his relations with the *philosophe*. After decrying the

[33] *J. de T.* (Dec.1748), pp.2824–25.   [34] M.xxiii.266.

attitude found in the *Connaissance des beautés et des défauts de la poésie*—the anonymous author had depreciated the ancients and placed Voltaire in first place—as being offensive to Voltaire inasmuch as the great poet had always shown a high regard for the ancients[35], the Jesuit editor turned to the preface of *La Tragédie de Sémiramis*, in which Voltaire exposes his views on the theatre. Passing over the section in which the poet compares the Italian opera to the ancient Greek tragedies, to the advantage of the latter, Berthier considers Voltaire's arguments against Brumoy's theory[36], and then concurs in the *philosophe*'s opinion. The Jesuit historian had stated that the poet should not invent his themes or his characters because 'the spirit of the spectator is revolted; everything seems unbelievable to him, and the play fails in its effect, due to lack of probability.' Voltaire refutes this by pointing out that to the spectator a fictional subject is the same as a true one which is unknown. The *Journal* concludes: 'Il faudra se ranger à l'opinion de m. de V. et reconnaître que la tragédie n'exclut point les sujets de pure fiction. . . . Il en résulte que dans la question présente, le p. Brumoy a été plus sévère qu'Aristote; que cet endroit par conséquent de son discours sur le parallèle des théâtres, ne doit pas être pris pour règle ni suivi à la lettre. Du reste il faut dire qu'en le critiquant m. de V. témoigne bien de l'estime pour son livre, "son travail et son goût".'[37]

When Voltaire undertook to disprove the authenticity of the political testament of cardinal Richelieu, the relations between the author and the *Journal de Trévoux* underwent a further strain. In answer to the *philosophe*'s attack, the maréchal de Richelieu invited the public to inspect the manuscript which was in his possession, and the *Journal* printed a 'Réfutation du sentiment de m. de Voltaire qui traite d'ouvrage supposé, le testament politique du cardinal Richelieu.' In the article, the editor, after pre-

---

[35] *J. de T.* (Nov.1749), pp.2350ff.
[36] Brumoy had been on the editorial staff of the *Journal* between 1722 and 1739. His *Théâtre des Grecs* was translated into several languages. Samuel Johnson translated it in England.
[37] *J. de T.* (Jan.1750), pp.183ff.

senting detailed proofs of the manuscript's authenticity, concludes by saying that the affair is closed and 'if someone henceforth wished to maintain the forgery of the famous testament, it would be apparently to say of himself like Horace, "Frontis ad urbanae descendi praemia".'[38] As the testament was generally accepted as authentic, it seemed that the question was ended. The *Journal* for the following month returned to its earlier review of the *Tragédie de Sémiramis* on the occasion of the printing of a new edition of Brumoy's *Théâtre des Grecs*, which Berthier describes as too hastily prepared and in need of corrections. The article begins by stating: 'Pour prouver au public que le *Théâtre des Grecs* a besoin de corrections, nous plaçons ici la lettre suivante, où l'on verra que le p. Brumoy a pu induire m. de Voltaire en erreur sur un endroit d'Euripide. On a déjà vû par notre Journal de janvier que le même m. de V. a reproché justement et sensément une opinion fausse à l'auteur du *Théâtre des Grecs*. Présentement c'est peut-être celui-ci qui égare l'auteur de la *Tragédie de Sémiramis*'.[39]

Voltaire had preferred Racine's portrayal of Phèdre's despair upon discovering her rival, to Euripides's use of a satire by Hippolytus on learned ladies which makes the hero appear as a 'wretched comic character.' Berthier points out that this critique, made by Brumoy and repeated by Voltaire, derives from a misunderstanding of the term 'femmes savantes.' The critics, explains the Jesuit editor, are using the term in the modern sense, as given by Molière, whereas 'the expressions of Hippolytus merely indicate "women who have intelligence", or also if you wish, "women who are cunning and intriguing".' This interpretation would invalidate the criticism made by Brumoy and Voltaire and would make Hippolytus's speech fit the circumstances, he asserts. When Voltaire states that the ghost in Shakespeare's *Hamlet* is preferable to that appearing in Aeschylus's *The Persians* because Darius in Aeschylus appears only to announce the misfortunes of his family,

---

[38] *J. de T.* (Feb.1750), p.360. [39] *J. de T.* (March 1750), p.743.

the editor suggests that Darius has many more functions than that given him by Voltaire. This is not to say that the *philosophe* is not justified in preferring Shakespeare in this matter, explains Berthier, but he wishes only to show that the critic overlooks much of the significance of the role of Darius[40].

In the meantime Voltaire had not abandoned his stand on Richelieu's testament but had reiterated his position by adding to his *Oreste* two chapters on 'printed lies,' in which he again attacked the authenticity of the document. In an article announcing the play, the *Journal* exclaims: 'Le mépris extrême que témoigne m. de V. pour le Testament politique pris en lui-même (l'auteur à part) nous surprend beaucoup .... M. de V. remplit son nouvel écrit de raisons négatives, de conjectures, d'explications arbitraires qu'il sait tourner habilement au désavantage du Testament politique'.[41]

The following month, the *Journal de Trévoux* returned to *Oreste* to praise the author in his zeal for the ancients. The article begins with the announcement that Voltaire declares himself to be an admirer and disciple of the Greek tragedians. This is an excellent choice of masters, observes Berthier, for it results in a simple plot suitable for inspiring compassion, and it excludes the 'insipid and idiotic love motif which has so long dishonored our theater.'[42] Having noted that the preface is written 'ingeniously and nobly,' the editor enters into a comparison between Sophocles's *Electra* and Voltaire's *Oreste*, in which the former is favoured as being 'more sustained and more moving,' although the role of Aegisthus is preferred in Voltaire's play. The review concludes with the

[40] *J. de T.* (March 1750), p.743.
[41] *J. de T.* (May 1750), p.1136. Voltaire remained unmoved in his stand. As late as 1764 Bachaumont remarks: 'On vient de réimprimer le Testament politique du Cardinal de Richelieu.... Il paraît désormais prouvé par les faits que cet ouvrage, malgré les raisons fortes et supérieures de m. de Voltaire, est réellement de ce grand ministre....

On y trouve dans les bibliothèques les différents manuscrits originaux, dont m. de Voltaire, ignorait l'existence' (*Mémoires secrets*, ii.105). Voltaire, undaunted, printed the following year another attack against the testament in the form of a brochure entitled, *Doutes nouveaux sur le testament attribué au cardinal de Richelieu*.
[42] *J. de T.* (June 1750), ii.1443-44.

remark that in *Oreste* 'la diction est belle; qu'elle est toutefois magnifique, sublime et inimitable peut-être dans l'auteur Grec, qu'enfin M. de Voltaire mérite les plus grands éloges pour son zèle à imiter les Anciens, et pour son courage à écarter du théâtre français le langage ridicule des héros de roman'.[43]

A few months later an anonymous brochure (by Gaillard) appeared comparing four Electras, including that of Voltaire in his *Oreste*. The author belittles the other three and says that not only is he going to 'have m. de Voltaire thrash Sophocles,' but he also intends to 'crush Sophocles and Euripides.' The *Journal* decries this attitude and reminds its readers that Voltaire in his *Epitre à mme la duchesse Du Maine* has given 'striking evidence of his regard for the ancients and for Sophocles in particular,' and therefore he would not wish to suffer 'these base flatteries.' The article concludes: 'M. de Voltaire has conquered enough territory in the empire of letters not to wish to invade the possessions of others; his reputation is too great to need the petty resources contained in an odious parallel.'[44]

If we except the disagreement on Richelieu's testament, and Berthier's obvious preference for the ancients, the relations between the *Journal de Trévoux* and Voltaire up to 1750 had been as friendly as could be expected between an author and a critical journal[45]. While the *Lettres philosophiques* might have caused the Jesuits some apprehension as to the possible future development of Voltaire's thinking, the author had not pursued that interest further but had turned to scientific and literary subjects—preoccupations which were praised and encouraged by the *Journal de Trévoux*, perhaps in the hope that they would distract Voltaire

[43] *J. de T.* (June 1750), p.1472. For a more detailed view of Berthier's attitude toward the theatre, see Chapter III, dealing with J. J. Rousseau.

[44] *J. de T.* (August 1750), pp.1840ff.

[45] Pellisson tells us that, in general, writers looked upon the journalist as 'un censeur souvent malin, parfois malveillant, presque toujours incommode. Comment auraient-ils été disposés à voir en lui un confrère? Bien plutôt il devait leur paraître un concurrent, même quand il n'était pas un adversaire' (*Les Hommes de lettres au 18ème siècle* [Paris 1911], p.257).

from his metaphysical speculations and prevent his drifting further away from the church. With his sojourn in Prussia, however, Voltaire returned once more to his early interest in philosophical speculation, and such works as *La Voix du sage et du peuple* (1750) and *Idées de La Mothe Le Vayer* (1751), attacking convent life and dogmatic religion, began to appear. With the publication of *Micromégas* in 1752, the worst fears of the Jesuits seemed to be materializing; Voltaire was going further 'dans le travers,' as Brumoy had phrased it earlier. When reviewing the work in the *Journal*, Berthier begins by expressing the hope that Voltaire is not really the author of *Micromégas*, which he describes as 'good neither for the republic of letters, nor for religion.'[46] He goes on to give a resumé of the book, pointing out such objectionable passages as that in which the academician talks against princes who wage war, a view which evokes the comment: 'Here is a rash criticism of sovereigns.' The editor then turns to religious matters, attacking as materialistic the statement that we do not know the essence nor all of the attributes of matter, and as Spinosism, the definition of death as 'giving back our bodies to the elements and renewing nature under another form.' What is this 'other form,' asks the Jesuit editor, if not 'another modification whose sole substance, nature, in Spinoza's system, is the whole foundation.'[47] In deference to the author, Berthier adds: 'We attack here only the sentiments and the book, not the person whose name appears on the titlepage,' and he concludes: 'Ajoutons, sur ce petit roman de *Micromégas*, qu'il a aussi le défaut de ne ménager pas assez les intérêts de la pudeur; qu'il présente quelques traits licencieux qui blessent un lecteur modeste: défaut inexcusable, liberté qu'un auteur ne doit pas se permettre et qu'y a-t-il de plus aisé de ne pas tomber dans cet écueil, quand on a des mœurs, quand on sait le respect dû au public! Que si l'on manque de ces deux qualités, pourquoi écrit-on?'[48]

[46] *J. de T.* (April 1752), i.757.
[47] *J. de T.* (April 1752), pp.757-58.
[48] *J. de T.* (April 1752), pp.757ff.

A short contribution by Voltaire to Bachaumont's *Essai sur la peinture, la sculpture, et l'architecture*, is received with more favour when it appears in the same year. When the editor comes to the passage at the end of the *Essai* entitled, 'On what is not done and what could be done,' he announces that this portion written by Voltaire has some excellent suggestions for beautifying Paris under the guise of Rome, and 'a few sprinklings of critiques make these four or five pages very piquant, not to mention the added colour of the style which is never lacking in the author.'[49]

Two years later, Berthier turns reluctantly to Voltaire's *Abrégé de l'histoire universelle* to tell his readers that it is written in a very light and very bold style, and he begins his criticisms by saying: 'Two things would be desirable: first, that a respect for religion had governed this pen; secondly, that fewer errors had been inserted in the historical accounts.' The first of these is by far the most important, he insists, and 'we have the sorrow of seeing that almost no consideration has been given this point in that work.'[50] When religion is attacked, pursues Berthier, 'how could we remain silent on procedures of this nature?' As in the case of *Micromégas*, the editor again suggests hopefully that Voltaire did not write this *Abrégé*: 'The author is named at the head of the book: it is of his own admission? Is it not rather one of those typographical frauds of which there are so many examples?' In any case, continues Berthier, some of the pitfalls in the work must be exposed, but he reiterates his intention of remaining within the bounds of moderation by declaring: 'La modération, dont nous ne devons pas nous écarter, resserrera nos critiques dans les bornes du pur nécessaire; nous en séparerons les reproches, les termes contentieux, les soupçons désavantageux. L'exposition des faits avec la réfutation des principes, suffira pour convaincre le public qu'il règne ici un grand abus des talents'.[51]

The journalist then proceeds to refute some of the statements found in the *Abrégé*. He first upholds the authenticity of an eighth-

[49] *J. de T.* (Oct.1752), p.2478. [51] *J. de T.* (Feb.1754), p.283.
[50] *J. de T.* (Feb.1754), i.282.

century Chinese monument showing that Christian missionaries had been sent there from Syria in A.D.636, and which Voltaire had called 'one of those pious frauds which they have always too easily allowed themselves.' Berthier then turns to an attack on the Koran which he sees as an implied allusion to the Bible: 'On peut demander à qui en veut l'auteur, et s'il ne prétend point qu'à cause du silence de nos écritures touchant les systèmes de physique, comme l'attraction, les forces vives, les monades et autres inventions pareilles, on est en droit de contredire la divinité de ces saints livres?'[52] When God gave us his revelation, he asserts, 'his aim was not to make physicists out of us, but to attach us to himself.' He told us that he created the world and not how he did it, and 'he will judge us not on our observations in physics, but on our good works.' Scripture and science are not contradictory, he continues, but have different fields of investigation, nor does scripture ever contradict the incontestable discoveries of science. Berthier then condemns Voltaire's 'method' which consists in placing on the same level true religion and everything which is false and despicable[53]. As an example of this method, he points out the statement that religious dogmas have caused seditions and have divided the Christian world whereas the pagan world did not have such differences because the pagans did not have any dogmas. They did not have any dogmas, retorts Berthier, because 'the divinity had not manifested itself to them,' and they had 'neither revelations nor prophecies, nor miracles, nor promises: which is assuredly not the position in which the Christians find themselves.'[54] The article continues with the exposition of various irreligious passages, noting: 'We would be very prolix if we wanted to point out here everything which the author hazards on what is most respected in the Catholic church.' Berthier concludes the review by promising to consider the second volume of the *Abrégé* at another time, 'always with the distress inspired by a work so against good order.'[55]

[52] *J. de T.* (Feb.1754), i.296–97.
[53] *J. de T.* (Feb.1754), p.301.
[54] *J. de T.* (Feb.1754), p.309.
[55] *J. de T.* (Feb.1754), p.309.

In the meantime, Voltaire had disavowed the *Abrégé* and volume two of the *Journal* for February announces a 'Lettre de m. de Voltaire au sieur Jean Neaulme libraire,' wherein the author repudiates the work. After quoting the letter, the editor states: 'M. de Voltaire a raison de s'élever avec force contre un ouvrage où la religion et la vérité ne sont nullement respectées. Comme nous avons cru qu'il était de notre devoir d'indiquer dans nos *Mémoires* (Voy. Fevr. 1 vol.) quelques-uns des écueils où a donné l'auteur, nous publions aussi très-volontiers le désaveu de m. de Voltaire; et nous nous félicitons d'être entrés dans ses vues en faisant la critique de ce livre si peu digne d'un Chrétien, d'un Catholique, et d'un homme de lettres'.[56]

The following month Berthier returns to the second volume of the *Abrégé* and states that its author quotes liberally from an *Histoire des croisades* which the *Journal* had already refuted in 1750[57]. After answering objections and pointing out historical inaccuracies in the *Abrégé*, particularly in connection with the popes, the editor concludes: 'This is what we had to say about this history, which has earned the indignation of virtuous men, the criticism of men of letters, and the disavowal of the one whose name appears on the titlepage'.[58]

Berthier no doubt knew Voltaire to be the author of the *Abrégé*, and that it had been disavowed to avoid impending condemnation[59]. If the Jesuits had entertained any hope of winning back the errant philosopher, it must have seemed clear after 1750 that the writer's brilliant genius had definitely been committed to enmity with the church. Ever since the *Lettres philosophiques* had appeared, he had been under a cloud of suspicion. For a time it

[56] *J. de T.* (Feb.1754), ii.558.
[57] A letter to the editor had declared of the *Histoire des Croisades*: 'Elle porte le nom de m. de Voltaire mais comme ce poète célèbre s'est récrié une infinité de fois contre des livres qu'on lui attribuait faussement, je ne crois pas que celui-ci soit sorti de sa plume'

(*J. de T.* [Oct.1750], p.2269). The work is also refuted in the Nov.1750 issue, i.2470-88.
[58] *J. de T.* (March 1754), pp.655ff.
[59] it is at this time that Voltaire had received communion at Easter in Colmar.

seemed as if the author had decided to confine himself to literary matters and forego more dangerous subjects, but with the publication of *Zadig*, *Micromégas* and the *Abrégé*, there could be no further doubt of his intentions. At a time when the intellectual struggle had reached a point where neutrality was no longer possible—the Prades affair had forced men to take sides in 1751, the *Encyclopédie* had been suppressed in 1752 and its editors were now striking back effectively—it was clear to Berthier that Voltaire had committed himself irrevocably against the church. The one factor which probably decided the Jesuit editor to attack the *philosophe* openly as an enemy of religion was Voltaire's decision to ally himself with the Encyclopedists. Berthier had already declared himself an adversary of Diderot and had been instrumental in the suppression of the *Encyclopédie*[60]. The appearance of volume v of that work, containing articles by Voltaire[61], must have convinced Berthier that his was no longer an independent voice. Conciliation would henceforth be futile toward this new and formidable addition to the Encyclopedic 'conspiracy.' The *Journal de Trévoux* for December 1755 reflects this change in attitude in the blunt tone used by the Jesuit editor in referring to the *philosophe*.

In the course of an article reviewing a work entitled *Lettres critiques*, which refutes modern writings against religion, Berthier breaks his silence on Voltaire's *Lettres philosophiques* and declares: 'On sait que les *Lettres philosophiques* sont d'un célèbre auteur qui, presque dans tous ses écrits, attaque directement ou obliquement le Christianisme: s'il en loue quelques sectes, ce sont toujours celles qui sympathisent le plus avec le tolérantisme.... Les anecdotes historiques ne se placent guères dans ces *Lettres* qu'autant qu'elles fournissent des traits odieux contre notre religion: les observations mêmes les plus philosophiques, sont semées de

---

[60] see Chapter IV dealing with Diderot and the *Encyclopédie*.

[61] The *Nouvelles ecclésiastiques* for 20 February 1756 announced the appearance of the fifth volume of the *Encyclopédie*, and informed its readers that Voltaire had contributed the articles 'esprit,' 'éloquence,' and 'élégance.'

réflexions critiques sur nos dogmes'.[62] When Voltaire praises English writers, continues the article, it is only those writers most favourable to incredulity. The *Lettres* are dictated 'by a hatred for Christianity; a hatred as blind as it is furious, as unjust as it is opinionated.' The editor then enters into a lengthy refutation of Voltaire's views on the immortality of the soul, and in particular, the writer's statement that we do not know all the properties of matter and therefore do not know if the soul is material. To this Berthier replies that while we do not know all the properties of matter, we do know enough to distinguish it from the soul, and he adds: 'Sur la nature de l'âme, nous avons assez de lumières pour nous convaincre de sa spiritualité et de son immortalité. Si cette lumière nous découvre nos devoirs essentiels, devoirs de société, devoirs de religion, etc., que faut-il de plus pour parvenir à la fin qui nous est destinée? Pourquoi des ténèbres qui nous restent, nous faire un bandeau qui nous aveugle sur ces devoirs et sur cette fin? La lumière qui nous manque, doit-elle éteindre le flambeau qui nous éclaire?'[63]

The editor then turns to Voltaire's attacks on Pascal and decries the *philosophe*'s method, stating that witticisms, antitheses and epigrams may display a fine wit but they should not be resorted to in a serious critique. 'If they cover up its weakness in the eyes of narrow minds,' asserts the editor, 'they betray it in the view of serious intellects.'[64] The calling of Pascal's distrust of reason and his fear before the uncertainty of eternity 'fanatisme', evokes a defense of the author of the *Pensées*. There is nothing more important to man than to know whether everything ends or does not end with this life, begins Berthier. Should not the uncertainty of such problems bring on disquietude, fears and alarms? In such a cruel uncertainty, he continues, 'the confidence of the *philosophe* can only be compared to the enthusiasm of the fanatic.' After discussing some of the errors which the author of the work under review points out in Voltaire's criticism of Pascal, Berthier

[62] *J. de T.* (Dec.1755), p.2939.   [64] *J. de T.* (Dec.1755), p.2950.
[63] *J. de T.* (Dec.1755), p.2948.

concludes that other critics had already presented Pascal's errors. Voltaire, however, although capable of discerning them, is unable to correct them because his corrections, 'bearing constantly the imprint of the unfortunate prejudices which he has accepted as his principles, could not help being more faulty than Pascal's text.'[65]

Voltaire's irreligious writings again come under the scrutiny of the editor of the *Journal de Trévoux* when two years later, in connection with a long article refuting various objectionable books, Berthier turns to the *philosophe* and declares emphatically: 'Cet écrivain se donne pour l'ami du genre humain, il est encore plus l'ennemi du Dieu que nous adorons. Apôtre d'une philosophie dont la date est récente, il emprunte les armes qu'elle a forgées contre la révélation: il regarde cette révélation sainte comme une chimère fondée sur des monuments incertains, sur des oracles supposés et sur de faux miracles: il la représente tantôt comme un fantôme dont le fanatisme ensanglante les autels, tantôt comme une superstition dont l'extravagance fait rougir le sens commun, et quelquefois comme un monstre dont l'hypocrisie et l'ambition ont accrédité l'imposture'.[66] The Jesuit editor then enumerates some of Voltaire's attacks against Christianity, such as the claim that all sects are false, and only natural law is true; that faith is useless and 'probity is all the religion that is necessary'; that there is no eternal punishment in hell; that human liberty is only an illusion of pride; and that before the fifteenth century 'we had as history only ancient fables and old women's tales'; assertions which cause the editor to exclaim: 'Such is the point to which this author claims that "the love of humanity and the horror of fanaticism" have conducted his pen.'[67] Having reaffirmed his belief that 'natural religion not only is in agreement with revealed religion, but that it requires its profession,' Berthier turns to the methods used by 'this legion of unbelievers who, reunited against us by the hatred they bear against the holiness of our dogmas and

[65] *J. de T.* (Dec.1755), p.2954.   [67] *J. de T.* (Jan.1757), pp.102–3.
[66] *J. de T.* (Jan.1757), i.101.

divided among themselves by the diversity of their systems, have not yet been able to form a uniform sect,' and he remonstrates: 'After all, if this faith is so vain and so vile why do its enemies expend so much energy against it and why do they accumulate so many chronological and historical errors?' Are these obscenities and sophisms which are used to attack the gospels the weapons of a wholesome and pure philosophy? he queries. Are these the teachings which will help our youth overcome its wildness and weaknesses? 'We have only to look at the testimony of our society,' he concludes[68].

Berthier did not limit himself to this forceful declaration against the *philosophes*, but he organized a staff to write a refutation of their works. Voltaire, when he heard of it, wrote to d'Alembert asking: 'Je vous demande en grâce de me dire ce que c'est qu'un livre contre ces pauvre déistes, intitulé *La Religion vengée*, et dédié à monseigneur le dauphin, dont le premier tome paraît déjà, et dont les autres suivront de mois en mois, pour mieux frapper le public'.[69] That same month (January 1757) d'Alembert answered his friend that the work was being prepared by a group of churchmen and that 'the Jesuit Berthier, great and celebrated director of the *Journal de Trévoux*, is at the head of this fine enterprise,' and he added: 'Quelqu'un qui lit le *Journal de Trévoux* ... me dit hier que, dans le dernier journal, vous étiez nommément et indécemment attaqué: "Ce poète, dit-on, qui s'appelle l'ami des hommes, et qui est l'ennemi du Dieu que nous adorons." Voilà comme ils vous habillent, et voilà ce que m. de Malesherbes, le protecteur déclaré de toute la canaille littéraire, laisse imprimer avec "approbation et privilège".'[70]

[68] *J. de T.* (Jan.1757), pp.104ff. In connection with Berthier's statement regarding the inability of the *philosophes* to form a 'uniform sect,' the following words of Voltaire written to d'Alembert in 1765 are of interest: 'C'est bien dommage, encore une fois, que Jean-Jacques, Diderot, Helvétius et vous, *cum aliis ejusdem farinæ homi-* *nibus*, vous ne vous soyez pas entendus pour écraser *l'inf* ....Le plus grand de mes chagrins est de voir les imposteurs unis, et les amis du vrai divisés' (M.xliii.457).

[69] M.xxxix.159.

[70] M.xxxix.163. Mourret states that *La Religion vengée* was written by Lefranc de Pompignan (*A History of*

In April of the same year, the *Journal* continues the review of the *Lettres critiques* begun in its earlier issue, and the editor turns to Voltaire's *Histoire universelle*. He shows his reluctance to attack the *philosophe* by stating as a preface to his criticisms: 'It is sad for us to find here a living author whose talents we admire, and to have to deplore the use he makes of them; he abuses them in the most essential matters.'[71] The historical errors in Voltaire's work are not the result of ignorance, begins Berthier, but are deliberate distortions of truth to place the church and religion in an unfavourable light: 'Quelque étranger que soit m. de V. dans les antiquités chrétiennes, ces méprises qui se trouvent dans le cours de son histoire, ne sont point les bévues d'un ignorant: ce sont des hostilités contre l'église et la religion. Abattre l'une et l'autre, élever sur leur débris un édifice philosophique, un temple dédié à la licence de penser, et consacré par l'indépendance de toute autorité, asservir et restreindre le culte et la morale à une philosophie purement humaine et profane; voilà, ce semble, le projet ou le complot formé par l'auteur de cette *Histoire universelle*'.[72]

After quoting some of the criticisms presented in the *Lettres critiques* under review, Berthier charges Voltaire with being an unreliable historian because in a true historian, 'impartiality requires that one give an account of the virtuous actions which have made the church illustrious, with as much fidelity as one indicates the weaknesses which have afflicted it,' and the natural conclusion which it would be fitting to draw from the scandals 'is to admire the divine providence which has preserved its religion among so many storms.'[73] Berthier then turns to the *Poème sur la religion naturelle* and accuses the author of unintentionally furnishing arms to atheism: 'Ce poème paraît destiné à réfuter l'athéisme; mais entraîné par ses préjugés et par son zèle contre la

the Catholic church, vi.534), but this is not the same work. Pompignan's *La Religion vengée de l'incrédulité par l'incrédulité même* was published in one volume in 1772, while the enterprise mentioned by d'Alembert was published periodically in 21 volumes, beginning in 1756.

[71] *J. de T.* (April 1757), ii.1078.
[72] *J. de T.* (April 1757), p.1079.
[73] *J. de T.* (April 1757), p.1087.

religion révélée, l'auteur, en creusant les fondements du naturalisme se propose de saper ceux du Christianisme. Dans ce plan,
il entre donc deux objets qui demandaient un écrivain également
versé dans la métaphysique et dans la théologie, matières aussi
étrangères à m. de V. que lui sont familières toutes celles qui sont
du ressort de la poésie et de la belle littérature. De là vient que
sans le savoir, comme sans le vouloir, aux athées qu'il combat, et
aux théologiens qu'il attaque, il fournit des armes contre ses
assertions'.[74]

The chief of these weapons is Voltaire's suggestion that thought
can be a property of matter. This, declares Berthier, is the basis
of atheism: 'Thus, materialism comes of itself and places itself on
the foundation which m. de V. has prepared for naturalism, without that poet's having reserved for himself any means of excluding it from his system.'[75] In reality, continues Berthier, the stress
on natural religion alone weakens the whole structure because
natural religion and revealed religion 'form an immutable edifice.'
Revealed religion 'rises up on natural religion as upon its absolute
base, and it becomes its rampart and perfection.' The editor then
considers the refusal of the *philosophes* to accept the doctrine of
hell, a stand which 'reassures the most hardened culprit,' and he
explains: 'La plupart des déistes, pour s'en épargner la frayeur,

[74] *J. de T.* (April 1757), p.1088.
[75] *J. de T.* (April 1757), ii.1089.
When in 1749 Voltaire had taken issue
with the materialistic viewpoint of
Saunderson in Diderot's *Lettre sur les
aveugles*, the author, no doubt recalling Voltaire's suggestion in his essay
on Locke (*Lettres philosophiques*, 1734)
that matter could have been endowed
with thought by the creator, had reminded his critic that the blind man's
position is strengthened by the writings
of Voltaire himself. After presenting
Saunderson's arguments in a letter to
the *philosophe*, Diderot adds: 'Quelle
force n'ajouterait point à ce raisonnement l'opinion qui vous est commune
avec Locke que la pensée pourrait bien
être une modification de la matière'
(Best.3403; xvii.91). Fundamentally,
of course, Diderot was right in his
assertion, and this becomes all the more
clearly apparent when we read in a
letter dated July 1757 from Voltaire to
d'Alembert concerning the *Encyclopédie*: 'Je prie l'honnête homme qui
fera "Matière" de bien prouver que le
je ne sais quoi qu'on nomme "matière"
peut aussi bien penser que le je ne sais
quoi qu'on appelle "esprit"' (M.xxxix.
237). See also *Micromégas* (1752) for a
similar view by Voltaire.

aiment mieux se figurer dans Dieu une bonté qui, sans exiger ni pénitence ni satisfaction, pardonne le crime, ou se lasse de le punir. De là dans leurs systèmes les idées les moins homogènes se confondent, comme celles de l'intolérance et de la persécution'.[76]

If the aforementioned works of Voltaire had furnished Berthier occasion for attack, the *philosophe*'s imprudent poem on Jeanne d'Arc laid him completely open to some of the journalist's most vehement criticism. When he comes to the *Poème de la Pucelle d'Orléans* the Jesuit editor cannot contain himself as he exclaims: 'Never has hell vomited up a more deadly plague.'[77] Irreligion boldly raises its most licentious banner in this work, he affirms, and 'voluptuousness impudently displays here the most lewd pictures; obscenity borrows the language of the market place for this work; the basest buffoonery seasons its impiety. . . . The odour given off by these verses is enough to infect and corrupt every age and every condition in society.'[78] The editor forsees dire consequences for the future when such poems are permitted to be printed, and he cries out: 'Religion, pudeur, modestie, bienséances, décence, qu'êtes-vous devenues dans un siècle où de pareils attentats contre l'innocence des mœurs publiques osent se produire? Quels vices, quels forfaits ne souilleront pas les âges et les climats qui donneront un cours libre à de pareils écrits?'[79] The appearance of this attack against Voltaire's writings evoked another letter from d'Alembert to his friend the same month, in which he notes: 'I recommend to you Garasse Berthier who, so they tell me, has again harassed you in his latest journal. These are the works which should be curbed by "declarations".'[80]

Berthier's decision to expose the irreligion he found in Voltaire's works, a decision arrived at with some reluctance, as we have seen, did not blind the Jesuit editor to the literary merits of the

[76] *J. de T.* (April 1757), ii.1092.
[77] *J. de T.* (April 1757), p.1097.
[78] *J. de T.* (April 1757), p.1097.
[79] *J. de T.* (April 1757), p.1098.
[80] M.xxxix.200. Garasse had been a churchman who wrote against unbelievers in the seventeenth century. Voltaire and d'Alembert frequently use this name in referring to Berthier.

author. Thus, when he reviews a book entitled, *Réflexions philo-sophiques et littéraires sur le Poème de la religion naturelle*, he praises its author for his moderation and his recognition of the literary ability of Voltaire, remarking: 'The factor which increases his merit is that he is not carried away by his zeal: even when dealing with an unbeliever, he respects a man of talent, a man who has made a great name for himself, even though he misuses it; he praises when one should praise.'[81] But Berthier is as firm in his critiques of the *philosophe*'s unorthodox statements. Before considering specific points, the editor shows his uneasiness at the weapon of satire utilized by Voltaire when he says of the 'caustic darts' which the writer likes to 'hurl against holy things and holy people': 'darts all the more capable of impressing a superficial reader because they are thrown as if in passing and jokingly, and they are dipped in the salt of ridicule and seasoned with that decisive and cutting tone, both of which take the place of reasons and arguments for the multitude.'[82] This mode of attack is decried by the Jesuit editor and he expresses surprise that 'a philosophical poet places in opposition to the most serious truths of religion, to the strongest arguments of theology, only witticisms or even sorry jokes.' Turning to the critic's refutation of various objectionable statements made by Voltaire, Berthier pauses at the *philosophe*'s belittling of the immortal soul and points out that here is 'the pitiful contradiction of our free-thinkers. There has been no century in which men have been so proud of the right to think and in which they have been so bent on decrying and debasing that part of ourselves which does the thinking.'[83]

When the author of the *Réflexions* under review suggests that Voltaire is slowing down as a poet, Berthier interrupts his review

[81] *J. de T.* (Sept.1757), p.2146. The previous month Berthier had reviewed a brochure entitled, *Examen du Volté-ranisme* and had stated: 'L'auteur a prétendu combattre le *Poème de la religion naturelle* de m. de V., entreprise louable si elle n'avait eu pour objet que de rappeler ce bel esprit à la religion révélée; mais on s'élève ici presque également contre la loi naturelle, le Christianisme et le matérialisme' (*ibid.* [Aug.1757], p.2095).
[82] *J. de T.* (Sept.1757), p.2150.
[83] *J. de T.* (Sept.1757), p.2157.

to remark that if his faults were only stylistic, Voltaire would still be a great poet. The few negligences brought up by the critic are 'ingenious' and could easily be forgotten. 'If we were permitted to criticise the critic himself, we would say that in several places the reflexions of the observer seem to us to be too severe.' It is not the poetry which is bad, specifies the editor, 'but it is principally because of the subject matter, and the manner of treating it that this poem is reprehensible.' Returning to the poem, Berthier again shows his aversion to Voltaire's mode of attack by insisting: 'On demande de quel côté est l'"imbécile ignorance", ou de l'homme qui paie de raisons, ou de l'homme qui ne répond que par des invectives, des traits caustiques, des mépris insultants, et des saillies brusques? On crie à l'imposture: le sage Chrétien, le vrai Catholique ne juge, ne damne personne; il s'attendrit sur les malheureux qui s'égarent, et laisse à Dieu le soin de les juger. Fondé sur des preuves solides, il croit à la révélation qui n'admet qu'une Religion, et exclut les autres: c'est donc la révélation même, et non pas lui qu'on veut attaquer'.[84] In conclusion Berthier quotes Voltaire's verses:

> Que conclure à la fin de tous mes longs propos?
> C'est que les préjugés sont la raison des sots.

And the editor adds: 'To discover who are these "fools," we should examine on which side the prejudices are to be found.'[85]

Voltaire remained silent before the Jesuit editor's attacks, and, having made his points against the author, Berthier no longer mentioned him until the *philosophe* printed a reply to the *Journal de Trévoux* after a delay of four years. If Voltaire had not chosen to answer Berthier's attacks until 1759 it was not because he was unaware of them. We have seen that d'Alembert had written to his friend informing him of the incriminating articles in the *Journal*. What decided the *philosophe* to answer his critic at that time? Several explanations have been offered. Paillet de Warcy, for example, states that Voltaire, in a fit of rage because Berthier had

---

[84] *J. de T.* (Sept.1757), p.2171.   [85] *J. de T.* (Sept.1757), p.2171.

'refused to recognize him as the Homer and the Sophocles of France,' removed the portrait of father Porée, his former Jesuit teacher, from his wall at Ferney and thereafter attacked Berthier and the Jesuits[86]. Gustave Desnoiresterres, on the other hand, points to the editor's unflattering review of the *Panégyrique de Louis XV*, plus the later attack in 1757 on the *Histoire universelle*, as the reason why the *philosophe* became his 'equally violent and indefatigable enemy.'[87] Finally, d'Alembert, in his *Eloge de Crébillon*, suggests the reason for Voltaire's break with his former teachers when he writes concerning the Jesuits: 'Voltaire eut longtemps à se louer d'eux; et durant tout ce temps leur donna des témoignages publics et multipliés de sa reconnaissance. Ils eurent enfin, par cette fatalité qui les poursuivait dans les dernières années de leur trop long règne, le malheur ou la sottise d'attaquer dans leur journal de Trévoux et ailleurs, cet homme célèbre, et de l'attaquer, non-seulement comme écrivain, mais ce qui était plus propre à lui nuire, comme ennemi de la religion et de l'état. Ce procédé fit taire à l'instant toute la reconnaissance de leur ancien disciple, qui se vengea de ses anciens maîtres, devenus ses ennemis, par des épigrammes en vers et en prose, telles qu'il les savait faire'.[88]

All these reasons probably contributed to Voltaire's break with the editor of the *Journal de Trévoux*. Yet even d'Alembert's account infers that the *philosophe* reacted immediately and in a sudden burst of anger, whereas in reality there was a four-year period of silence on the part of Voltaire before he answered in 1759 the attacks begun by Berthier in 1755. One reason for this silence could be that Voltaire might have considered the journalist's opposition to be too ineffectual to be taken seriously. Despite Berthier's attacks, the *Encyclopédie* had renewed publication after the temporary suppression in 1752. It seemed that the storm had been weathered, and the Jesuits had become more circumspect in

---

[86] *Histoire de la vie et des ouvrages de Voltaire*, i.152.

[87] *Voltaire et la société au XVIIIᵉ siècle*, v.414.

[88] d'Alembert, *Œuvres*, viii.402–3.

dealing with the enterprise. D'Alembert had reflected this point of view in the *Avertissement* to volume iii of the *Encyclopédie* upon its renewed publication in 1753. Four years later he wrote to Voltaire expressing his conviction that the opposition could not stop the movement, remarking: 'They have just published a declaration inflicting the "death penalty" on all who publish writings "tending" to attack religion; but with a little toning down, all will go well, no one will be hanged, and the truth will be told.'[89] Voltaire reflects a similar attitude of aloofness mingled with annoyance when he tells d'Alembert of the activities of the Jesuit Marie, who was preaching against the *philosophes* in Marseilles: 'I do not yet know whether the absurdities of those people should make me burst with laughter or indignation. It is better to laugh; but there are still so many fools that it angers one.'[90]

It is possible that, had it not been for the urgings of d'Alembert, Voltaire might not have engaged so actively in a campaign against the Jesuits. Although the *Journal de Trévoux* had ceased to attack the *Encyclopédie* after its reappearance in 1753, the encyclopedist must have suspected that the Jesuits' opposition had not ceased for that, and he had continued his efforts to enlist the literary talents of his friend against him. Nor did his fears prove to be unjustified. The attempted assassination of Louis xv by Damiens in 1757 had evoked suspicions that the republican doctrines of the encyclopedists, by undermining respect for the authority of the king, had been responsible for the crime[91]. There followed an outbreak of anti-encyclopedist brochures and a renewed movement for more repressive measures against the publication. It began to appear that the earlier optimism had been premature. In addition to *La Religion vengée* and such brochures as Moreau's *Mémoire pour*

[89] d'Alembert states that some Jesuits had attempted to arrange a reconciliation between Voltaire and the society (M.xxxix.199).

[90] M.xxxix.229.

[91] Voltaire, when he heard of the attempt, wrote to d'Alembert that the authors of *La Religion vengée* would probably accuse the would-be assassin of being a Philosophe, adding: 'J'ai bien peur que Pierre Damiens ne nuise beaucoup à la philosophie' (M.xxxix. 159).

servir à l'histoire des Cacouacs, a sermon against the encyclopedists was preached before the king, and it was rumoured that the
Encyclopédie would be more severely censored. After the many
letters received from d'Alembert before this event, in which the
encyclopedist frequently referred to Jesuit activities against the
Encyclopédie, it is not surprising that Voltaire should suspect his
former teachers when the renewed attacks against the publication
were intensified in late 1757. Recalling d'Alembert's reference to
Berthier's role in the publication of *La Religion vengée* he writes
to Thieriot on 5 January 1758: 'Je ne sais pas comment les supérieurs des jésuites... peuvent souffrir de telles impertinences dans
leurs bas officiers. Ils se font des ennemis irréconciliables.... Voilà
de plaisants marauds, de croire soutenir la religion par des libelles
diffamatoires, et de mériter le pilori en prêchant les bonnes mœurs!
Les prédicateurs de Genève seront plus sages, et je crois qu'ils se
garderont bien de s'exposer au ridicule en attaquant l'*Encyclopédie*'.[92]

Voltaire's concern for the *Encyclopédie* is evident here, and it
seems that with sufficient encouragement from d'Alembert, he
would go all-out in its defense. He writes to Diderot urging him
to stand firm in the face of the renewed attacks[93], and when he
learns of d'Alembert's withdrawal from the editorial staff, he en-
treats him to reconsider, writing at the same time to Diderot to

[92] M.xxxix.352.

[93] Raymond Naves cites this letter to
uphold his statement that Voltaire, in
writing to Diderot, 'lui envoie un vi-
brant appel au combat, et ce combat
doit s'engager contre les jésuites, à qui
il attribue les *Cacouacs*' (*Voltaire et
l'Encyclopédie* [Paris 1938], p.53).
While Voltaire banteringly refers to
himself here as a 'cacouac' he does not
attribute the publication to the Jesuits.
He does make a reference to the authors
of 'une libelle périodique contre vous,'
which is more likely *La Religion ven-*
gée, a series of volumes which, in fact,
was published periodically and of which
d'Alembert had already made him
aware in his letters. The letter reads in
part: 'Mandez-moi, je vous prie, les
noms de ces malheureux .... On dit
que ces monstres veulent faire les plaisants, et qu'ils prétendent venger la
religion, qu'on n'attaque point, par des
libelles diffamatoires qui devraient servir à allumer les bûchers de leurs sodo-
mites prêtres, si on n'avait pas autant
d'indulgence qu'ils ont de fureur'
(M.xxxix.364).

enlist his aid in reversing the ex-editor's decision[94]. When on 20 January 1758 d'Alembert writes him defending his position, Voltaire's attitude changes completely, and he abandons the publication—a fact which illustrates clearly the influence of d'Alembert on the *philosophe*. To Voltaire d'Alembert was the chief force on the staff of the *Encyclopédie*[95], and his defense of the enterprise was prompted in part by a sense of loyalty to his friend.

While Voltaire's ties with the Jesuits had all but been severed by 1758, he still seemed to blame their 'bas officiers,' rather than the Society in general, for the strong opposition to the *Encyclopédie*, and Berthier is looked upon as the real culprit. Thus, when a year later the news reached him of the arrest and imprisonment of Portuguese Jesuits in connection with the attempted assassination of their king, Voltaire's first reaction, despite a tinge of sarcasm at their expense, is one of disbelief. In a letter to Tronchin dated February 1759 he declares: 'The resident does not believe the news about the Jesuits; nothing has been sent to him from Versailles; therefore it is very suspect.' But he adds rather ironically—it will be recalled that he had ascribed the attempted murder of Louis xv alternately to the Jesuits and the Jansenists: 'It is apparently some Jansenist who probably invented these horrors, of which all Jesuits have always been incapable, as everyone knows.'[96] A week later Voltaire continues to maintain that the Jesuits are innocent of the crime by writing in the same vein: 'It is quite understandable that they may have encouraged an assassination and that they may have prayed for the success of that holy action; but the fact that they were brought to prison in

[95] in 1757 mme d'Epinay complains of this to Grimm when she tells him of her visit to Voltaire, exclaiming: 'Croiriez-vous qu'on ne parle que de d'Alembert lorsqu'il est question de l'*Encyclopédie*?' (M.xxxix.333). This attitude was understandable when we consider that Voltaire's chief contact with the publishers was through his friend's letters. It will be recalled that it was d'Alembert who first approached the *philosophe* in the name of the enterprise when he wrote Voltaire thanking him for taking the abbé de Prades into his home at Potsdam in August 1752.

[96] M.xl.35.

bins like bundles of laundry seems to me suspicious, and makes me tremble for the truth of what is being charged against them.'[97] The correspondence of the *philosophe* reveals a progressive acceptance of the charges against the Jesuits of Portugal but with fluctuations between a wait and see attitude and outright accusations of their members as 'assassins of kings.' This seems to be a period of indecision. One has the impression that, although near the point of exasperation, Voltaire still retains a certain regard for his former teachers, and would be willing to overlook past attacks against him provided the *Journal de Trévoux* desist from further provocations. In a letter to d'Alembert dated February 1759, he states: 'I must know, my dear and great philosopher, if brother Berthier continues to stuff his "monthly purges" of Trévoux with insults and stupidities against honest men who are not thinking of him.'[98] D'Alembert replied somewhat vaguely that although he no longer read Berthier's *Mémoires de Trévoux* he has heard that 'they have not degenerated.'[99]

[97] Voltaire's suspicion was justifiable because according to Ludwig Pastor the Portuguese minister (the marquis of Pombal) had wished to expel the Jesuits as defenders of papal policies, to make way for a state-controlled church patterned after that of England (*History of the popes*, xxxvi.371). The Jesuits had already been denied access to the court, where they had been confessors to the royal family, and Pombal had attacked their activities in Paraguay as dangerous to the nation, when the attempt was made on the king's life. The deed occurred while Joseph I was returning with the young marchioness Teresa de Tavora, with whom he was on intimate terms, and was ascribed to the desire of her family to avenge its honour. An official report issued 4 September 1758 announced that the king had fallen down a flight of stairs and injured his shoulder. Pombal evidently saw in the incident an opportunity to remove the greatest obstacle to a severance of the Portuguese church from Rome and, three months later, the old marquis of Tavora was arrested with his family and domestic staff, twelve of the eighteen defendants being executed. Ten Jesuits, including Malagrida, Tavora's confessor, were arrested as instigators of the plot and sentenced without trial. Malagrida was imprisoned, and two years later burned by the inquisition for heresy and subversive doctrines, the Jesuit order was expelled from Portugal, and a rupture with the papacy was effected shortly thereafter; see Pastor, xxxvi.3–11, 308ff, and Ranke, *History of the popes*, ii.489.

[98] M.xl.40.

[99] M.xl.45. Actually, Berthier had not attacked Voltaire since his article in the September 1757 issue of the *Journal*.

The storm against the encyclopedists was made more intense upon the appearance of Helvétius' *De l'esprit*. Linking his name with the *Encyclopédie*, the authorities implicated Diderot and his staff as sharing the deterministic views expressed in *De l'esprit*. There followed an official condemnation on 8 March 1759, not only of *De l'esprit* and the *Encyclopédie*, but also of Voltaire's *Lettres philosophiques* and *Poème sur la loi naturelle*. This second suppression of the *Encyclopédie*, and the condemnation of some of his own works apparently made a strong impression on Voltaire, and no doubt reinforced his decision, arrived at after d'Alembert's resignation from the staff of the *Encyclopédie*, to withdraw from polemic activity against the Jesuits. In a letter to Bertrand dated 22 March 1759 he writes: 'Je crois que l'*Encyclopédie* se continuera; mais probablement elle finira encore plus mal qu'elle n'a commencé et ce ne sera jamais qu'un gros fatras. J'ai eu la complaisance d'y travailler lorsqu'il y avait encore un peu de liberté dans la littérature; mais, puisque les assassins des rois coupent les ongles aux gens de lettres, il faut se contenter de penser pour soi, et laisser là le public qui ne mérite pas d'être instruit'.[100]

This attitude, reflecting a momentary discouragement perhaps due to an exaggerated idea of the power of the Jesuits as manifested in the recent condemnation[101], was to be short-lived. This had not been simply another storm against the encyclopedists; it seemed to be a final, concerted assault meant to silence them once and for all. D'Alembert had frequently made Voltaire aware of Berthier's role against the *Encyclopédie*. By May 1759 the *philosophe* was convinced that he must take an active part in this crucial struggle. He announces his intention to reply to their mutual enemies when he writes to d'Alembert: 'What! You are answer-

[100] M.xl.65.
[101] an indication of Voltaire's conviction at this time that the Jesuits were invincible may be seen in a letter to Bertrand three weeks after the condemnations of 8 March 1759. Referring to the yet undecided fate of the Jesuits in Portugal he writes: 'Les jésuites échapperont, n'en doutez pas; et peut-être dans un an ils seront tout-puissants en Portugal comme ils le furent en France après l'assassinat de Henri IV' (M.xl.71).

ing that madman Rousseau....You embolden me; *I* am answering
brother Berthier and "tutti quanti" and you will see with what
audacity.'[102]

The promised answer, in the form of a prose addition to the
Ode sur la mort de la markgrave de Bareith, far from being merely
a personal reprisal against its author's critics, is in fact a public
announcement that henceforth, those who attack the encyclopedists must answer to Voltaire[103]. Referring to the *Journal de Trévoux*'s accusations that the *Encyclopédie* is dangerous to church and
state, he asks whether the *philosophes* had anything to do with
past religious wars or with the recent attempt on the life of the
king of Portugal. Berthier, a 'Jesuit pedant who is compromising
the society of which he is a member,' as well as other journalists,
are doing all this to earn a few crowns. He makes an exception of
the *Journal des savants* and Bayle, adding: 'J'excepte encore mes
amis; mais je ne puis excepter frère Berthier, principal auteur du
Journal de Trévoux, qui n'est point du tout mon ami. Il faut savoir
qu'il y a non seulement un *Journal de Trévoux*, mais encore un
Dictionnaire de Trévoux: par conséquent il y a eu un peu de jalousie de métier entre les ignorants qui ont fait pour de l'argent le
Dictionnaire de Trévoux et les savants qui ont entrepris le *Dictionnaire de l'Encyclopédie*, je ne sais pourquoi'.[104] While Berthier
is still presented as an individual assailant, the Jesuits are not
spared in Voltaire's consideration of their quarrels with the Jansenists, and it is clear that this is his final ultimatum to the society
which Berthier represented: 'Que le gazetier de Trévoux ne force

[102] M.xl.89.

[103] the *Ode* probably appeared
toward the end of May. In a letter to
d'Argental dated 3 June 1759, Voltaire
refers to it saying: 'Que dites vous de
l'avis à frère Berthier et à "monsieur"
des *Nouvelles ecclésiastiques*?' (M.xl.
112). Beuchot (M.viii.467–468) states
in a footnote that he believes this 'avis'
to be an answer to the *Journal*'s article
on the *Ode* rather than a reference to

the prose addition to the *Ode* itself.
Inasmuch as the letter pertaining to the
'avis' is dated 3 June, and the *Journal
de Trévoux* review of the *Ode* did not
appear until July, the 'avis' more probably refers to the prose addition to
the *Ode*.

[104] M.viii.477. For a complete treatment of this accusation concerning the
Dictionnaire de Trévoux, see chapter IV
below.

point les hommes éclairés à une récrimination juste et terrible; que ses supérieurs mettent un frein à son audace. J'estime et j'aime plusieurs de ses confrères; c'est avec regret que je lui fais sentir son imprudence, qui lui attire de dures vérités. Quel emploi pour un prêtre, pour un religieux, de vendre tous les mois à un libraire un recueil de médisances et de jugements téméraires!'[105]

The July 1759 issue of the *Journal de Trévoux* includes a lengthy article answering the charges made by Voltaire in his *Ode*, and it was clear that the 'gazetteer of Trévoux' was not going to heed the *philosophe*'s warning. Referring briefly to the *Ode* itself, the Jesuit editor states that while there are a few 'harsh or unharmonious verses,' the poem as a whole lacks neither fire nor elevation, but that in eulogizing natural law, the poet should not have forgotten that there is also a revealed religion which should guide men as well[106]. Berthier then turns to the prose dissertation at the end of the poem, and to Voltaire's complaint that false editions are constantly being attributed to him. Even the editions which have not been disavowed by the author contain very reprehensible statements dealing with religion and truth, replies the editor. The reader has only to consult *La Religion vengée* 'whose object is to refute all impious works,' and he will realize this. Only those editions avowed by Voltaire are refuted in this work, continues Berthier, and will the author disavow these too when he sees them refuted? But the gentlemen on the staff of *La Religion vengée* will not be satisfied with that, he promises; they will ask the author to disavow not only the edition of his works but also the impieties they contain, and not only those impieties in general, 'but specific passages on materialism, fatalism, pyrrhonism, deism, universal toleration, etc.'[107]

Turning to various charges made by Voltaire, the Jesuit editor says of the *philosophe*'s accusation that the *Journal* is a 'collection

---

[105] M.viii.478. In addition to this attack in the *Ode*, Voltaire satirized Berthier by introducing a character named Bertios in his play *Socrate* which appeared in June 1759.

[106] *J. de T.* (July 1759), i.1687.

[107] *J. de T.* (July 1759), p.1690.

of falsehoods' that, on the contrary, he is constantly being accused of being too indulgent toward authors and their works, adding:
'Il n'y a que les livres contraires à la religion, aux mœurs, à l'honnêteté et à la paix publique, qui ne méritent aucune indulgence.
Si le *Journal de Trévoux* s'est acquitté de son devoir à cet égard,
quel peut être son crime? Et si l'on se trouve dans le cas de la censure, n'est-il pas juste qu'on s'impute à soi-même les sentiments
et les écrits qui auront pu y donner lieu?'[108] If Voltaire does not
consider the journalist his friend, continues Berthier, that is assuredly a misfortune, and he will try to practice friendship without
friendship in return because religion tells us to love those who do
not love us. The editor will therefore continue to interest himself
in Voltaire's peace and happiness and to hope that 'that holy religion, not only the natural, but the Christian and Catholic one in
which he was born, will occupy the remaining moments which
providence is allowing him in the contemplation of the days in
eternity!'[109] When Voltaire remarks, 'what a business for a priest!,'
Berthier expresses his dislike for his position as editor and agrees
that 'this business, it is true, of being the "gazetteer of Trévoux"
is neither beautiful nor agreeable,' adding: 'Cependant si cette
"gazette" se borne à censurer fortement les livres pernicieux; à
rendre compte honnêtement des ouvrages composés avec sagesse;
à tempérer, dans les cas indifférents ou purement littéraires, la critique par des éloges, il serait difficile d'assurer que la sainteté du
sacerdoce ou de la profession religieuse est blessée par un tel
emploi'.[110]

Berthier then becomes apologetic for entering into such personal details but he explains, 'It is after all necessary to allow us
these discussions, since m. de Voltaire enters into details which
are almost domestic'; and when the author says he will teach the
Jesuit editor 'some harsh truths,' the journalist replies calmly:
'The gazetteer of Trévoux does not consider as "harsh" towards
him what is merely a small attack of ill-humour in this man of fine

[108] *J. de T.* (July 1759), pp.1693-94.   [110] *J. de T.* (July 1759), i.1695-1696.
[109] *J. de T.* (July 1759), p.1695.

talent whose château has ceased to be a place of "Délices", since chagrin has entered it.'[111] Answering briefly the charge dealing with the *Dictionnaire de Trévoux*, 'which is the work neither of the journalists nor of the society of which they are members,' Berthier turns to the accusation that the journalist 'persecutes philosophy and the philosophes,' and he remarks: 'Il n'est point difficile, au reste, de deviner qui sont les "philosophes" dont m. de Voltaire entreprend de venger les droits, et qui sont les "persécuteurs" contre lesquels il tonne. La mode s'est comme établie d'appeler "philosophe" ceux qui attaquent la religion révélée, et "persécuteurs" ceux qui combattent pour sa défense. On prodigue, en même temps, à ces derniers les titres de "superstitieux," de "fanatiques," de "fourbes," de "pédants," de "factieux," etc. M. de Voltaire épuise toute cette nomenclature'.[112] Refuting several other points in Voltaire's *Ode*, the editor ends his article with the announcement that there will be printed in Volume ii of the July *Journal de Trévoux* an extract of a book entitled, *L'Oracle des nouveaux philosophes, pour servir de suite et d'éclaircissement aux œuvres de m. de V.*

The promised article, forty pages in length, begins with the announcement that Voltaire's works will be considered only in regard to the author's treatment of the Christian religion. An exposition is then made of the main tenets of Voltaire's beliefs, including the stand that only natural religion is valid, all others being the result of superstition, barbarism and fanaticism, and instituted by imposture. Voltaire's plea for tolerance and liberty are then described and the editor points out: 'That is the oracle's whole doctrine,' a doctrine which he has been preaching for the past fifty years, embellishing it with 'all the ornaments which dazzle the superficial mind.' When exposing this doctrine, continues Berthier, 'his fertile pen has always been able to compensate for the extreme dearth of proofs by a prodigious abundance of charm.' But this is not the way one should try to convince a rea-

[111] *J. de T.* (July 1759), i.1698.   [112] *J. de T.* (July 1759), i. 1700–1701.

sonable man, he insists: 'Ce n'est ni la variété, ni la légèreté du style; c'est la force et la solidité des principes et des raisons qui doit décider en pareille matière. Quand il s'agit d'intérêts si sérieux, ce n'est pas la beauté du génie, c'est la bonté de la cause qui doit captiver et emporter tous les suffrages'.[113]

The editor then considers in detail Voltaire's views, turning first to the author's belief that one religion is the same as another. If Christ is not divine, replies Berthier, Christians are wrong in considering him as such, while if he is indeed God, how could he look with the same eyes on those who accept him and those who insult him? 'Between truth and imposture,' concludes the editor, 'especially in matters of cult and dogma, we cannot conceive that God could be indifferent.' Similarly, the *philosophe's* denial of the dogma of hell is refuted with the reflection that Voltaire would remove from God all sense of justice and have him regard the believer who adores him sincerely and the unbeliever who blasphemes him as equally worthy of everlasting glory. Voltaire's defense of natural religion meets with more favourable comment, and when he refutes the Hobbesian view that man's notion of justice was merely a social convention acquired in passing from the state of nature to that of social organization, Berthier states that the *philosophe*, in reaffirming the divine inspiration of natural law, is on firmer ground. In this matter, he tells his readers, 'l'oracle semble se métamorphoser et devenir aussi bon Philosophe qu'il est grand poète, puisque, dans son poème de la religion naturelle, il y a peu de vers aussi beaux, comme il n'y en a point d'aussi vrais, que ceux où il établit l'inspiration de la loi naturelle. On les rappelle ici avec complaisance'.[114]

Because Voltaire refuses to take the logical step from natural religion to revealed religion, continues the article, it is necessary to demonstrate the insufficiency of natural law and the necessity of a revelation if any certainty is to be had as to exactly what God desires of men. There follows a discussion of the validity and

[113] *J. de T.* (July 1759), ii.1812–1813.   [114] *J. de T.* (July 1759), *loc. cit.* ii.1812–1813.

certainty of the Christian revelation as proved historically through prophecies and miracles, and the editor then turns to the question of tolerance.

To the accusation that the church attempts to force men to believe against their wills, Berthier declares that such a project would not only be tyrannical but it is above the power of tyranny to execute, and he adds: 'Ce projet est une supposition odieuse qu'on prête à l'église Chrétienne. Ce n'est point par la contrainte, comme le Mahométisme et tant d'autres sectes, c'est par la voie de la persuasion et de la conviction la plus éclairée et la plus raisonnable que le Christianisme s'est établi et étendu. Ce n'est point encore autrement qu'il garde ses conquêtes et qu'il en fait de nouvelles. Le cri qu'on élève contre la crainte et la persécution, est donc un cri d'injustice et de calomnie. On ne violente, on ne force personne à professer le Christianisme'.[115]

In taking this position, Berthier, although he never mentions it, must have been aware that there had been and there was still going on in some countries, coercion by the combined ecclesiastical and secular powers, but he seems genuinely opposed to it. Nor was this enlightened position reflected by Berthier that held by all French Catholics of his day; rather, it illustrates the adherence of the Jesuits to ultramontane policies despite national sentiments. Better to understand this position, the religious and political controversies of the time should be taken into account. The struggle for temporal power between the papacy and the Bourbon courts of France and Spain had reached its climax during the reign of Louis XIV. The French king, in fostering his position as absolute monarch, had sought to exclude papal authority from his kingdom not only in temporal but in spiritual matters as well. Rallying the French clergy to his position, he had caused a declaration of Gallican immunities to be drawn up in a convocation held in 1682. Pope Innocent XI denounced this document darticularly because of article IV, which curtailed his spiritual

---

[115] *J. de T.* (July 1759), ii.1820.

authority in the French church, and he refused to grant spiritual sanction to those chosen by the king for episcopal sees. To prove his orthodoxy, the French monarch, in the name of the church, revoked the edict of Nantes which granted religious liberties to the Huguenots. The Papal court, however, had abandoned the policy of coercion—perhaps made wiser through its experience with the Spanish Inquisition[116]—and therefore decried the action of Louis XIV. Leopold von Ranke describes the king's action as follows: 'He believed himself to be rendering a great service to the church. It has indeed been also affirmed that Innocent XI was aware of his purpose and had approved it, but this was not the fact. The Roman court would not now hear of conversions effected by armed apostles. "It was not of such methods that Christ availed himself: men must be led to the temple, not dragged to it".'[117] This latest gesture rejected, and the pope having refused to change his stand toward Gallican liberties, Louis XIV took possession of Avignon and caused the papal nuncio to be shut up at Saint-Olon. Relations worsened between the monarch and the pope, and there was talk of a schism, and the possible appointment by the king of the archbishop of Paris, Harlai, as patriarch of France. Alexander VIII, who had succeeded Innocent XI as pope in 1689, maintained the

[116] the Spanish Inquisition, although established with the approval of Sextus IV, functioned independently of papal authority as a political institution, and is illustrative of the struggle of the Bourbons to exclude papal influence even in the ecclesiastical affairs of their respective nations. Despite condemnations by the popes of the cruelties and injustices of the Inquisition, it was frequently used as a pretext to do away with political enemies or to replenish the royal treasury by confiscation of the property of wealthy citizens. Papal impotence reached the point where at times books approved by Rome were condemned in Spain, and even saints Teresa of Avila and Ignatius Loyola were investigated for heresy. Cf. Ludwig Pastor, *The History of the popes* (St. Louis 1898), iv.400.

[117] *The History of the popes during the last four centuries*, ii.465. Ranke quotes the above from a Vatican manuscript dated 1689. John Alzog states of the revocation: 'It is worthy to mention that pope Innocent XI disapproved of these severe measures, but not being himself on amicable terms with the French king, requested James II of England to interpose his good offices in behalf of the oppressed Protestants' (*Manual of universal church history*, iii.284).

unyielding attitude of his predecessor toward the Gallican declaration, and Louis XIV finally gave in and in 1693 retracted the
offending articles.

In the meantime a quarrel between the Jansenists and the Jesuits
was further dividing the clergy of France. The doctrine on grace
of Baius, condemned by Rome in 1567 and 1579, had been revived
by Jansenius through the translations of the Dutch professor's
work by abbé de Saint-Cyran. Jansenius expounded a doctrine of
grace and predestination close to that of Calvin. In addition,
opposing the council of Trent's decision, upheld by the Jesuits,
which urged frequent reception of the sacrament of holy eucharist
to strengthen the soul against sin, Jansenius declared it to be a
reward for, rather than a means to perfection, and the refusal of
this reward was all the more meritorious. The new doctrine also
called for a restoration of the old discipline of bodily penances
before granting absolution for sins in the sacrament of penance.
The doctrine was condemned and, after numerous delays and
negotiations, the Jansenist bishops were required by Rome to
sign a formula of condemnation of five proposals of Jansenius as
heretical. The dispute between the king and the holy see soon
overshadowed the controversy and Jansenism seemed to disappear.

In 1684 there appeared an edition of the *New testament* by
Pasquier Quesnel which contained commentaries replete with
Jansenist doctrines. Quesnel's bishop, de Noailles (later to become
cardinal, and archbishop of Paris), approved the book but when
Clement XI condemned it, he sought to avoid retracting his approval. There followed twenty years of disputes and condemnation, the Jansenists appealing to the principle of Gallican liberties
as one reason for refusal and the Jesuits upholding papal authority. Finally, through the urgings of the Jesuit Le Tellier, the pope
issued the famous bull *Unigenitus* in 1713, denouncing Quesnel's
heretical doctrine. By thus adopting the Jesuit tenets as opposed
to the Jansenists, says Ranke, 'it is certain that the papacy... succeeded in attaching to its interests that powerful order, which
from that time proved itself the most vigorous defender of ultra-

montane doctrines and the papal claims.'[118] Cardinal de Noailles submitted in 1728, and Jansenism was officially dead, but it survived in the spirit of the ruling classes and the parliament, and thenceforth the Jesuits were singled out for destruction.

The Jesuit defense of papal authority was one of the chief reasons for the suppression of their order not only in France but in Spain and Portugal as well. At a time when the Bourbon monarchs were engaged in a struggle with the papacy for power over the spiritual as well as temporal authority in their realms, the society could only be viewed as an enemy force working against the national interests. In France the order's downfall was precipitated by the enmity of the Jansenists, whose official condemnation had been engineered by the Jesuits. But it is significant to note that the two main charges brought against the Society of Jesus were on nationalistic grounds, their persistent opposition to the four Gallican propositions, and their obedience to their general in Rome. According to Ranke, the Jesuits were attacked by both the *philosophes* and the parliaments because 'that order stood forth as the chief bulwark of the ultramontane principles.'[119]

Berthier's rejection of force as a means of conversion cannot, however, be ascribed entirely to his adherence to papal policies. He seems to have been sincerely convinced that 'the true Catholic does not judge nor condemn anyone; he pities the unfortunate ones who go astray and leaves the task of judging them to God.'[120] If a man should not be forced to accept Christianity against his will, it does not follow that the Jesuit editor believed that he

[118] *The History of the popes*, ii.483.
[119] *ibid.*, ii.485. After the suppression of the Jesuits in France and Spain, continues Ranke, 'the hostility of the Bourbons did not end there. From the persecution of the Jesuits, they proceeded to a direct attack on the holy see. It was proposed to invade the states of the church and starve out Rome.' In 1769 the Neapolitan, Spanish and French ambassadors to the papal court

demanded the suppression of the whole order. When Maria Theresa of Austria refused to come to the aid of the pope because it was not a religious but a political affair, the pontiff's resistance was broken. In 1773 Clement XIV dissolved the society (*ibid.*, ii.493-4).
[120] *J. de T.* (Sept.1757), p.2171. For a more detailed treatment of Berthier's defense of censorship, see Chapter VI below.

should be permitted to attack it when it was the religion of the state. After declaring in his July 1759 article dealing with Voltaire that 'no one is being forced to profess Christianity,' he concedes that in nations where that religion reigns, unbelievers are not permitted to attack its profession and that their books are banned, but that is because 'scandal and license would have disastrous consequences for the public good and the public tranquility.'[121] But it shows 'downright bad faith' and a 'cunning disguise,' he affirms, when 'the *philosophes* who are enemies of religion feign to confuse intolerance enclosed within just limits, and coercion.' On the accusation of coercion, the editor declares: 'On ne vous force pas de partager le dépôt dont nous sommes héritiers; mais on vous défend de le violer et de le profaner. On ne vous oblige pas de vous glorifier dans la foi qui est notre trésor, ni dans l'espérance qu'elle nous donne pour une autre vie; mais on ne permet pas que notre foi et notre espérance soient pour vous un objet de mépris et de dérision. Si vous ne voulez pas prendre part à nos avantages que vous ne pouvez contester, au moins ne leur insultez pas par des écrits scandaleux, dont vous pouvez vous absentir'.[122] Berthier then concludes his remarks on intolerance with the statement: 'Unbelievers, you accuse us of a fanaticism which we do not even have a semblance of possessing, while the hatred which animates you against our religion inspires in you a fanaticism whose too-apparent excesses are inconceivable.'[123]

The article turns once more to the manner in which Voltaire 'exposes his plan of war against Christianity,' and states that this is done not through reason but by relying on 'the indecency of the mockery and on the maliciousness of the sarcasms' with which he fills his work. Similarly, the historical works of the author disfigure the facts 'with the view to combatting Christianity.' The editor then concludes with the remark that Voltaire 'declares himself tolerant of all the religions in the world, except Christianity.'[124]

[121] *J. de T.* (July 1759), ii.1822.
[122] *J. de T.* (July 1759), ii.1822–23.
[123] *J. de T.* (July 1759), ii.1823–24.
[124] *J. de T.* (July 1759), ii.1829.

Berthier probably knew only too well that such outspoken denunciations of Voltaire would not go unanswered, and when we consider the attacks already made on him not only by Voltaire, but by Diderot in the *Encyclopédie*[125], his decision to include the above articles in the July 1759 issue of the *Journal* reveals an unusual steadfastness of purpose. This is particularly so if we are to believe d'Alembert. In a letter to Voltaire in February 1759, he states that 'brother Berthier and his accomplices dare not appear on the streets these days for fear that people will throw Portuguese oranges at their heads.'[126] Berthier's reaction to the attacks on the Jesuits is revealed in a letter to the marquis de Cambis-Velleron dated July 1759. He begins by apologizing for his long delay in writing, explaining that 'all the storms we have undergone during more than six months caused me to renounce all communication with the outside,' and he continues: 'Je me suis borné au train de nos Mémoires que j'aurais encore abandonné de bon cœur si j'en avais été le maître. Vous savez, monsieur, ce que la calomnie et la fureur ont fait inventer, dire, et publier contre nous; l'Europe entière a été inondée de discours et de papiers. Que faire au milieu d'un orage si impétueux? sinon se taire, se cacher, posé et attendre une meilleure vie'.[127]

If Berthier had thought that he had cause to lament he was soon to learn that the 'storm' of which he wrote was but a prelude, because his articles in the July issue of the *Journal* evoked from Voltaire in November of the same year his most devastating satire—the *Relation de la maladie, de la confession, de la mort, et de l'apparition du Jésuite Berthier*. In Swiftian style, the author begins his *Relation* as follows: 'Ce fut le 12 octobre 1759 que frère Berthier alla, pour son malheur, de Paris à Versailles avec frère Coutu, qui l'accompagne ordinairement. Berthier avait mis dans la voi-

---

[125] see Chapter IV below.

[126] d'Alembert, *Œuvres*, xv.95. This was not due exclusively to the attacks of the *philosophes*. The news of the imprisonment of the Jesuits of Portugal for allegedly having plotted the attempted assassination of their king had spread through Europe by this time and was being utilized to discredit the Jesuits of France.

[127] Bibliothèque Calvet, Avignon, MS.3467, f.302.

ture quelques exemplaires du *Journal de Trévoux*, pour les présenter à ses protecteurs et protectrices; comme à la femme de chambre de madame la nourrice, à un officier de bouche, à un des garçons apothicaires du roi, et à plusieurs autres seigneurs qui font cas des talents. Berthier sentit en chemin quelques nausées; sa tête s'appesantit: il eut de fréquents bâillements. "Je ne sais ce que j'ai", dit-il à Coutu, "je n'ai jamais tant bâillé". "Mon révérend père", répondit frère Coutu, "ce n'est qu'un rendu". "Comment! que voulez-vous dire avec votre rendu?" dit frère Berthier. "C'est", dit frère Coutu, "que je bâille aussi, et je ne sais pourquoi, car je n'ai rien lu de la journée, et vous ne m'avez point parlé depuis que je suis en route avec vous." Frère Coutu, en disant ces mots, bâilla plus que jamais. Berthier répliqua par des bâillements qui ne finissaient point. Le cocher se retourna, et les voyant ainsi bâiller se mit à bâiller aussi; le mal gagna tous les passants: on bâilla dans toutes les maisons voisines. Tant la seule présence d'un savant a quelquefois d'influence sur les hommes!'[128]

Following this extremely effective introduction, the condition of the Jesuit editor is described as growing worse, and upon examination he is found to have been poisoned. When the doctor asks the coachman if he has been transporting packages for an apothecary, the latter replies that the only package he has in the coach is that containing two dozen copies of the *Journal de Trévoux*. 'Well, gentlemen,' exults the doctor, 'was I wrong?' The package is burned and Berthier is given a page of the *Encyclopédie* in a glass of wine as a remedy. A priest is called to confess the dying editor, and the interrogation by the confessor affords Voltaire an opportunity to bring up a series of scandals involving Jesuits, including several authors in the society whose books had been condemned, and the imprisonment of the Jesuits in Portugal as accomplices in the attempted assassination of the king. When the priest hears that Berthier is editor of the *Journal*, he begins recounting the evils it has caused and refuses the Jesuit absolution unless he promises to abandon the publication. At that moment

[128] M.xxiv.95–96.

Coutu interrupts to tell the dying man that his confessor is none other than the editor of the Jansenist *Nouvelles ecclésiastiques*, a bitter foe of the Jesuits. The shock of this discovery causes Berthier to admit that he has been a bore, a fanatic and that he has written many hateful and idiotic things, but, he says, the Jansenists are no better. There follows a clever monologue in which, through the editor's dying words, Voltaire attacks both the Jesuits and the Jansenists: 'Nous voulons dominer partout, je le confesse; et toi, tu voudrais tout brouiller. Nous voudrions séduire toutes les puissances; et toi, tu voudrais exciter la sédition contre elles. La justice a fait brûler nos livres, d'accord; mais n'a-t-elle pas fait aussi brûler les tiens? Nous sommes tous en prison dans le Portugal, il est vrai; mais la police ne t'a-t-elle pas poursuivi cent fois, toi et tes complices? Si j'ai eu la bêtise d'écrire contre des hommes éclairés qui dédaignaient jusque-là de m'écraser, n'as-tu pas eu la même impertinence? ne nous tourne-t-on pas tous deux également en ridicule? et ne devons-nous pas avouer que dans ce siècle, l'égout des siècles, nous sommes tous deux les plus vils insectes de tous les insectes qui bourdonnent au milieu de la fange de ce bourbier?'[129] With this avowal, the Jesuit editor dies to the consoling words of Coutu who exclaims: 'Ah! reverend father, you are a saint, . . . you are the first author who has ever admitted that he was boring; now, die in peace . . . and you can be sure that you will work miracles.'[130]

---

[129] M.xxiv.101.

[130] M.xxiv.101. That the *Relation* was not intended merely as a means of giving vent to the author's personal animosity toward Berthier is evident not only from the *Relation* itself with its denunciation of the Jesuits in general, but from Voltaire's correspondence as well. When writing to mme d'Epinay in October 1759, Voltaire mentions the success of his brochure and speaks of his projected *Apparition du jésuite Berthier* adding: 'L'Apparition pourra bien valoir l'agonie. Petit caractère et net, afin de tenir peu de place . . . . Il faut rendre "l'infame" ridicule, et ses fauteurs aussi. Il faut attaquer le monstre de tous côtés, et le chasser pour jamais de la bonne compagnie' (M.xl.196). In another letter the following month, the author again reflects this attitude when he tells mme d'Epinay of the *Relation*: 'Il m'a paru pourtant qu'il y a un peu de gros sel dans la première partie; mais tout est bon pour les jésuites' (M.xl. 242).

Berthier, as we have seen in the letter already quoted, had decided on a policy of silence during the 'storm' which had broken against him and his society. The *Relation* no doubt reinforced this resolution, and Voltaire was never again mentioned by name in the *Journal de Trévoux*. Two works by Voltaire, but published anonymously, received brief mention by the Jesuit editor in the ensuing years. The first, the *Panégyrique de saint Louis*, is presented to the readers of the *Journal* as follows: 'En général l'auteur, quel qu'il soit, s'élève ou s'échauffe difficilement. Il prend bien des mesures avant que d'en venir aux grands traits d'éloquence: mais nous remarquons avec plaisir que, quand il est parvenu à se dégager des préliminaires, et à se livrer au pathétique, il met véritablement beaucoup de feu et d'intérêt dans sa manière'.[131]

Voltaire's brochure, *Projet aussi utile aux sciences et aux lettres, par Sadoc Zorobabel*, evokes a brief mention in May 1762, when the editor says that it is 'only a pleasantry.' The remark that ecclesiastics are more rigid toward simony when they have the least hope of obtaining benefits, is described as being 'of a piquant malignity,' and the article concludes by noting that 'this whole plan is scattered with lightly malicious remarks which will have no other effect than to amuse for a moment idle readers. We believe that in truth Sadoc Zorobabel is capable of writing something better than a caviling brochure.'[132]

Having once committed himself to an active campaign against the Jesuits, and particularly against their spokesman Berthier, Voltaire, as was his custom with those against whom his animus was aroused, seized upon the editor of the *Journal de Trévoux* and pursued him relentlessly. Commenting on this, Diderot wrote of the editor in the article 'Jésuite' in the *Encyclopédie*: 'Il a bêtement irrité contre sa société notre de Voltaire, qui a fait pleuvoir sur elle et sur lui le mépris et le ridicule, le peignant, lui, comme un imbécile, et ses confrères tantôt comme des gens dangereux et méchants, tantôt comme des ignorants, donnant l'exemple et le

---

[131] *J. de T.* (Jan.1760), ii.355.   [132] *J. de T.* (May 1762), pp.1183ff.

ton à tous nos plaisants subalternes'.[133] In addition to attacks on the Jesuits in general, such as the famous cry of 'Let us eat Jesuit, let us eat Jesuit,' in his masterful satire *Candide* (1759), there flowed from the pen of Voltaire a constant stream of writings against Berthier. In 1760 he published an addition to the *Relation de la maladie du Jésuite Berthier* in the form of a *Relation du voyage du frère Garassise, continuateur du Journal de Trévoux*. In the same year the editor was again satirized in the poem, *Dialogue d'un Parisien et d'un Russe*. An attempt by his Jesuit neighbors near Ferney to expand their lands at the expense of six brothers who owned property adjoining theirs, furnished Voltaire a further opportunity to show his anger toward Berthier. The six brothers Desprez de Crassy had heavily mortgaged their property to a Genevese official, and the Jesuits of Ornex had purchased the debt from the original mortgagee. By proving that the debtors were unable to pay, the Jesuits obtained title to the property. Voltaire, as he was later to do in such cases of injustice as those involving Calas, Sirven, La Barre and others, came to the rescue of the brothers, and forced the Jesuits to return the property to its rightful owners[134]. The *philosophe* relates the incident to d'Argental as follows: 'Amusez-vous de cet imprimé, et voyez comme on trouve des jésuites partout: mais aussi ils me trouvent. Je leur ai ôté la vigne de Naboth. Il leur en coûte vingt-quatre mille livres: cela apprendra à Berthier qu'il y a des gens qu'on doit ménager'.[135]

In December 1761 the Jesuit editor is satirized under the name of Bathos in *Les Chevaux et les ânes*, while a few months later the new edition of *La Pucelle* contains a number of verses against 'the author of the *Journal de Trévoux*.' By May 1762 Voltaire was obliged by his health to reduce his literary activity[136]. He

[133] Diderot, *Œuvres*, xv.284.

[134] Desnoiresterres, vi.59–61. Desnoiresterres states that in the case of the brothers Desprez de Crassy, Voltaire was motivated more by 'l'envie de prouver aux Berthier, aux Kroust et "tutti quanti," qu'il ne fait pas bon s'attaquer à lui' (p.61).

[135] M.xl.177.

[136] in April 1760 he had written to d'Alembert, 'J'avoue que je ne suis pas mort, mais je ne peux pas dire que je suis en vie; Berthier se porte bien, et je suis malade' (M.viii.365).

complains of this to de Cideville, stating: 'The work which was my consolation has been forbidden me. I can no longer make sport of brother Berthier, de Pompignan and Fréron.'[137]

Further attacks were unnecessary, in any case, because in 1762 the Jesuits were suppressed and Berthier ceased to be the editor of the *Journal de Trévoux*. D'Alembert kept his friend posted as to Berthier's activities, and after writing several letters mentioning the rumour that the ex-editor was to be named tutor to the children of the king, he writes in September 1762: 'Brother Berthier, according to what he said, felt like going to a Trappist monastery, and he ended up wanting to go to Versailles . . . . They say he will be active in the education [of the king's children] without having any title.'[138]

The expulsion of the Jesuits had aroused the pity even of those who had been violently against them, relates de Tocqueville, 'and those Jesuits who remained in France saw the most respected houses open to them. It became in good taste to have one's Jesuit as an habitual guest.'[139] It would seem that Voltaire had not been exempt from this general movement of compassion at the suppression of the Jesuits because his friend d'Alembert writes to him on 25 September 1762: 'Savez-vous ce qu'on me dit hier de vous? que les jésuites commençaient à vous faire pitié, et que vous seriez presque tenté d'écrire en leur faveur, s'il était possible de rendre intéressants des gens que vous avez rendus si ridicules. Croyez-moi, point de faiblesse humaine; laissez la canaille janséniste et parlementaire nous défaire tranquillement de la canaille jésuitique et n'empêchez point ces araignées de se dévorer les unes les autres'.[140]

While Voltaire no doubt was concerned over the fate of the Jesuits it was probably less out of pity for them than for fear of the consequences of their suppression in France. Despite his attacks

---

[137] M.xlii.117.
[138] d'Alembert, *Œuvres*, xv.220–22.
[139] *Histoire philosophique du règne de Louis XV* (Paris 1847), ii.345. In this respect Voltaire was in the fashion, for he too had his Jesuit, father Adam.
[140] M.xlii.248.

on them he had always admired their educational system of which he himself had been a product. Thus in 1763 he tells Bianchi concerning the Jesuits: 'Les jansénistes ont tant fait qu'ils ont fermé leurs théâtres. On dit qu'ils fermeront bientôt leurs écoles. Ce n'est pas mon avis; je crois qu'il faut les soutenir et les contenir: leur faire payer leurs dettes quand ils sont banqueroutiers; les pendre même quand ils enseignent le parricide; se moquer d'eux quand ils sont d'aussi mauvais critiques que frère Berthier. Mais je ne crois pas qu'il faille livrer notre jeunesse aux jansénistes, attendu que cette secte n'aime que le *Traité de la Grâce,* de saint Prosper, et se soucie peu de Sophocle, d'Euripide, et de Térence'.[141]

A further consideration was the fear that the Jansenists, having crushed their greatest opponents, would now devote all their energies against the *philosophes.* Voltaire reflects this concern when he writes to d'Alembert: 'The jesuits were necessary, they were a diversion; we made fun of them, and we are going to be crushed by pedants who will only inspire indignation.'[142]

D'Alembert did not seem to share Voltaire's concern over the expulsion of the Jesuits of France. Indeed, he sought to have them suppressed in Prussia as well. In a letter dated 29 December 1763 he tells Voltaire that he is trying to convince Frederick that he should expel them from his kingdom[143]. Voltaire replied that if he wished to lower himself to expelling the Jesuits of Silesia he would probably succeed but 'you will not have the pleasure of chasing French Jesuits; Luc [Frederick] got rid of them a long time ago.'[144] The project proved a failure and d'Alembert tells his friend that the monarch has refused to expel the Jesuits, saying that 'he will leave it to a bellicose nation like France' to fight

[141] M.xli.573. René Pomeau, in his article 'Voltaire au collège,' states: 'Si maître Arouet eût confié son cadet aux messieurs jansénistes de Saint-Magloire qui avaient élevé l'aîné, Voltaire eût été un autre Voltaire. L'élève du P. Porée a subi "l'emprise"; il l'a reconnu lui-même, dans des déclarations à la fois intéressées et sincères' (*Revue d'histoire littéraire de la France* [janvier–mars 1952], lii.1).
[142] M.xliii.185.
[143] M.xliii.63.
[144] M.xliii.82.

them[145]. The Encyclopedist's obstinate pursuit of the Jesuits is understandable when we consider that it was they, and Berthier in particular, who had been most consistently opposed to the *Encyclopédie* and had been instrumental in its suppression[146]. There is a possibility that, as when d'Alembert had influenced Voltaire to attack the Jesuits openly in 1759, he may have succeeded in enlisting the aid of the *philosophe* in his campaign to have them expelled from Prussia. De Tocqueville states that when in 1764 Voltaire asked Frederick not to accept ex-Jesuits in his kingdom, the monarch reminded the author of his debt to the Jesuits, pointing out: 'Souvenez-vous, je vous prie, du père Tournemine, votre nourrice (vous avez sucé chez lui le lait des muses), et reconciliez-vous avec un ordre qui a porté, et qui, le siècle passé, a fourni à la France des hommes du plus grand mérite'.[147]

Berthier, in fact, was not so far away from Voltaire in his personal views as their enmity might suggest. As we have already seen, the Jesuit editor was a man of the enlightenment, sharing the views of many of the *philosophes* regarding the monarchy, experimental science, and even tolerance, insofar as he decried the use of physical violence in combatting irreligion and recognized the futility of trying to influence men into accepting Christianity through any other means than persuasion through reason. What placed him at odds with Voltaire and the *philosophes* in general was his determination to defend his faith and the values of Christianity of which he was so firmly convinced. In this defense, he

---

[145] M.xliii.180.

[146] see Chapter IV below.

[147] *Histoire philosophique*, ii.349. The same letter is also quoted by de Warcy, *Histoire de Voltaire*, i.198. In the *Œuvres* of both Voltaire and d'Alembert, as well as in Koser and Droysen's *Briefwechsel*, there are no letters between the monarch and the *philosophe* between 31 October 1760 and 1 January 1765. Moland states that a letter from Voltaire to Frederick dated

9 December 1764 has been lost (M.xliii. 421). In any event, one reason for the coolness between them had been the king's refusal to commit himself completely to the cause of the encyclopedists. When d'Alembert wrote in 1764 that he would like to see Voltaire and Frederick reconciled, the *philosophe* replied: 'If he had done what he had so often promised me in the past, to lend a vigorous hand to crush *l'inf* . . ., I could forgive him' (M.xliii.313.).

upheld the censorship of the press on the grounds that since France was a Catholic nation, any attack on its religion was an attack on the government, and if allowed it would result in revolt and civil strife. It was because the accusation of irreligion was closely linked with that of conspiracy and sedition against the nation that the *philosophes* were particularly endangered by the attacks against them in the *Journal de Trévoux*. These attacks were all the more redoubtable because Berthier refused to engage in personalities but tried to limit himself to a refutation of the ideas he found objectionable, while recognizing even in the writings he most strongly condemned the genius of the author who produced them. This moderate tone, together with Berthier's constant appeal to reason, probably carried more weight with his readers than personal vituperation would have done. His attempt to limit his quarrels to the issues under discussion did not spare him from the fate of those who incurred the wrath of Voltaire. Like Fréron and Lefranc de Pompignan, he was to be mercilessly plagued with the brilliant and unrelenting satire of his most persistent adversary, and was thereby to achieve a dubious immortality.

III

Jean Jacques Rousseau

The relations between Jean Jacques Rousseau and the *Journal de Trévoux* were more cordial than those enjoyed by most of the *philosophes*. One reason for this may be found in Rousseau's writings themselves. Presenting as they did arguments for virtue and religion, they seemed to emanate from a well-intentioned author who now and then went astray from orthodoxy only through a misguided zeal for moral values. Such a solicitude for virtue would necessarily strike a responsive chord in the editor of the *Journal*, who felt that the vices decried by Rousseau were only too real[1]. While concurring in the *philosophe*'s revulsion from the vices of courtly life, as we have seen, Berthier was far from ascribing them to the same cause suggested in the *Discours sur les sciences et les arts*.

In 1747 Berthier had already decried the 'injustice of those who ascribe to the arts and sciences, the personal faults of the scholars, of the artists, the ridiculous customs they have assumed, and the abuse which they have made of their talents.'[2] Four years later,

---

[1] this is particularly true of Rousseau's early writings, but the favourable impression they created persisted throughout his career. As late as 1775, when the *philosophe* had already shown clearly in his *Emile* that his was not an orthodox concept of Christianity, Chaudon, a bitter anti-*philosophe*, could still praise Rousseau's zeal for morality, and indicate his hope for the author's conversion by adding: 'Plaise à ce Dieu qui lui a dicté un si bel éloge de la morale évangélique, lui inspirer plus de foi pour ses dogmes, et ouvrir ses oreilles à la voix de la grâce, et ses yeux à la lumière de la vérité!' (*Anti-Dictionnaire philosophique*, ii.336). Even at the beginning of the nineteenth century Feller bemoans the fact that those who claim to be defending the church against the doctrines of the encyclopedists invariably omit Rousseau from their attacks even though he is as irreligious as the *philosophes*, and indeed, continues the critic, they even go so far as to praise Rousseau for his solicitude for religious values (*Mélanges de politique de morale et de littérature* [Louvain 1822], i.36off).

[2] *J. de T.* (Sept.1747), p.1807.

when Rousseau's first discourse appeared, the Jesuit editor reflected the same attitude. In considering the *Discours*, Berthier preludes his review with the following remark: 'On a dit du p. Malebranche que "l'imagination servait un ingrat"; et le moins qu'on puisse dire, après avoir lu le discours qui s'annonce ici, c'est que l'auteur, en le composant, ne songeait guères aux services qu'il recevait actuellement des lettres et des sciences. Cependant comment pouvait-il ne pas voir tous les trésors de l'éloquence et du génie prodigués en sa faveur? Comment se rendait-il insensible à la différence extrême que la Littérature met entre lui et le vulgaire ignorant?'[3] This discourse seems capable of causing a revolution in commonly accepted ideas, continues the article, and a lengthy passage is quoted beginning with the words 'O Fabricius!' Pausing to admire its 'virile and vigorous beauty,' the editor answers the exhortation to destroy the products of art by asking what crimes those statues and edifices have committed, or what guilt can be ascribed to the rich libraries, the sanctuaries of erudition and the famous schools which the author would destroy.

When Rousseau strikes out at those who smile with disdain at the words 'nation' and 'religion,' and who use their talents to destroy 'everything held sacred among men,' he evokes a more favourable reaction from his critic, who comments: 'We can only applaud these marks of zeal; and the author merits praise in the detail of his discourse; not to mention the literary glory which is due his fine intellect and his powerful eloquence.' But does he always avoid confusing science itself with what is only its abuse? asks the editor. And he underlines his remarks by asking whether iron should be abolished from agriculture because it has been used as a weapon to kill citizens, or whether all religion should be abolished simply because some unscrupulous individuals profane

---

[3] *J. de T.* (Feb.1751), p.506. Voltaire was to write a similar reminder to Rousseau when, upon receiving the *Discours sur l'origine de l'inégalité*, he wrote: 'Les lettres nourrissent l'âme, la rectifient, la consolent; elles vous servent, monsieur, dans le temps que vous écrivez contre elles; vous êtes comme Achille, qui s'emporte contre la gloire, et comme le père Malebranche, dont l'imagination brillante écrivait contre l'imagination' (M.xxxviii.449–450).

it by using it as a pretext to veil their passions. Enumerating some of Rousseau's arguments, the Jesuit editor remarks: 'All these reasons when justly evaluated attack only the disorders, the excesses, the digressions.' He concludes his review on a light note by commenting that 'in general, this whole discourse is of such taste, of such force as to make one wish that the author may no longer quarrel with the muses: they would lose too much from it, and what should they not do to win him over to their side!'[4]

When Rousseau wrote an answer to the critics of his first discourse, Berthier could not help but admire its author's talent, and making known Rousseau's answer, the editor announces to his readers: 'Nous ne ferons point remarquer que l'auteur tire toutes sortes d'avantages de son sujet, soit pour se dégager des objections personnelles qu'on lui fait, à des contradictions qu'on lui reproche, soit pour dire quelque chose d'obligeant à son adversaire. Il y a bien de l'esprit dans tout ce procédé et l'on sent cela d'autant mieux qu'on est plus instruit des qualités de l'agresseur et des talents de celui qui est sur la défensive. Quelle modestie d'ailleurs dans ce dernier, quel ton vertueux, quelle sincérité; et en même temps quelle adresse à remettre les sciences sous le glaive de la critique!'[5] Then, in the same bantering tone he had used in reviewing the *Discours*, Berthier points out several contradictions he finds in Rousseau's defense of it, such as the statement that, while the arts and sciences corrupt a nation, yet each individual in that nation can be a learned and honest man. 'There must be some sort of metaphysics in this,' the editor remarks, 'and we do not know how a scholarly nation will be corrupted while each individual scholar can be or even is virtuous.'

When he touches on the matter of religion, however, Berthier becomes more serious, and he recognizes the potential influence of Rousseau's prose on religious sentiment when he comments: 'Inasmuch as the interests of religion are involved in this controversy, m. Rousseau deals with this matter with a force, with an

[4] *J. de T.* (Feb.1751), pp.519ff.   [5] *J. de T.* (Dec.1751), pp.2541-42.

elevation of genius and style which can make a great impression on his readers.' Summarizing Rousseau's arguments from the Bible, including the assertion that Christ did not choose philosophers but simple folk as his disciples, Berthier concludes: 'Here is an excellent passage and one finds there some great truths; but still a little too much in that general, exclusive, absolute tone which touches one of the extremes.'[6]

A 'Lettre de J. J. R. de Genève à m. Grimm', written by Gautier, appearing the following month in the *Journal de Trévoux* affords Berthier another opportunity to consider the controversial Rousseau. After comparing him to Hannibal because in his attack against literature he shows 'neither truce, nor peace, nor settlement, nor modification, nor moderation,' the Jesuit editor speculates jocosely on what the writer would do if he were not at war against the arts and sciences. No doubt, he suggests, Rousseau would become embroiled in some other controversy, and it could be so much the worse for his adversary because he has all the talents of the most famous lawyer in pleading his cause. Such promptness in replying, and such fire, he concludes, perhaps can be found in him alone[7]. While Berthier indulges in a few chuckles over the author's extreme stand, he cannot but show his admiration for this hitherto little known writer's genius, and in the same issue of the *Journal*, in the course of a review of the *Encyclopédie*, he expresses his high regard for Rousseau. Upon reviewing favourably his article 'Accompagnement,' Berthier asserts: 'Il est honorable à l'*Encyclopédie* d'avoir su s'attacher cet homme de lettres et ce bon écrivain. Il dira sans doute du ton ferme, entier et absolu qu'on lui connaît, qu'il n'en aime pas plus les études et l'érudition. Mais quels que soient ses sentiments, il n'empêchera pas que le concours de ses lumières n'ajoute au mérite de l'*Encyclopédie*'.[8]

By April the *Journal* remarks that Paris is beginning to tire of the dispute over the arts and sciences[9], but the following month,

---

[6] *J. de T.* (Dec.1751), pp.2545ff.
[7] *J. de T.* (Jan.1752), pp.137ff.
[8] *J. de T.* (Jan.1752), p.161.
[9] *J. de T.* (April 1752), p.926.

when Jean Jacques answers still another critic, the Jesuit journalist returns to the controversy to point out that Rousseau is still defending his cause as Cato defended that of the republic, that is, without hope of winning, but with no desire to surrender; still, he continues, this reply, which is a masterpiece of force and eloquence, should be read. A virtuous tone dominates the latest rebuttal, but it is sometimes mingled with bitterness, it is noted. If this affair had been a political or military quarrel, concludes the editor, blood would have been shed. 'Fortunately, it is all being handled with the pen.'[10]

Although the *Journal de Trévoux* usually ignored current theatrical productions, the preface to Rousseau's play *Narcisse, ou l'Amant de lui-même* is mentioned briefly in connection with the author's attempt to justify his literary productions in view of his earlier writings against literature. He cries out against literature, the article begins, but he does not stop writing verses, music and plays. When the preface justifies this by emphasizing that, since everything has been corrupted by letters, one must make use of them to prevent the evil from spreading, Berthier quips that we may now console ourselves since letters are like medicines which benefit the patient who indulges in them[11]. It is obvious from these reviews that the Jesuit editor does not take the quarrel over the arts and sciences too seriously and that, mingled with his raillery, there is a certain admiration for this controversial figure. Thus, when an anonymous defender of the arts stoops to invectives against Rousseau, Berthier denounces such practices and remarks: 'Nous souhaiterions qu'on traitât cette matière "des avantages" ou "des dangers" de la littérature avec tout le sang-froid et tous les égards qu'un si beau sujet mérite. Ce sera une des meilleures justifications de la science, si elle n'inspire que de la douceur et de la politesse à ses défenseurs'.[12]

In the fall of 1753 Rousseau's *Lettre sur la musique française* rekindled a quarrel which had by then begun to subside. French-

[10] *J. de T.* (May 1752), pp.1146–47. [12] *J. de T.* (June 1753), i.1523.
[11] *J. de T.* (March 1752), pp.750ff.

men were divided into two camps over the question whether French music was to follow the tradition of Lully, which stressed simplicity of composition and made music subservient to the poet, or whether it was to follow the innovations of the Italian opera, which stressed melody and made the librettist the hand-maid of the composer. In February 1752 Grimm had published in the *Mercure* a violent attack on French music, upholding the supremacy of the Italians. Several patriotic Frenchmen rose to defend French music, and Rousseau came to Grimm's rescue in a *Lettre à m. Grimm.* The controversy was brought to its peak with the appearance in Paris the same year of an Italian 'opera buffa' troupe. In this quarrel, enlivened by the buffoons, the Encyclopedists upheld the Italians while Fréron and others defended French music. In January 1753 Grimm renewed his attack on French music in a brochure entitled *Le Petit prophète de Boehmischbroda*, in which the destruction of the Academy of music is prophesied if the French do not revitalize their decadent music by following the lead of the Italian Pergolesi. There followed a flurry of brochures and pamphlets on both sides, and the controversy reached its height in February 1753. The following month Rousseau wrote his opera *Le Devin du village*, which seemed to settle the quarrel in favour of Italian music. Soon there-after interest in the controversy died down[13].

Throughout this phase of the buffoons' quarrel the *Journal de Trévoux* had remained silent, but as early as 1746 Berthier had shown himself to be very close to the position which the Ency-clopedists were to champion several years later. In reviewing Bollioud de Mermet's *De la corruption du goût dans la musique française*, which was a plea for maintaining the *status quo* in French music as represented by Lully, and which denounced the 'corrupting' influence of Italian music on that of France, Berthier criticized this stand and took the opportunity to expound his own

[13] see A. Richard Oliver, *The Ency-clopedists as critics of music* (New York 1947), pp.89–95.

ideas on the matter. In the first place, he notes in his review of the work, if composers of today are without verve, it is not that they have drifted from Lully but that they lack genius. Genius is rare, and there were more poor poets and musicians in ancient times than good ones. Indeed 'Molière and Despréaux had as much difficulty in avoiding as in combatting the poor taste or the lack of genius of their contemporaries.' We preach in vain about good taste; it would be more profitable to teach those who are without genius a distaste for and abstention from the arts[14]. Reflecting on the growing disgust of the French for their traditional music, Berthier asks why one should insist on maintaining the standards of Lully? Music needs variety, and if Lully did not use chromatics and harmony, then that is all the more reason for us to use them. Music has to be varied 'unless we want to say that our good taste consists in boring all Europe with the same song with which we ourselves are really bored.'[15] In profane or indifferent arts, why limit intelligence and talent to servile imitations or to a cold and insipid copying? Monotony is the greatest plague of good music. There exist enough compositions by Lully, Lalande and the rest to satisfy those preferring that type of music, he continues, so let us have something new. The best course to follow is to develop a universal taste. Even Turkish and Chinese music contain some good. What we call 'taste for simplicity' or 'taste for what is natural' is equivocal; it is even injurious when it attempts to exclude the richness of nature and of art[16].

It is true that Lully's compositions are models of simplicity, the editor proceeds, but today the range of the keyboard has been extended. The increase in the range of modern instruments has

[14] *J. de T.* (Dec.1746), pp.2037ff.

[15] *J. de T.* (Dec.1746), pp.2638–39. Cahusac reflects the same state of French music in the Encyclopedia article 'Débiter' when he states that foreigners are weary of French music (*Encyclopédie* [Paris 1754], iv.652).

[16] *J. de T.* (Dec.1746), pp.2639ff.

The Encyclopedists also fought prejudices against foreign music. Oliver tells us that they 'taught the French to appreciate the masterpieces of musical composition that were being created abroad, without regard for national barriers or prejudices' (*The Encyclopedists as critics of music*, p.168).

extended our music and our faculties. Why should we not take advantage of the richer and more varied expression now at our command? The organ, for example, should not be limited to a simple accompaniment of the serpent or to the narrow and almost monotonous repetition of the plain chant when of all instruments it is the richest and most varied[17]. Turning to the crux of the controversy, Berthier places himself categorically on the side of Italian music when he asserts: 'The Italians, why hide it, have always been better musicians, and perhaps more inventive than we are.' When Mermet complains that French taste is being corrupted by imitating foreigners, the Jesuit editor replies that if the Italians are better musicians than we are, they should be followed. Our fault is not in imitating them but in doing it badly[18]. He then points out that Mermet makes an exception of Corelli in his criticism because the composer is more 'French.' Thirty years ago, counters Berthier, Mermet would probably not have excepted him. Then Corelli was completely 'Italian' and we were completely 'French.' If our author finds him now to be 'French,' pursues the editor, is it not that he himself has become Italianized to that extent? As for Locatelli, Handel, Hess, Telemann and other foreigners who have residential rights in Paris, those who find them too difficult to follow will probably conclude that these composers 'still reflect the soil of Italy, Germany, or England.'[19] Berthier then concludes his review by answering Mermet's question as to why Frenchmen prefer the taste of foreigners: 'Cela vient, pourquoi non? de ce que le Français a du goût pour toutes sortes de bonnes choses, de ce qu'il a de l'intelligence pour les connaître, de ce qu'il a même une certaine modestie impartiale et pleine d'équité, pour ne pas se croire parfait, et pour sentir que les Italiens le sont plus que lui en ce genre. Que faire? Si la vicissitude des choses humaines a rendu l'Italie l'arbitre et le modèle des

[17] *J. de T.* (Dec.1746), pp.2642–44. The encyclopedists propounded essentially the same theory on the greater perfection of modern musical instruments to explain why Lully wrote simpler music. Cf. Oliver, pp.29, 69.
[18] *J. de T.* (Dec.1746), p. 2647.
[19] *J. de T.* (Dec.1746), p.2648.

beaux arts, comme elle le fut autrefois de l'empire et de l'univers, à l'exclusion de ces mêmes arts, dont elle laissait modestement alors l'empire à la savante Athènes'.[20]

During the renewed furor caused by Rousseau's *Lettre sur la musique française*, the *Journal de Trévoux* attempted to maintain a neutral position in spite of the editor's leanings in favour of much of the *philosophe*'s thesis. The review of the *Lettre* in the January 1754 issue begins in the light manner which Berthier had used in previous reviews of Rousseau's works: 'Voici un ouvrage qui pourra faire croire que l'auteur est bien près de se réconcilier avec les arts et les sciences. Voyez... le pouvoir de la musique.... Celui qui regardait l'étude des lettres ... comme la source des plus grands désordres, nous parle aujourd'hui très sérieusement et en philosophe, d'harmonie et de mélodie ... et autres bagatelles qui sont à la littérature, ce que le clinquant est aux habits de théâtre. Mais si ce fameux censeur des sciences s'intéresse une fois aux objets subalternes, aux connaissances de pur amusement, qui peut désespérer de le voir un jour partisan des grandes choses, de l'éloquence, de l'histoire, &c'.[21]

After chiding Rousseau in this vein Berthier speculates on the reasons which might have led the writer to indulge in the arts which he had previously attacked. In view of such firm assertions in the first discourse, it is pointed out, he could not have changed completely. Either he still has the same convictions—in which case this new article only indicates that he speaks in good faith but conducts himself improperly—or the *Discours* was only a 'purely theoretical thesis or a theory mingled with facts which should not be gone into too deeply.'[22] Turning to the *Lettre* itself, whose contents are described as 'very forceful, not very tactful, very false according to many people,' Berthier gives a

[20] *J. de T.* (Dec.1746), p.2649.
[21] *J. de T.* (Jan.1754), p.111. The placing of music in the category of 'objets subalternes' reflects a prevalent attitude of the period. D'Alembert, in the 'Discours préliminaire', for example, 'gives music the last place among the arts of imitation' (Oliver, p. 62).
[22] *J. de T.* (Jan.1754), p.114.

lengthy resumé of Rousseau's views without venturing an editorial comment, after which he concludes: 'M. Rousseau trouvera des adversaires; il n'en sera pas étonné; il leur répondra peut-être, et il ne changera point de sentiment. Mais quelle que soit la fortune de notre musique il faudra toujours reconnaître deux choses; la première qu'elle est attaquée ici par un écrivain de la plus grande force; la seconde qu'il ne serait pas à propos de mettre, dans cette controverse, plus d'intérêt que de sang froid et de bonne humeur'.[23]

The adversaries of whom the Jesuit editor had spoken were not long in answering. The *Lettre* produced 'no less than 25 works by way of reprisal.'[24] Eight such replies are mentioned in an article in the *Journal de Trévoux*, and in this instance, the editor comes to the defense of Jean Jacques. In answering de Bonneval's apology for French music Berthier concedes that French music may be pleasing to Frenchmen but, he suggests, that does not prove that it is better. France may still be in its childhood when it comes to music, and children admire everything because they have no idea of anything superior. This does not mean that the editor wishes to take Rousseau's side, he adds, but he does not think the critic has proven his point, nor does he approve of the methods employed in defending French music against its adversary: 'On s'y permet quelques personnalités contre lui; mauvaise ressource encore, et capable de faire croire que nous pourrions bien n'avoir point de musique, puisque notre façon de prouver que nous en avons une est si défectueuse'.[25]

The journalist then turns to a letter from Grimm, 'who last year was prophesying against our French music,' and indicates his disapproval of the German critic's attack, which takes the form of a personification of 'French music,' which speaks on its own behalf. Calling the vilification of a nation and its writers an 'equally senseless and base manner of avenging oneself,' Berthier refutes the arguments presented, which are found to be full of

[23] *J. de T.* (Jan.1754), p.131. [25] *J. de T.* (Feb.1754), i.264–5.
[24] Oliver, p.95.

'personal remarks and insults,' and he concludes that 'French music' would have done better to hire a lawyer than to plead for itself in this manner[26]. Bâton's letter agreeing in part with Rousseau but proposing a method for the amelioration of French music is the most pleasing to the Jesuit editor because it tries to formulate a reasonable view without using invective, and its contents are displayed at greater length than those of the other pamphlets. Volume ii of the *Journal* for February continues the review of the works of anti-Rousseau critics, noting in passing that the quarrel between French and Italian music must be of some consequence since so many persons are taking part in the strife. Here, the editor indicates that he does not accept Rousseau's view that there is no hope for French music. The abbé Laugier, whose *Apologie* reflected a view similar to that of Bâton, is commended for combining courtesy and good sense in his arguments. Rousseau, explains Berthier, thought the French incapable of music. His system was merciless, it destroyed both the tree and its fruit, it removed all resources, sentiments and courage under the pretext that there was no hope for French music. His critic, it is found, is more humane in that, while recognizing many of Rousseau's statements to be true, he suggests reforms and the means of implementing them. The review ends with a plea for moderation and for less 'bitterness, pride, fewer threats and injurious expressions.'[27]

The violent attacks made on Rousseau's works seem to have changed Berthier's attitude toward him from one of detached amusement mingled with admiration, to a more sympathetic treatment, and to a greater esteem for a writer who could arouse such a storm. Thus, five months later, the appearance of an anti-Rousseau work by Travenol evokes the comment from the journalist that the subject of French versus Italian music has been worn threadbare, and he makes use of this brief mention of the controversy to praise the *philosophe*. He announces to his readers

[26] *J. de T.* (Feb.1754), i.270.   [27] *J. de T.* (Feb.1754), ii.541.

that he wishes to make a reflection, and he hopes it will not offend anyone, namely, that twice this citizen of Geneva has aroused our literary world by proposing two sorts of paradoxes, and that is certainly not the mark nor the characteristic of a poor writer; and he pursues: 'Cent autres eussent raisonné, comme lui, sur les sciences et sur notre musique, sans exciter la moindre rumeur dans l'empire des lettres. Ses deux brochures au contraire ont mis les imaginations en feu; ont armé tous nos littérateurs; ont fourni, pendant des années entières, un aliment continuel aux presses typographiques. Encore une fois, qu'est-ce que cela prouve, et que doit-on penser des talents d'un tel auteur? Le public attend une troisième brochure sur quelque autre sujet, pour voir si le 'tergiminis tollere honoribus' aura lieu par rapport à m. Rousseau'.[28]

This admiration did not prevent Berthier from disagreeing with the author of the *Lettre sur la musique française* when he thought his theory too extreme. When Pergolesi's *La Serva padrona* was presented in Paris with French words adapted to the Italian composer's music, the editor concluded, first, that Italian music merits the greatest praise because it reaches 'the true goal of art, which is to paint, to move, to interest, to please', although it should have been used for a less frivolous subject; secondly, the fact that m. Beaurans has succeeded in substituting the French language for the Italian shows that 'our prose is not an invincible obstacle to the progress of musical art among us.'[29] Then, as if to indicate that this is his final word on the subject, the editor concluded: 'Il faut bien sentir que la traduction qu'on nous donne prouve plus, en quelque sorte, qu'il n'était nécessaire pour terminer la controverse des Français et des Italiens. C'est de très-bonne musique italienne qu'on adopte; c'est du Français très chantant qu'on met en œuvre; c'est du Français presque aussi chantant que l'Italien, puisqu'il se combine parfaitement avec la musique italienne: doit-il rester désormais aucun sujet, aucune branche de controverse?'[30]

[28] *J. de T.* (July 1754), ii.1912.
[29] *J. de T.* (Nov.1754), pp.2876–77.
[30] *J. de T.* (Nov.1754), pp.2877–78.

Up to this time the *Journal de Trévoux* had not had any serious disagreements with Rousseau. His writings, while they had frequently been treated in a jocular tone, had obviously evoked the admiration and sympathies of the Jesuit editor. The appearance of the *Discours sur l'origine de l'inégalité*, however, was greeted with a strong attack from the *Journal*. Berthier, and the orthodox in general, could accept the author's thesis that men should listen to nature, if by 'nature' he meant 'reason.' But it was clear in this second discourse that by 'nature' Rousseau meant only man's instincts and physical inclinations, and law and right could not be based on this purely physical concept[31]. The *philosophes* generally had praised the essential goodness of the passions in opposition to the orthodox view that due to original sin man's passions inclined him towards evil and were to be suppressed by reason. Before this time, Rousseau had seemed to reflect traditional Christian principles, going astray at times through an excess of zeal. When he had become a contributor to the *Encyclopédie* Berthier may have had some fears as to the influence such a relationship with Diderot might have on the Genevan. With the publication of the second discourse, reflecting as it did some of the tenets of the *philosophes*, it must have seemed to the Jesuit editor that the writer had been won over by the encyclopedists and must now be regarded as an enemy of the church.

The first mention by the *Journal de Trévoux* of the *Discours sur l'inégalité* is found in an article refuting 'various modern writings against religion.' Presenting a lengthy resumé of Rousseau's doctrines, the article declares: 'Toute cette doctrine . . . est un tissu de paradoxes inconcevables. Qu'on en dépouille la surface de ces ornements étrangers qui imposent, de ce style figuré qui séduit, de ces traits ingénieux qui éblouissent, alors l'attention la plus légère suffira pour rejeter un système que l'histoire dément, que la physique réprouve et que la raison déteste'.[32] Refuting the author's contentions that primitive man was only more or less

---

[31] cf. Palmer, *Catholics and unbelievers*, p.175.

[32] *J. de T.* (Sept.1757), p.2186.

different from the beast, that natural law falls into the category of arbitrary conventions, that organic instinct was man's 'certain and invariable principle,' and that natural law has only served to lead him astray and deprave him[33], Berthier exclaims: 'Is it possible to imagine a more dangerous, a more licentious, a more unreasonable system?' Rousseau, continues the editor, breaks all the ties of society, of humanity, of religion. He invites men to flee a few vices by forgetting all exemplary virtues, to recapture the complete liberty of savage life by satisfying the appetites of brute instinct. If the author had offered us this mixture of erudition and misanthropy simply as an amusing fable, we might excuse his license; but, concludes the article, his tone is too serious for us not to recognize in this discourse 'the cry, the signal of a philosophic conspiracy against any type of government and religion.'[34]

This was indeed a serious charge, and Rousseau, fearing the power of the Jesuits as he did[35], could not ignore it. It is probably

[33] in the 18th century, as today, the term 'natural law' had various meanings. The 'natural law' attacked by Rousseau was that which Voltaire was later to defend in his *Poème sur la loi naturelle* (1756). For this natural law, which was envisaged as the moral law implanted by God in every man, and which could be arrived at through reason, Rousseau substituted the natural law which relies on natural instincts and physical inclinations as a guide rather than on rational moral concepts. As we have seen in the preceding chapter, Berthier upheld the concept defended by Voltaire. When an anonymous brochure attacking the *Poème sur la loi naturelle* declared that it is doubtful that man was made for reason, the Jesuit editor had declared: 'Mais quel guide veut donc suivre l'auteur?"L'instinct": c'est ce qu'il substitue à la raison, à la religion, aux lois, à la puissance des souverains. Il n'y a rien de

plus faux et de plus impie que cette première épître' (*J. de T.* [Aug.1757], p.2096).

[34] *J. de T.* (Sept.1757), p.2193. In 1754 Fréron had made a similar remark concerning a philosophical conspiracy when, upon noting Diderot's praise of Rousseau in the former's *Pensées sur l'interprétation de la nature*, he had stated: 'Ils sont associés avec quelques autres pour ce commerce d'encens. Ces puissances philosophiques ont conclu entre elles une ligue offensive et défensive' (*L'Année littéraire*, i.14).

[35] for instance, when the publication of Rousseau's *Emile* had been delayed, perhaps remembering their role in the suppression of the *Encyclopédie*, he had ascribed the delay to Jesuit interference in spite of Malesherbes's assurances that they were in too grave a danger themselves to be concerned with a book 'où il ne s'agissait pas d'eux.' 'Je ne voulus jamais croire,' he tells us,

following this article that he presented himself in person to speak with the editor of the *Journal*. Berthier recounts this interview as follows: 'Un jour, on vint me demander à la maison professe: le portier indique ma chambre; on heurte: une personne que je n'avais jamais vue se présente. Que désirez-vous de moi? lui demandai-je.

— Est-ce que vous ne me connaissez pas?

— Je n'ai pas cet honneur-là.

— Oh! pardonnez-moi, vous me connaissez; et moi aussi je vous connais, père Berthier. Nous nous connaissons beaucoup, je vous assure. Je ne vous cacherai pas que vous m'avez fait passer plus d'une mauvaise nuit; et si, à votre tour, vous voulez être sincère, peut-être avouerez-vous que je vous en ai fait passer aussi plus d'une mauvaise.

— Je vous proteste, monsieur, avec la plus grande sincérité, que je n'ai pas l'honneur de vous connaître.

— Je suis Jean Jacques Rousseau, et je viens causer un peu avec vous.

— Oh! m'écriai-je alors en lui présentant un siège, combien je suis honoré de la visite que vous voulez bien me faire.

Nous causâmes en effet un peu, c'est-à-dire deux grandes heures. Vous pensez bien que nous ne fûmes pas d'accord ni pendant ni après la conversation; mais j'eus infiniment à me louer de l'extrême honnêteté de m. Rousseau; et je n'avais jamais été si bien à portée d'aimer la beauté de son génie'.[36]

'que les jésuites fussent en danger . . . . Leurs succès passés, qui ne s'étaient jamais démentis, me donnaient une si terrible idée de leur puissance, que je déplorais déjà l'avilissement du parlement' (*Confessions*, p.531).

[36] quoted by Montjoye, *Eloge*, p.67. The date of the interview is not given, but the period following Berthier's review of the *Discours sur l'inégalité* was chosen for the time of the meeting because it was felt that no review prior to this one would have warranted the statement from Rousseau, '. . . vous m'avez fait passer plus d'une mauvaise nuit,' whereas the accusation of conspiracy against the government and religion would have caused enough disquietude on the part of Rousseau to warrant a visit to the accuser. A further complication is added by a reference in the *Confessions* to Berthier according to which the author would have met the Jesuit editor in 1748. Rousseau

The mutual admiration engendered by their meeting is one factor which may have contributed to the cordial relations between Rousseau and the editor of the *Journal de Trévoux*. The emotional attachment of the *philosophe* to the Jesuits, in spite of his fear of their power, may also have had an influence on those relations. In the earlier years at Les Charmettes, when the young Rousseau had been strongly influenced by Jansenism[37], it was through his friendship with his Jesuit confessor, father Hemet, and his companion father Coppier, that he finally rejected the Jansenist doctrines. Speaking of the two Jesuits who visited him frequently, Rousseau states: 'J'allais aussi les voir à Chambéri; je me familiarisais peu à peu avec leur maison; leur bibliothèque était à mon service. Le souvenir de cet heureux temps se lie avec celui des jésuites au point de me faire aimer l'un par l'autre; et, quoique leur doctrine m'ait toujours paru dangereuse, je n'ai jamais pu trouver en moi le pouvoir de les haïr sincèrement'.[38] When the citizen of Geneva arrived in Paris in 1741, it was to the Jesuit Castel that he turned with the manuscript of his opera, probably attracted to him because of his famous ocular harpsichord[39].

says: 'Je cessai de voir le p. Castel et par là d'aller aux Jésuites, où je ne connaissais que lui seul. D'ailleurs l'esprit tyrannique et intrigant de ses confrères . . . me donnait tant d'éloignement pour leur commerce, que je n'en ai vu aucun depuis ce temps-là, si ce n'est le p. Berthier, que je vis deux ou trois fois chez m. Dupin, avec lequel il travaillait de toute sa force à la réfutation de Montesquieu' (p.301). This could mean that Rousseau *saw* Berthier without having been introduced to him or without having spoken to him, because at this time Jean Jacques was employed as mme Dupin's secretary; her husband, being much older than she, and opposing the *philosophes* as he did, would probably not have frequented her salon since it boasted such

guests as Fontenelle, the abbé de Saint-Pierre and Voltaire (cf. Rousseau, *Confessions*, p.269). In any case, if we assume Montjoye's account of the meeting between Berthier and Rousseau to be correct, the interview would probably not have occurred in 1748, since the *Journal de Trévoux* had never mentioned him before 1751.

[37] 'Les écrits de Port-Royal et de l'Oratoire, étant ceux que je lisais le plus fréquemment, m'avaient rendu demi-janséniste' (*Confessions*, p.226). The Oratorians by this time had been 'won over by the Jansenist error' (Mourret, *History of the Catholic church*, vi.532).

[38] *Confessions*, pp.226–27.

[39] Bertrand states that Castel 'l'accueillit, l'encouragea de son mieux, le

Castel formed a good opinion of the young composer and in a letter on music he pauses to remark: 'J'ai l'honneur de connaître m. Rousseau, de le connaître homme d'esprit, bonne personne même. On l'a peut-être trop poussé, trop entêté; on n'a pas assez accueilli peut-être l'opéra tout de sa façon (poésie et musique) qu'il me présenta en arrivant de province, de Genève, où j'entrevis bien du bon sur le papier'.[40]

While Rousseau was on friendly terms with Berthier, several sources tend to exaggerate their friendship because of a confusion of Berthiers. The *philosophe* enjoyed a close friendship with a father 'Berthier de l'Oratoire', of whom he writes occasionally in his *Confessions*[41]. Most authorities, including Plan's *Table de la Correspondance générale de J.-J. Rousseau*, published in 1953, confound Berthier the Oratorian with Berthier the Jesuit editor, and list all references to father Berthier under the former name. Joseph Etienne Berthier, the Oratorian, was born in 1710 and died in 1783. He was a partisan of Cartesian physics as expounded by Malebranche, and was professor of physics in the college of the Oratorians in Paris[42]. One of his works, the *Physique des comètes*, was dedicated to Rousseau in 1760.

conduisit chez quelques personnes qui devaient l'aider à faire valoir son projet' (*Le Père Castel*, p.19). See also Rousseau, *Confessions*, p.266.

[40] Quoted by Fréron, *Année littéraire* (1754), i.338. Bertrand states that in spite of Castel's good offices toward Rousseau, 'l'amitié ne pouvait se conclure entre eux. . . . Le père ne s'accommoda point de l'âpre misanthropie du philosophe' (*op. cit.*, p.19). Rousseau, for his part, conceived suspicions of Castel and ceased to see him (*Confessions*, p.301).

[41] *Confessions*, pp.471–72. See also *Correspondance*, v.90, 149; vii.220, 251.

[42] Chaudon states that the Oratorian, who was known at Versailles as 'l'homme aux tourbillons,' because of his adherence to cartesian physics, was a member of the Royal society of London and the correspondent of the Academy of Sciences in Paris (*Dictionnaire universel*, ii.518). Rousseau's friendship for the Oratorians, as for many others, soured in his later years, and he lists them as his enemies who 'seront à jamais implacables' (*Rêveries*, p.13). The editor of the *Journal de Trévoux* and the Jesuits were among those who fared no better. Describing his fears that the Jesuits were plotting against him, Rousseau explains: 'J'avais toujours senti, malgré le patelinage du p. Berthier, que les jésuites ne m'aimaient pas, non-seulement comme encyclopédiste, mais parce que tous mes principes étaient encore plus op-

After the *Journal de Trévoux* review of the second discourse, we find no specific mention of Rousseau until the appearance of his *Lettre sur les spectacles*. If Berthier had not been able to accept all the doctrines expounded in the other literary works of this author, here was a thesis which reflected perfectly the attitude held by the Jesuit editor. What was more, Rousseau in this latest work had denounced Diderot and had thus publicized his break with this 'dangerous' group, and his espousal of a cause which had already been championed by Berthier in his writings must certainly have brought the two men closer and increased Berthier's admiration for Jean Jacques. As early as 1750 the *Journal* had called for a reform of the theatre and the total exile of illicit love from the stage[43]. During the quarrel over French versus Italian music Berthier had declared that if operas and musical theatrical productions were mentioned in the *Journal*, it was only because they were of interest to the arts and sciences, the chief subject matter of the *Mémoires*; but he had indicated his disapproval of the deplorable morals which were too often shown in those 'profane spectacles.'[44]

The most complete exposition of his views on the theatre had been made in the course of a review of Desprès de Boissy's *Lettre sur les spectacles* in 1756. The author advanced a view similar to that expounded later on by Rousseau, and his *Lettre*, favourably reviewed by Berthier, afforded the editor the opportunity to introduce his own arguments in support of the author. Voltaire's assertion in his *Siècle de Louis XIV* that the censorship of plays is due to rigorism, is criticized, and the journalist quotes Voltaire's statement that out of 400 tragedies presented in France only ten or twelve are not founded on 'a love plot . . . . It is a perpetual flirtation.' How can the condemnation of this situation be called rigorism, queries the article, when women neglect domestic pursuits to ornament their persons and seek 'the glory of having a

posés à leurs maximes et à leur crédit que l'incrédulité de mes confrères' (*Confessions*, p.531).

[43] *J. de T.* (Feb.1750), p.513.
[44] *J. de T.* (Nov.1754), p.2872.

court which they flatter themselves into believing is due solely to their charms.'[45] The principles of Christianity and the theatre cannot be reconciled, declares the editor, and the clergy quoted by Voltaire as being in favour of the theatre would soon withdraw their support if they were asked to put it in writing. Turning to the opera, Berthier counsels that it is not the music which should be attacked—on the contrary, he asserts, music is capable of elevating the soul and can be a source for good—but the libretto is made up entirely of the language of profane love and this deserves 'a wise and total suppression.'[46] A new edition of de Boissy's *Lettre* is reviewed two years later and the editor once more affirms his stand by concurring in the author's thesis: 'Le théâtre, en effet, n'offre presque toujours que des passions folles et criminelles; il perd la plupart des jeunes gens qui le fréquentent; il rend inutile, par le mélange ou l'addition des farces, le fruit qu'on pourrait retirer des pièces sérieuses ou édifiantes; il n'a jusqu'ici corrigé que des ridicules et fomenté des vices; il a contre lui l'autorité des raisons et l'exemple des hommes vertueux'.[47]

As in the case of the *Lettre sur la musique française*, the *Journal de Trévoux* did not speak of the *Lettre sur les spectacles* directly, but introduced the subject by refuting several letters criticizing Rousseau's position. These included three articles which had appeared in the *Mercure* in refutation of the author of the *Lettre*. In his article, Berthier defends 'the learned Genevan' and concludes that 'Christian life excludes forever the theatre and all its circumstances.'[48] When, three months later, Gresset, the author of the plays *Sidney* and *Le Méchant*, sent a letter to the *Journal* repenting his 'false glory' and renouncing the theatre in the name of religion with the words, 'the sanctuary and the theatre are two incompatible objects,' Berthier concurs and exclaims: 'Religion has finally opened his eyes . . . . He is leaving forever that bewitching career.'[49] Such a stand could not fail to evoke criticism,

[45] *J. de T.* (April 1756), i.842–44.
[46] *J. de T.* (April 1756), p.848.
[47] *J. de T.* (Feb.1758), p.561.
[48] *J. de T.* (April 1759), i.854ff.
[49] *J. de T.* (July 1759), p.1711.

and the Jesuit editor was soon obliged to answer an article which appeared in the *Mercure* maintaining that the theatre was compatible with Christianity, and citing the plays given in the Jesuit schools as an example of this fact. In his reply, Berthier admits that plays could be compatible with Christianity if the morals they presented could be rendered edifying by the good examples proposed in the play, by the conduct of the actors and by the intention of the spectators, but, he points out, the drama is still very far from that ideal and it is questionable whether it would ever reach it. As to the plays presented in Jesuit schools, he continues, they are only exercises destined to give young people a facility for public speaking and they do not enter the problem. But even these should be 'rare, strongly purged, and conducted by very wise persons.'[50] The article ends by suggesting that the church's doctrines be studied and it would be seen that theatre plays were not in accord with these teachings[51]. No further mention is made in the *Journal* of the controversy caused by the *Lettre sur les spectacles* except for a passing reflection in connection with a remark made by Trublet that it is to be feared that the theatre might ridicule virtue and thus disgust the spectator with it, to which Berthier replies: 'That is not only to be feared, but it happens very often; and that is one of the main objections we have against stage plays.'[52]

From this time on very little was printed in the *Journal de Trévoux* concerning Rousseau. Even when Berthier might have mentioned him he refrained from doing so in deference to the *philosophe*. An example of this is the matter of Rousseau's *Lettre sur la providence*. When in 1756 Voltaire had sent Rousseau a volume

[50] *J. de T.* (Aug.1759), pp.2084–86. Even these plays came under Berthier's criticism. When the Jesuit college at Rouen presented a production entitled *Le Plaisir sage et réglé*, the editor strongly attacked it declaring: 'Ce programme ou placart est répréhensible, et dès qu'il a paru sous nos yeux, nous avons cru devoir le critiquer; nous sommes même autorisés à le réprouver du ton fort et polémique que nous voudrions n'être jamais obligés de prendre vis-à-vis de personne' (*ibid.* [Sept. 1750], p.2098).

[51] *J. de T.* (Aug.1759), p.2086.

[52] *J. de T.* (Feb.1760), p.485.

containing his *Poème sur la loi naturelle* and his *Poème sur le désastre de Lisbonne*, the latter had written a refutation of the poem on the Lisbon earthquake in the form of a *Lettre sur la providence*. The letter had not been published nor did Rousseau desire its publication without the consent of Voltaire. But in 1760 a copy was somehow obtained and printed in Prussia. Trublet wrote its author informing him of the fact and stating that he would do nothing until he heard from Rousseau, adding: 'En attendant, je n'ai voulu prêter mon exemplaire à personne; j'en excepte le p. Berthier qui me le renvoya le lendemain. C'est un homme d'une probité parfaite, et si vous avez lu ceux des articles du *Journal de Trévoux* où il a rendu compte de vos ouvrages, vous savez combien il vous estime'.[53] Rousseau replied that he did not wish the letter made public, and Trublet again wrote him promising to remain silent and answering for Berthier's cooperation in the matter[54].

When *La Nouvelle Héloïse* appeared in the following year, it too was passed over in silence, but when Formey announced an expurgated version entitled *L'Esprit de Julie*, Berthier, now in his last month as editor of the *Journal*, took this final opportunity to show his continued regard for Rousseau. In mentioning the original work, the editor comments: 'C'est un excellent livre quand il est bon, c'est un ouvrage pernicieux quand il cesse d'exciter l'admiration. Il est comme cet arbre planté dans le jardin des délices lequel enseignait le bien et le mal. Le mieux serait de n'y point toucher, de peur d'être aveuglé par de fausses lumières; mais les hommes sont curieux, les femmes le sont encore plus; les jeunes gens le sont sans mesure et sans précautions'.[55] The six volumes were already absorbing European youth, continued the editor sadly, and m. Formey's solicitude seems superfluous. The impression has already been made, and although the book abounds in good principles, they appear to have been overshadowed by

---

[53] Rousseau, *Correspondance*, v.127.
[54] *ibid.*, p.153. See also *Confessions*, pp.504ff.
[55] *J. de T.* (May 1762), p.1321.

the evil. Turning to Formey's text, the Jesuit editor notes that it contains all the wise, sublime and heroic maxims found in the novel, but since they are disconnected they are not so pleasing as the original work which has 'the charm of narration and the enthusiasm of sentiment.' Nevertheless, concludes the journalist, there is so much brilliance even in these disconnected maxims that they still make agreeable reading[56].

By the time *Emile* appeared, the Jesuits had been suppressed and the *Journal de Trévoux* was no longer under the direction of Berthier. Had he still been editor-in-chief, he might have chosen to ignore the new work, or, if he had attacked its unorthodox statements, it would probably have been with more circumspection than that shown by his successor Jolivet. The new editor attacked the *Emile* with a vengeance. After announcing the work as a reprehensible, chimeric treatise on education whose early ridiculous and cynical scenes were like so many similar writings, Jolivet expresses amazement at the 'horrible dénouement'. His tone then becomes personal and he states that if Rousseau does not mind, he is going to tell him a few things. A lengthy resumé of Volume i is followed by a mock dialogue in which the editor sarcastically tells the author that the 800,000 inhabitants of Paris will leave for the woods and perhaps Rousseau will want to arrange for their subsistence. Jolivet ends the dialogue with the words:'TAIS TOI JEAN-JACQUES!'[57] The following month the review of *Emile* is continued in the same taunting manner and the editor asks Rousseau: 'Etes-vous tranquille m. Rousseau, tandis que nous vous parlons? L'humeur atrabilaire n'entre-t-elle pas en effervescence? ... Quoique vous rangiez tous les Européens dans la classe des "bêtes féroces" ... ils ne se croyent point en droit d'user de représailles en insultant à l'espèce de Lycanthropie qui vous arme contre eux'.[58]

In his *Confessions* Rousseau relates the storm of criticism aroused by his *Emile*, saying: 'Toutes les gazettes, tous les journaux,

[56] *J. de T.* (May 1762), p.1322.
[57] *J. de T.* (Oct.1762), pp.2617ff.
[58] *J. de T.* (Nov.1762), p.2813.

toutes les brochures sonnèrent le plus terrible tocsin . . . . J'étais un impie, un athée, un forcené, un enragé, une bête féroce, un loup. Le continuateur du *Journal de Trévoux* fit sur ma prétendue lycanthropie un écart qui montrait assez bien la sienne'.[59]

Although he was no longer in charge of a journal, Berthier, when he read the *Contrat social*, felt it necessary to refute this dangerous work, and he immediately began writing his *Observations sur le Contrat social*. He had already reached book III, chapter 12, of the *Contrat social* when 'the book was proscribed and a writ prepared against the author. Then father Berthier did not think he should continue his critical observations against a man already punished and very unhappy.'[60] His denunciation of Rousseau's philosophy is reminiscent of many of the editorials he had written for the *Journal de Trévoux*, but in spite of the nature of his writing, the ex-Jesuit still has a few good words to say of Jean Jacques: 'Cet écrivain est estimable par les qualités de son style, qui manque néanmoins en quelques endroits, de clarté, de suite, de facilité. Il voit quelquefois des vérités, et il les énonce avec force. Mais l'amour des singularités le jette souvent dans des écarts manifestes. Sa religion est, comme sa philosophie, pleine de hardiesses et de faussetés . . . . Mon intention est de faire voir combien il s'égare, afin d'empêcher les lecteurs du *Contrat social* de s'égarer avec ce dangereux auteur'.[61]

The basic issue in Berthier's criticism of the *Contrat social* is the question whether the instincts or passions are the best guides of men, as suggested by Rousseau, or rather, whether the only true guide of man is his reason, the passions being essentially evil, a stand taken by Berthier. Thus when the statement is made that men are in chains, the former editor retorts that a man is not a slave because he accomplishes his duties. Actually 'the sway of the passions and the reign of vice is slavery. No one is less a master of himself than the ambitious man, the miser, the sensual

[59] *Confessions*, p.554.
[60] 'Avertissement de l'éditeur,' *Observations sur le Contrat social* (Paris 1789), p.v.
[61] *Observations sur le Contrat social*, p.i.

man, the jealous man.'[62] Nor is the social order the basis of all rights, the critic continues. It is true that convention determines the form of government chosen, but even before this choice, reason and natural law existed, and the basic relationships essential to social order had already been determined by these two guides. Rousseau is always excessive in his assertions, it is noted, and he confuses valid dependency with slavery. After defending the monarchy as the ideal form of government, Berthier attacks the assertion that in forming the social contract each member must surrender all his rights to the community. While it is agreed that the individual must consent to be less free than he was, it does not follow that he must 'alienate himself with all his rights.'[63] When Rousseau propounds the idea that man in the state of nature acts selfishly on physical impulses and instinct, but that the civil state gives him the morality he lacked before, Berthier calls it very false, and maintains that independently of the civil state or political conventions, man has his reason and his liberty. He is not reduced to instinct, physical impulses and appetites. He is capable of moral actions, the establishment of the civil state is in itself a proof of this[64]. Nor can it be said that the general will is always right, continues the critic. Reason is always right. Sometimes the passions becloud men's reason, and ambitious men or usurpers are then accepted by the people. The chapter dealing with suicide is presented as containing 'things well perceived and well said,' but when the author tries to reason on laws 'he begins to go astray.' For example, the reflection that in the state of nature men do not owe each other anything they have not promised, is challenged. Even in the state of nature, replies Berthier, the law of charity is valid. 'In the state of nature all men are still brothers, still members of the great family which is the human species.'[65]

[62] ibid., p.5.
[63] ibid., p.48.
[64] ibid., p.54.
[65] ibid., p.80. The remainder of the Observations deals with various political systems as already discussed in

part 2, chapter 1, above. It should be noted that Berthier's authorship of the work ends on page 213. The anonymous continuator of the Observations, the abbé Bordier-Delpuits, changes the method of reasoning employed by

It is probable that any contact Berthier may have had with Rousseau ceased with the suppression of the Jesuits. Although he had been drawn to the writer by the similarity of many of their views and by the apparent regard of the author for religious values, the editor was no less firm in his denunciation of Rousseau's writings when he found it necessary to do so. While Jean Jacques, as we have seen, later called Berthier's friendliness toward him 'wheedling,' the Jesuit editor's refutations of his ideas when he thought them to be wrong seem to nullify this charge, while the regretful tone and the circumspection used in those attacks reveal a sincere admiration and regard for the man he once referred to as 'the learned Genevan.'

Berthier and leans heavily on moral and theological arguments with frequent quotations from the Bible. For example, after an introductory paragraph revealing the change in authorship, he begins by stating: 'L'auteur dit que "le souverain n'a d'autre force que la puissance législative"; mais si je demandais à saint Paul (qui est un moraliste bien plus éclairé que tous les jurisconsultes du monde) quels sont les droits du prince, il me dirait que c'est de faire des lois . . .' (p.213).

IV

Diderot and the Encyclopédie

The relations between Diderot and the *Journal de Trévoux* are in sharp contrast with those enjoyed by Rousseau. Here was not a naïve 'étourdi' whose heart was in the right place in spite of his errors: it was seen almost at once that Diderot was not simply a gifted writer but a dangerous enemy of church and state who would bear watching.

When Diderot's *Essai sur le mérite et la vertu* appeared, he was still comparatively unknown, but the *Journal de Trévoux* when reviewing the work recognizes the author's superior mind and gives his work a favourable review. It is pointed out that the anonymous author has taken the essay of Shaftsbury, has decomposed it in his own way, and has presented original reflexions in addition to those of the Englishman. Both the English author and his interpreter are presented as 'profound, penetrating, systematic and, especially, very serious.' The reader is reminded that this is not simply an amusing or passing brochure. Rather, it is reminiscent of Locke discussing morality[1]. The article concludes by remarking of Diderot's *Essai*: 'Les richesses y sont répandues à pleines mains; richesses d'idées, de sentiments, de développement, d'expression. Nous ne voudrions pas en garantir tous les axiomes, mais nous pouvons bien assurer qu'il n'y a qu'un très-grand philosophe qui ait pu renfermer tant de choses dans un si petit volume; avec cela, peu de personnes le liront, parce que le sérieux et le sublime y tient partout le premier rang'.[2]

With the appearance of the *Pensées philosophiques* in 1746, it was clear that here was a dangerous thinker indeed, and a man to be reckoned with[3]. The *Journal de Trévoux* chose to ignore

[1] *J. de T.* (Feb.1746), p.200.
[2] *ibid.*, p.220.

[3] Diderot's parish priest had denounced him on 4 May 1745, but the

163

the *Pensées*, perhaps in the hope that if it were not given any publicity it would not attract too many readers. Apart from a few minor references to the *Pensées* in the course of articles on apologetics[4], no mention is made of this work until December 1755 —nine years later.

By the time the *Journal de Trévoux* reviewed Diderot's *Mémoires sur différents sujets de mathématiques*, he was already a marked man. His *Bijoux indiscrets* had caused him difficulties with the authorities, and the *Promenade du sceptique* had been nipped in the bud. Reminding his readers that 'an intelligent man like Diderot never undertakes such a difficult thing without some profit to the arts,' Berthier, in his review of the work, discusses the author's project for accurately fixing a tone so that a musical composition can be played in different locations in exactly the same tone. It is a bold project worthy of a lofty intellect, remarks the editor with a slight tinge of irony, to fix something on this earth, and that is even more true of sound, which is essentially fleeting[5].

Turning to Diderot's considerations of the involute of a circle, the Jesuit editor notes that geometricians should be thankful to the author for showing them that all their speculations are not useless but can be employed in the life of the citizen and in society. The project for a new type of organ which can play a number of parts at once by means of a cylinder over which is passed a perforated roll, evokes the following observation: 'Comme M. Diderot déclare qu'il aime passionnément la musique, qui est

police chief to whom he had written was changed soon afterwards and no action was taken. The curé wrote a second, more detailed letter on 22 June 1747, and from that time on until his arrest in 1749 Diderot was under police surveillance (Venturi, *Jeunesse de Diderot*, p.170).

[4] the *Journal* for May 1748 mentions Diderot's refusal to accept miracles and states that he demands geometry when it is simply a question of ascertaining the historical accuracy of an event (p.1050). The March 1750 issue discusses Diderot's assertion that he would not believe his own eyes if he saw a dead man rise (p.665). A refutation of the *Pensées* is announced in the 'Nouvelles littéraires' section of the *Journal* for December 1751, without any details (p.2655).

[5] *J. de T.* (April 1749), p.602.

la passion des belles âmes, mais qu'il ne la sait pas, ce qui lui est commun avec beaucoup d'honnêtes gens, et comme il est d'un esprit vif, curieux, inventif, on n'est surpris ni de lui voir tenter la chose, ni de la lui voir tenter un peu inutilement'.[6] The idea is somewhat belittled by likening Diderot's invention to the German hand organs and 'serinettes' of the time. Nevertheless, adds the editor, we can thank the author for having further developed these instruments.

The views of Diderot on the effect of the resistance of air on a pendulum receive no better treatment. Recalling Leibnitz's remark that to disprove any system one had only to show that it ends in perpetual motion, Berthier states rather satirically that Diderot's demonstration disproves Leibnitz's claim since if the only thing stopping the pendulum is the resistance of air, and if the pendulum, because of its natural movement, cannot of itself come to rest, then perpetual motion has been found[7]. The article maintains its lightly mocking tone to the end and concludes: 'On propose ce problème à tous les savants. Mais on serait spécialement curieux d'en avoir la solution de la part d'un homme aussi habile et aussi homme d'esprit que nous paraît l'être m. Diderot, dont nous devons aussi remarquer que le stile est aussi élégant, tranchant et naïf, qu'il est vif et ingénieux'.[8]

The pervasive tone of mockery utilized in reviewing Diderot's *Mémoires* on mathematics probably was adopted as a precaution against this author, obviously a brilliant and dangerous thinker about whom disquieting rumours were already in circulation. When two months later the *Lettre sur les aveugles* appeared, and

[6] *J. de T.* (April 1749), p.613.
[7] *J. de T.* (April 1749), p.619.
[8] *J. de T.* (April 1749), p. 620. Jean Pommier cites these words to substantiate his statement that Berthier's review was 'un compte rendu assez favorable,' adding: 'Peut-être les Jésuites n'avaient-ils pas encore perdu tout espoir de fournir des collaborateurs à l'*Encyclopédie*' (*Diderot avant Vincennes*, p.89). The tone of this article does not seem to be that of one who is currying favour with an editor in order to be invited to collaborate. If the Jesuits had ever entertained such a hope, Berthier's attitude would have frustrated it.

its author was immediately imprisoned as a result, Berthier must have felt that his judgment of Diderot had been accurate. Perhaps in order not to give this audacious writer any further publicity, the Jesuit editor refrained from mentioning the *Lettre* or its author at this time. When in 1751 the second prospectus for the *Encyclopédie* appeared under Diderot's editorship, it is not difficult to imagine the uneasiness which this name at the head of the enterprise caused the editor of the *Journal de Trévoux*[9]. If Diderot's imprisonment for the *Lettre sur les aveugles* had caused him to be suspected, it had also revealed to the authorities the importance of his position on the newly projected *Encyclopédie*. 'Diderot's imprisonment at Vincennes in 1749 might have had very serious consequences not only for him but also for the whole project,' state Gordon and Torrey, 'the publishers admitted that only he could make order out of the manuscripts, and they set up such a cry to protect their extensive investments that he was released after three months.'[10]

When the project for an encyclopedia had first been announced, it 'was widely supported even among men of the church, many of whom, like the laity, felt that they lived in an age of peculiar enlightenment, and thought it an advantage to have the knowledge brought together in one place.'[11] It has been pointed out that the original prospectus for the *Encyclopédie* which appeared in 1745 without the collaboration of Diderot, 'in contrast to the hostility shown against the later project ... was well received, analyzed and publicized even by the Jesuit periodical the *Journal de Trévoux*.'[12] This would, of course, throw doubt on the thesis

[9] Belin tells us that 'les Jésuites, qui flairent dans l'*Encyclopédie* un dangereux adversaire, sont peu enthousiastes' (*Le mouvement philosophique au XVIIIème siècle*, p.57).

[10] *The Censoring of Diderot's Encyclopédie*, p.14.

[11] Palmer, *Catholics and unbelievers*, p.118. Berthier reflects this belief that this was an age of peculiar enlightenment when he says: 'On peut assurer que, si notre siècle n'est pas plus fécond en génies d'un certain ordre que les précédents, il a du moins l'avantage de posséder plus d'hommes éclairés' (*J. de T*. [Jan.1752], p.122).

[12] Gordon and Torrey, p.10. Berthier's review of this prospectus states in part: 'A en juger par le prospectus que nous abrégeons, et qui cite quatre

that the *Journal*'s editor feared the *Encyclopédie* simply because it was an encyclopedia.

Inasmuch as several of the *philosophes* accused the editor of the *Journal de Trévoux* of being opposed to the *Encyclopédie* because its editors were fearful for their own *Dictionnaire de Trévoux*[13], it might be well at this point to consider the relationship between the *Journal* and the *Dictionnaire*. The *Dictionnaire universel français et latin*, commonly known as the *Dictionnaire de Trévoux* because it was printed in that city by order of 'S.A.S. monseigneur prince souverain de Dombes,' first appeared in 1704. Although a list of sources was indicated, no authors were announced. Perhaps because it was printed in a city whose name had been in the public mind chiefly because of the *Journal de Trévoux*, the *Dictionnaire* was linked with the *Journal*, and the Jesuits were suspected of having been its authors. The *Journal des savants*, while reviewing the *Dictionnaire* in its issue for 28 April 1704, attests to this by noting of the new publication: 'The rumour had spread that the authors of a learned society had had the direction of this work, and we were expecting to find the same spirit and the same sentiments reigning throughout it.' But, continues the review, after having gone through it, the editors of the *Journal des savants* have recognized that it is the work of different people with varying points of view. Indeed, the editors point out, the *Dictionnaire* sometimes has opposing theological viewpoints, which would indicate that it cannot be attributed to one group in particular[14].

articles pour servir de modèle, . . . il n'est rien de plus utile, de plus fécond, de mieux analysé, de mieux lié, en un mot de plus parfait et de plus beau que ce *Dictionnaire*; et tel est le présent que m. Mills fait à la France, sa patrie par adoption, en faisant honneur à l'Angleterre, sa vraie patrie. Il traduit fidèlement l'ouvrage de m. Chambers; il y ajoute de belles planches jusqu'au nombre de 120 au moins' (*J. de T.* [May 1745], p.937).

[13] see Voltaire's statement quoted on p.119.
[14] *Journal des savants* (28 April 1704), p.431. Although the *Dictionnaire* announced no authors, the *Journal des savants* lists father Plumier, m. de Barras and father Mourgues as authors of certain articles, while the 1771 edition of the *Dictionnaire de Trévoux*, edited by abbé Brillant, mentions the abbé Du Mabaret in its preface as an important contributor to its first editions.

The *Journal de Trévoux*, for its part, announced the following year that 'none of those who are working on the *Mémoires* have had the least part in the *Dictionnaire*.'[15] The plausibility of the suggestion that the two publications were linked in the public mind because they were both printed in Trévoux is reinforced by the fact that when the *Mercure de Trévoux* appeared in 1708, it too was attributed to the Jesuit journalists, who were obliged to announce that 'inasmuch as several persons have attributed this *Mercure* to us because it is being printed in the same place as our *Mémoires* and is distributed in Paris at the same book-shop, we feel it necessary to correct their error by declaring here that we have no part whatsoever in it.'[16] In spite of their earlier announcement in 1704, the editors of the *Journal* found it necessary three years later to repeat their denial of any connection with the *Dictionnaire*[17].

If the authorship of the first edition of the *Dictionnaire de Trévoux* had been uncertain, that of the second edition appearing in 1721 was less so because father E. Souciet, one of the editors of the *Journal de Trévoux*, had had an important part in the new edition. Souciet, however, 'did not wish to admit it because they had inserted certain things in it of which he disapproved.'[18] Thus the *Journal* printed in 1724 a letter attacking the authors of the *Dictionnaire de Trévoux* as the 'faithful copyists' of Furetière's dictionary printed in 1691, and correcting their article on 'Célestin.' The *Journal*'s review ended with an editorial comment disclaiming any part in the *Dictionnaire de Trévoux*[19]. In the same issue of the *Journal de Trévoux* there is an announcement in the 'nouvelles littéraires' that the periodical has again received mail meant for the *Dictionnaire*, and the editors repeat, 'since people do not tire of attributing to us a work in which we have no part, we must not tire of indicating that we have no claim to it.'[20] A further denial appears in the December issue when, upon receipt

[15] *J. de T.* (March 1705), p.555.
[16] *J. de T.* (May 1708), p.898.
[17] *J. de T.* (March 1711), p.554.
[18] de Backer, *Bibliothèque*, vii.1403.
[19] *J. de T.* (July 1724), pp.1286–88.
[20] *J. de T.* (July 1724), p.1342.

of another letter for the *Dictionnaire de Trévoux* addressed to the *Mémoires*, the editors declare: 'We esteem this *Dictionnaire* as much as it deserves; but we are not its authors: we have so often stated as much that it is surprising that people still attribute it to us.'[21] It would seem that these denials finally convinced the public, because no further mention is made of the confusion between the two publications until the appearance of the third volume of the *Encyclopédie*. In the introduction, d'Alembert, when answering the *Journal de Trévoux*'s charges of plagiarism, subtly links the *Journal* with the *Dictionnaire de Trévoux* by reminding Berthier that the *Dictionnaire* should not accuse others of plagiarism because it too has borrowed from its predecessors. At this, Berthier exclaimed: 'Est-ce que le *Dictionnaire de Trévoux* nous appartient? Les éditeurs de l'*Encyclopédie* penseraient-ils que nous leur sommes opposés, parce que le *Trévoux* étant notre ouvrage, nous avons eu en sa faveur la prédilection paternelle? Bruits populaires, idées conçues par des littérateurs peu instruits! Combien de fois n'avons-nous pas déclaré que ce *Dictionnaire universel* nous est totalement étranger? Qu'on lise nos *Mémoires* de Mars 1705, de Juillet 1724 en deux endroits, et le *Dictionnaire* lui-même à l'article "Trévoux". Qu'on y ajoute le *Journal des savants*, du 28 Avril 1704'.[22]

The only source so far encountered which lists the *Dictionnaire de Trévoux* as a Jesuit publication and names authors, is the *Nouveau Larousse illustré*[23] published in 1900. It lists the Jesuit fathers Buffier, Bougeant, Castel, Ducerceau and Tournemine as its chief authors, but does not state which edition is involved. If the original edition is meant, the listing is questionable, since Castel would have been only 16 years old at the time of its publication while Bougeant would have been 14. The *Dictionnaire théologique catholique* for 1950 states that the *Dictionnaire de Trévoux* 'is not, as

[21] *J. de T.* (Dec.1724), p.2183.
[22] *J. de T.* (Nov.1753), p.2675.
[23] *Nouveau Larousse illustré* (Paris 1900), *s.v.* 'Dictionnaire de Trévoux,'

p.710. While Ducerceau was a Jesuit, he was not an editor of the *Journal de Trévoux*.

has often been stated, the work of the journalists of Trévoux. It is certain however that Father Souciet had a great part in the 1721 edition.'[24] If the Jesuits were in fact the authors of the *Dictionnaire*, they might have denied this so as not to have it considered as representing the Jesuit position, since many of the opinions of its contributors were not necessarily their own. In any case, the view that Jesuit opposition to the *Encyclopédie* was based on considerations of profit out of fear of its competition with the *Dictionnaire de Trévoux*—an accusation, it must be remembered, made in the heat of battle when any weapon was considered valid—seems to be an oversimplification, and misses the whole drama of the struggle of ideas in the eighteenth century. Nor does it explain the abrupt and marked change from a favourable attitude toward the first prospectus of the *Encyclopédie* to one of hostility toward the publication once Diderot was announced as its chief. Given Berthier's attitude toward Diderot as observed in his review of the *Mémoires* on mathematics, and his preoccupation with the defense of his religion, it is difficult to substantiate the thesis that his opposition to the *Encyclopédie* was based simply on jealousy for the *Dictionnaire de Trévoux*[25].

If Berthier felt any apprehension on discovering that Diderot was to edit the *Encyclopédie*, he did not betray it in announcing the new prospectus in January 1751. He simply states that 'everyone has seen the outline of this great work and men of letters have found it to be very well written'; and noting that the editors, Diderot and d'Alembert, state that they have followed Bacon's system in preparing their own work, the Jesuit editor promises

---

[24] *Dictionnaire de théologie catholique* (Paris 1950), *s.v.*, 'Trévoux,' p.1516.

[25] this view seems to have been utilized, even by modern scholars, as a ready formula of explanation for want of a more thorough investigation of the question. Jean Pommier, for example, in the *Revue d'histoire littéraire de la France* for July-September 1951 states of the second prospectus of the *Encyclopédie*: 'Comment allait-il être accueilli par la puissante Compagnie dont le *Dictionnaire* dit de Trévoux en était à sa 5e édition (1743) et qui disposait d'un Journal aussi répandu que les *Mémoires* de Trévoux?' (p.267).

his readers a comparison of the prospectus with Bacon's *De la
dignité et de l'accroissement des sciences* for the next issue[26]. The
promised article, utilizing the same light touch of irony employed
in the review of the *Mémoires sur différents sujets de mathématiques*, reveals that Berthier is still hopeful of causing his readers
to lose interest in Diderot. The article begins by stating that
while Bacon had suggested that new books should be like the
serpent of Moses which devoured those of Pharaoh, that is, they
should supersede the older books and make them useless, we
must not expect one work, such as the newly announced *Encyclopédie*, to be the serpent which will destroy all our libraries[27]. The
editor then makes a detailed comparison between the prospectus
and Bacon's work, showing how the former is merely an imitation of Bacon's great treatise, and parallels it almost word for
word. But, it is pointed out, whereas Bacon had intended to
examine all sciences in order to ascertain what still remained to
be done in each field, the *Encyclopédie* does not intend to produce
anything new in the sciences but will simply collect the best of
what has already been said in each branch of knowledge. Ten
volumes are promised, notes the editor, but, he adds almost prophetically, thirty volumes would not be too much for such a
project, and the editors have probably been working at it for
years; in fact, it would not be surprising if they have already con-
secrated fifty years to its preparation. Berthier concludes, explaining: 'Nous disons tout ceci à cause de la grande idée que nous
avons conçue de cette vaste entreprise. Elle aurait pu être mal
exécutée, et demeurer encore dans un véritable état de possibilité;
mais puisque l'ouvrage est fini, puisqu'à en juger par le prospectus il est parfait, admirons les ressources de notre siècle, acqué-
rons des droits sur un si beau livre, et désignons-lui dès à présent
une place éminente dans toutes nos bibliothèques'.[28]

Palmer's statement that this review of the second prospectus
'makes no attack on the Encyclopedia, veiled or open,'[29] does not

[26] *J. de T.* (Jan.1751), i.188.
[27] *J. de T.* (Jan.1751), ii.303–4.
[28] *J. de T.* (Jan.1751), ii.327.
[29] *Catholics and unbelievers*, p.19.

seem justified. Berthier's irony and his sceptical attitude toward the claims of the editors seem evident enough, and his review, coming as it did at the very beginning of the enterprise, could do much in prejudicing the success of the *Encyclopédie*[30]. Diderot could not leave this unfavourable impression unchallenged, and he felt it necessary to answer Berthier in an equally ironical letter to the editor of the *Journal de Trévoux*. After stating that the Jesuit editor praises the least known writers, the *philosophe* accuses him of failing to read the prospectus through, otherwise he would not have omitted from his review in the *Journal* the philosophical branch of the prospectus, which is the most important of all and of which Bacon says almost nothing. Conceding that Berthier had spoken well of the prospectus when he first announced it in the *Journal de Trévoux*, Diderot none-the-less accuses the editor of having hidden it in the 'nouvelles littéraires' section of the *Journal*, so that no one would read it. If the editors of the *Encyclopédie* have failed to mention periodicals in their prospectus, continues the letter, this oversight will be rectified in the *Encyclopédie*, and Berthier and his *Journal* will be mentioned with the distinction they deserve. The article 'Journal' will also praise Berthier's predecessors, 'whose loss we regret more than you do.' In concluding his letter Diderot states: 'Si j'apprends, par ceux qui lisent vos mémoires, que mes lettres méritent quelque attention de votre part, je ne vous en laisserai pas manquer; grâces à Dieu et à votre journal, les matériaux en sont tout prêts. On m'a dit que, non content des bontés dont vous m'aviez comblé, vous vouliez encore vous écrire à vous-même, dans le premier journal, sur l'*Encyclopédie*. Je cherche, comme vous voyez, à vous en épargner la peine. Au reste, dans le petit commerce épistolaire que je projette, et qui pourra, cette année, former un volume de plus à vos mémoires, je ferai de mon mieux, mon révérend père,

---

[30] Belin says of the prospectus: 'Le *Journal de Trévoux* en fait dans son numéro de Janvier, un éloge assez ironique, qui n'est pas sans faire une grande impression sur l'esprit du public et sans inquiéter beaucoup les libraires' (*Le Mouvement philosophique*, p.57).

pour ne vous ennuyer que le moins qu'il me sera possible; j'en écarterai donc, autant que je pourrai, la sécheresse; vos extraits en seront le principal objet'.[31]

Diderot's letter must have had a strong effect on the Jesuit editor, because rather than wait for the following issue to answer it, Berthier rushed through an 'addition to these *Mémoires*,' which appeared at the end of the February 1751 issue. In answer to the promised 'commerce épistolaire,' Berthier gives a veiled threat which exposes his real concern over the *Encyclopédie*. After noting that the exchange of letters promised by Diderot will entertain the readers of brochures, and that it is always a pleasure to receive letters from Diderot, who is a man of intelligence, when such letters deal simply with literary matters, Berthier adds pointedly, 'other matters are too dangerous, and he knows it well.'[32] The *Journal*'s editors are not concerned with its reputation, continues the journalist, but only with working 'without clamour, without affectation, without hope, and we must also say, without offending customs or religion: which is our capital and essential concern.' Then, assuming a less serious style, Berthier answers various points in the letter with the same air of light mockery which Diderot had employed. He promises a distinguished place in the *Mémoires* for the *Encyclopédie* in gratitude for the promised article on 'Journal' and the mention of his publication in Diderot's future writings. At the accusation that the first announcement of the prospectus was buried in the 'nouvelles littéraires,' the Jesuit editor affirms that this section of the *Journal* lists only those works which are considered worth reading, but if he has done wrong in thus interesting his readers in the new publication, it will be easy to correct the fault when the *Encyclopédie* appears. Finally, the editor promises to keep his readers posted on Bacon, the prospectus, the Encyclopedia, and Diderot's 'commerce épistolaire.'[33]

Certain statements in the correspondence between Diderot and Berthier suggest that the encyclopedist did not limit himself to a

[31] Diderot, *Œuvres*, xiii.168.
[32] *J. de T.* (Feb.1751), p.569.
[33] *J. de T.* (Feb.1751), pp.569–78.

defense through an exchange of letters, but may have succeeded in preventing an attack against the *Encyclopédie* from appearing in the *Journal de Trévoux* by appealing to the censor. The abbé Fontenay, in his *Du rétablissement des Jésuites*, speaks of Berthier's attack on the *Encyclopédie* and says of its editors: 'Ils eurent recours à une manœuvre qu'ils ont mise en usage bien souvent dans la suite. Ils s'adressèrent au magistrat, alors chargé de l'inspection de la librairie, pour qu'il fît défense au p. Berthier de continuer la censure qu'il avait promise; et ce magistrat complaisant donna cette défense'.[34]

In the letter already quoted, Diderot could have been referring to the suppressed article when he had written to Berthier: 'Someone has told me that . . . you wanted to write to yourself, in the next issue, about the *Encyclopédie*. I am endeavouring, as you can see, to spare you the trouble.'[35] In his answer to this letter, the Jesuit editor discloses that in fact such a letter was to appear in the *Journal de Trévoux* but that the censor had prevented its inclusion, and he explains the suppression as follows: 'Un critique, qui nous est inconnu, voulait faire imprimer, ces jours derniers, un écrit à trois parties contre le grand dictionnaire encyclopédique; mais il a eu affaire au censeur royal qui approuve nos Mémoires; et cette circonstance a fait échouer les desseins de cet anonyme. Car le docteur judicieux et attentif s'est ressouvenu que nous

[34] quoted by Sommervogel, *Essai historique*, pp.lxxxvii–lxxxviii. In discussing the problems of the censor in eighteenth-century France, de Tocqueville states that it was common for writers who were attacked to demand from the censor that the attacks be suppressed, and he indicates by giving examples from Voltaire and d'Alembert that the *philosophes* were not above this practice. *Histoire philosophique*, ii.86–7.

[35] it is conceivable that the 'someone' who warned Diderot of the impending attack in the *Journal* might have been Malesherbes, the controller of publications, who was favourable to the *Encyclopédie*, and who was later to hide Diderot's manuscripts in his own home when the authorities sought to seize them. On another occasion Malesherbes had dealt a blow to the Jesuits by refusing to permit the publication of an article presenting their side of the controversy over the bull *Unigenitus*. Gordon and Torrey, pp.16–17.

avions donné son suffrage à notre extrait; et sur cela l'ouvrage de l'anonyme a été rejeté'.[36]

In his answer to the Jesuit editor's statement, Diderot first notes the warning concerning the danger of writing on subjects other than literature and remarks: 'It will not be long, my reverend father, before I convince you of that through yourself.' He then turns to the question of the suppressed article and implies that the unknown critic is Berthier himself and that he may have had other reasons than that mentioned for not printing his attack: 'Votre censeur qui, avec tant de jugement, a si bonne mémoire, ressemblerait peut-être davantage à certains voyageurs qui se "souviennent" de la meilleure foi du monde de ce qu'ils n'ont jamais vu. Le critique dont vous me parlez, et dont "vos grands éloges" ont fait arrêter le "grand écrit" à TROIS parties, ne m'est pas aussi inconnu qu'à vous. Je l'aurais deviné aux TROIS divisions. Il a de très-bonnes raisons pour médire de vive voix de l'*Encyclopédie*; mais il pourrait en avoir de meilleures pour n'en rien dire par écrit'.[37]

The suppression of his own article against the *Encyclopédie*, if indeed it was his, as seems likely, would have come as a shock to Berthier, and it would explain in part the change in his policy as reflected in the *Journal de Trévoux* the following month. No mention of Diderot's latest answer is made, but referring to the *philosophe*'s first letter, Berthier begins his article by noting that since it has been said in 'a well publicized letter' that Bacon's work contains 'almost nothing on the philosophical branch which is the most extensive and most important' in the *Encyclopédie*'s system, he finds it necessary to compare this branch of knowledge as presented in both works. The article then goes into a point by point comparison of Bacon's philosophical system and that

---

[36] *J. de T.* (Feb.1751), p.569.
[37] Diderot, *Œuvres*, xiii.168. The emphasizing of the 'TROIS divisions' is probably a reference to Berthier's earlier review of the prospectus in which the general principles of the *Encyclopédie* are presented under three headings: the faculties of memory, imagination and reason.

expounded in the prospectus, showing their similarity. Those sub-divisions of the prospectus which differ from or are in more detail than Bacon's are presented as being merely a more minute sub-division of his sections. What is most notable in the article is the absence of the irony which Berthier had used in his earlier articles on Diderot. At that time the *philosophe* had still been sufficiently unknown to permit the belittling of his works in the possible hope that the general public would consider them unworthy of attention. In the early part of his career, Diderot had been in too much trouble with the authorities to dare complain of this treat-ment, but by the time the second prospectus for the *Encyclopédie* had appeared, Diderot's position was considerably strengthened, and he felt secure enough to fight back. The recognition that this dangerous enemy was now a truly formidable foe must have caused Berthier to take stock, and contemplate a new course of action. A possible further consideration in the Jesuit editor's change in attitude was the realization that, by entering into a per-sonal quarrel with Diderot as he did, he had jeopardized his reputation for moderation and calm, impersonal critiques, and had embarked the *Journal de Trévoux* on the type of polemics which had discredited it under some of his predecessors. His deci-sion to discontinue the dispute on a personal basis is announced when he states in conclusion that to reply to the reproaches which have been made and which he has discussed in this article, he wishes to quote the words of Bacon: 'If we have . . . given occa-sion to someone to contradict, let him know that, as we do not seek to alienate ourselves from the opinions of others, neither do we intend to argue.'[38] If Diderot had won this round he was not yet rid of his adversary—Berthier would continue to keep a watchful eye on the editor of the *Encyclopédie*. As if to warn the *philosophe* of the consequences of remaining intractable, the Jesuit editor, still speaking through the quotation from Bacon, recounts the story of how the French army under Charles VIII when

[38] *J. de T.* (March 1751), p.737.

entering Italy during the conquest of Naples had marked the lodgings they had chosen with chalk rather than take them by force of arms: 'De même aussi, continue Bacon, nous souhaitons que la vérité entre paisiblement dans les esprits; qu'elle y marque, pour ainsi dire, avec de la craie, le lieu de son séjour, et qu'elle ne soit jamais obligée de prendre les armes pour s'en ouvrir le passage'.[39]

In the following month the *Journal de Trévoux* reviewed Diderot's *Lettre sur les sourds et muets* with the announcement that 'the author . . . is completely unknown to us.'[40] Actually, the author was certainly known to Berthier since Castel had wanted to write a review of both the *Lettre sur les aveugles*, and the *Lettre sur les sourds et muets*, but had been refused permission by the editor[41]. Castel was friendly with Diderot at this time and the encyclopedist had already appealed to him in the matter of his quarrel with Berthier exclaiming: 'But in the name of God, reverend father, what has father Berthier in mind in persecuting an honest man who has no other enemies in society but those he has made for himself through his attachment for the Society of Jesus,' and Diderot had gone on to show how he had refused a sum of money offered him if he would attack the Jesuits, saying: 'I shall know how to manage in my quarrel with father Berthier without the aid of anyone.'[42] The decision to present the *Lettre* as being

[39] *J. de T.* (March 1751), p.737.
[40] *J. de T.* (April 1751), p.841.
[41] Donald Schier, p.48.
[42] Diderot, *Œuvres*, xix.425. Donald Schier cites this letter to substantiate his statement that Diderot appealed to Castel 'to appease Berthier in the matter of the thesis of the abbé de Prades' (*L. B. Castel*, p.44). While the letter is undated, it was more probably written some time in 1751 or thereafter, since the author speaks of 'mon aveugle clair-voyant' and 'mon sourd-muet.' The letter is in answer to a communication from Castel concerning the

Lettre sur les sourds et muets. Diderot thanks Castel for his kindness in having written and says that he has known 'deux moments doux dans ma vie.' One was a letter from mme du Châtelet when the *Lettre sur les aveugles* appeared, and now, 'mon sourd-muet m'en vaut une autre de vous.' This would indicate that Castel's letter and Diderot's acknowledgement now under consideration were written shortly after the appearance of the *Lettre sur les sourds et muets*, and presumably before Berthier's review of the work in April 1751, because a subsequent letter from

by an anonymous author may have been made in order to deny Diderot any undue publicity, and to permit the critic to review the work in a more detached manner. Announcing that the material dealing with the author's linguistic theories is 'fairly precise' and 'rather well put together,' and suggesting that everyone should read it, Berthier remarks that those readers who do not read to learn but who simply seek easily grasped outlines will no doubt wonder exactly what these abstract 'traces of intelligence and erudition' really mean. They will wonder if there are paradoxes or arbitrary opinions in this theory. But philosophers must not think in this manner, they should enter with courage and zeal into the question of inversions[43]. The section dealing with the language of gestures is found to be 'quite extensive' but 'somewhat broken up by digressions,' so that readers may wonder if they have grasped the whole argument and whether deaf-mutes actually confirm the existence of inversions in the French language. 'This does not prevent us from deriving much enjoyment from the ingenious endeavours which are found here,' adds Berthier cautiously, 'particularly at the experiment of the deaf-mute presented before the ocular harpsichord.' Concluding his review of the *Lettre* with a comparison of the linguistic theories of the

Diderot to Castel, dated 2 July 1751, mentions the two *Lettres* and states: 'Je suis bien fâché que vous n'ayez pas été chargé de les faire connaître au public' (Diderot, *Œuvres*, xix.427). The Prades thesis, on the other hand, did not appear until November 1751, and it is not even mentioned in the *Journal de Trévoux* until June 1753. In this article as well as in those which followed it, Diderot was never connected in any way with the abbé's thesis. The only suggestion that Prades's ideas are not really his own appears in the July 1753 issue of the *Journal* where it is said of his 'Apologie': 'Nous y voyons, avec regret, ce théologien puiser toujours ses senti-ments et son langage dans des sources décriées, ... encenser trop libéralement des auteurs justement suspects, et vomir sur ses censeurs et sur d'autres théologiens, les flots d'une bile amère' (p.1621). Georges Roth comments on the letter from Diderot to Castel dated 2 July 1751: 'Diderot écrit au père Castel pour le remercier de son intervention conciliatrice dans le débat avec le r. p. Berthier' (Denis Diderot, *Correspondance* [Paris 1955], i.130). The letter is rather an expression of regret that Castel was unable to influence his colleague and, in particular, was not given permission to review Diderot's two writings.

[43] *J. de T.* (April 1751), pp.841–3.

abbé Batteux and Diderot in the latter's favour, the editor states of the encyclopedist's work: 'There are some keenly reasoned and well-expressed things in it,' but he does not agree with Diderot's view that someday the present generation would be looked upon as his contemporaries now look upon the ancients[44].

The article evoked an answer from Diderot which was reviewed by Berthier in July of the same year with the announcement: 'L'auteur anonyme de la *Lettre sur les sourds et muets* vient de publier des additions pour servir d'éclaircissements à quelques endroits de son ouvrage. Ces additions forment un petit volume dont la plus grande partie est en observations sur l'extrait que nous donnions de sa lettre dans nos derniers Mémoires d'Avril. Cette espèce de réponse est d'un style où la modération et la politesse se font reconnaître; il s'y trouve d'ailleurs des discussions ingénieuses, des développements qui décèlent un esprit bien exercé dans la méthode d'analyse. Nous sommes bien-aises que l'article de nos Mémoires sur les sourds et les muets ait fait naître cette nouvelle production'.[45]

The cautious and almost conciliatory note struck by the *Journal de Trévoux* in its review of Diderot's *Lettre* was a preview of Berthier's new policy towards the *Encyclopédie*. It is as if having regained his composure he had decided to assume an air of detachment and impartiality, and present his observations in the moderate tone he had generally adopted in his critiques of other literary works. Thus, three months after the appearance of the first volume of the *Encyclopédie*, the *Journal* published a lengthy review of the 'Discours préliminaire' which is announced as 'lacking neither in fire, nor elegance, nor the amenities.' Turning to the touchy subject of the general principles underlying the publication as repeated from the prospectus, the editor again compares them with Bacon's ideas but this time points out the reasons advanced by the *Encyclopédie* for differing from that author, noting that these reasons can also be appreciated because, 'in all of

[44] *J. de T.* (April 1751), pp.843ff.   [45] *J. de T.* (July 1751), pp.1677–78.

this, and in general the whole order and concatenation of our knowledge, there reigns and will always reign much of the arbitrary. We must propose what we imagine to be the best,' Berthier continues, 'without thinking that the system we suggest is the only system or the most excellent one.'[46] The review is reasonably objective but, upon occasion, the editor questions the accuracy of the *Encyclopédie*'s statements. For example, when illustrating how science was retarded in early times it is said that pope Zachary condemned a bishop for having guessed the existence of the antipodes six hundred years before Columbus discovered them, Berthier replies that in the first place it was not a bishop but a priest who was condemned, and secondly his crime was not that of having guessed the existence of the antipodes but for having taught that under the earth there existed 'another world, other men, another sun and another earth,' thus suggesting that there were other races of men apart from those decended from Adam, and that consequently, redemption was not universal.

When d'Alembert praises eighteenth-century men of genius, the Jesuit editor departs from his factual tone and interjects a note of irony, remarking: 'C'est un Philosophe qui loue; ainsi l'on doit croire qu'il n'exagère rien, qu'il choisit avec pleine et entière connaissance de cause et qu'il ne lui est pas venu en pensée de dire ce mot des femmes savantes: "Nul n'aura de l'esprit hors nous et nos amis".'[47] Following a promise of further articles on the *Encyclopédie*, the journalist expresses 'in advance, the satisfaction which several articles dealing with grammar, music, geometry, chemistry, botany and mechanics have given us.' The editor concludes with the suggestion that the writers should indicate the sources of the articles enumerated as borrowed, but this is offered, 'for the perfection of this work whose erudition, moreover, is beautiful and extensive.'[48]

[46] *J. de T.* (Oct.1751), p.2270.
[47] *J. de T.* (Oct.1751), p.2285.
[48] *J. de T.* (Oct.1751), p.2295. Alphonse Jobez asserts that when the

first volume of the *Encyclopédie* appeared the *Journal de Trévoux* 'attaqua avec violence le *Discours préliminaire*. D'Alembert répondit au père Berthier,

Having given this introduction to the first volume, the *Journal de Trévoux* then published five additional articles on the *Encyclopédie*, averaging forty pages each, and following the alphabetical order established by the publication. The first of these articles, appearing the following month, returns briefly to the quarrel over the prospectus and points out that the editors of the enterprise have admitted relying heavily upon Bacon's system for their 'encyclopedic tree', including the philosophical branch, thus confirming the critique made seven or eight months ago in reply to 'a letter' which had claimed that Bacon's work contained almost nothing of the *Encyclopédie*'s philosophical branch. But, adds Berthier by way of appeasement, this is true only of the prospectus. The *Encyclopédie* itself is a 'very lofty, very solid enterprise,' and when it has been completed its editors will justly be able to apply to themselves the words of the ode: 'Exegi monumentum aere perennius.'[49] The editor then outlines the method followed by the publication and points out a number of articles taken from Moréri's *Dictionnaire* and the *Dictionnaire de mythologie* by the abbé de Claustre. The tone of the article is detached and factual, but when the editor pauses at the article 'Aius-Locutius' in which is found a plea for the lifting of censorship against 'productions of incredulity' when such works are written in a learned language, and forbidding them in the vulgar tongue because they are to be feared only for the faith of simple folk, Berthier calls it a 'vain subterfuge' noting that it is not the country people, artisans or children who read these books but those who 'consider themselves to be superior,' and who can read the learned languages, and he emphasizes that 'the article "Aius-Locutius" should have had a judicial censorship of which no traces appear in this first volume of the *Encyclopédie*.' A footnote adds that approbations

principal rédacteur de ce journal, une lettre vive et hautaine' (*La France sous Louis XV*, iv.318). The *Journal*'s review of the 'Discours préliminaire' certainly does not seem 'violent' nor has there been preserved any letter from d'Alembert to Berthier on this or any other subject. Jobez may possibly be referring to Diderot's letter in reply to Berthier's attack on the second prospectus.
[49] *J. de T.* (Nov.1751), p.2423.

have been promised for the volumes to follow but it is unfortunate that they were not used in this one[50]. As if to make his position clear and show that he is not opposed to the publication as a literary work but as a medium of anti-religious propaganda, Berthier declares: 'No one is more disposed to recognize the fine sections of the Encyclopedia; we shall receive them with complaisance in our extracts to come; we shall point them out no matter what faculty, science, art or author they might come from.' Then, by way of illustration, he reviews an article on grammar written by Du Marsais and concludes: 'Quand nous rencontrons ici des articles sur cette matière, nous ne sommes point tentés de recourir aux autres lexiques, à celui de Trévoux par exemple, quoiqu'il soit destiné particulièrement à la langue; et la raison en est bien simple. Il règne dans cette partie du nouveau *Dictionnaire*, un goût de composition qu'on sent être primitif, original, venu de source, et portant l'empreinte d'un grand maître'.[51]

The promised surveillance of the *Encyclopédie* as arranged by Boyer had doubtless caused Berthier to feel that he could henceforth publicize the enterprise without fear of advertising unduly an irreligious work. But with the scandal aroused in November by the acceptance at the Sorbonne of the unorthodox thesis of the abbé de Prades, a contributor to the *Encyclopédie*, he may have wondered if the machinery of censorship could halt the growing strength of this 'conspiracy' against the church and the government. A movement for the suppression of the publication must have been initiated at this time, for in his journal the marquis d'Argenson noted on 11 December 1751: 'On se remue beaucoup touchant la thèse de Sorbonne qu'a soutenue l'abbé de Prades, un des écrivains du *Dictionnaire encyclopédique*, et l'on dit que ce livre va être défendu. Le président de la thèse et le prieur de Sorbonne vont être repris aussi pour avoir signé cette thèse sans

---

[50] *J. de T.* (Nov. 1751), p.2448. After the appearance of the first volume, Boyer 'had succeeded in having his own censors, the Jesuit abbés Tam-ponnet, Millet and Cotterel, appointed to examine all articles in the succeeding volumes' (Gordon and Torrey, p.15).

[51] *J. de T.* (Nov.1751), p.2450.

l'avoir lue'.[52] Two weeks later he writes that 'there is a great storm against the *Dictionnaire encyclopédique*, and that storm comes from the Jesuits.'[53]

It may be that the Jesuits had decided to await the appearance of volume ii of the *Encyclopédie*, and thus ascertain the effectiveness of Boyer's censors before undertaking any further action on the suppression of the publication. If Berthier was alarmed by the course of events, he did not show it in the *Journal*'s review of the *Encyclopédie* in December. Maintaining the same moderate tone he had assumed after his quarrel with Diderot the previous year, the Jesuit editor continued his review of volume i by exposing with methodical calm those articles which had been borrowed from other works without indicating the sources, and those which were inaccurately transcribed. He indicates articles copied from such works as the *Dictionnaire de médecine*, Monnier's *Institutions astronomiques*, the *Dictionnaire de Trévoux*, the *Dictionnaire de Chomel* on cookery, Calmet's *Dictionnaire de la Bible*, and others, sometimes quoting from both the *Encyclopédie* and the work plagiarized. Those articles which do give credit to the sources are praised, and the honesty of their authors is pointed out. Thus Daubenton's admission in his article 'Abeille' that some of his material came from Réaumur's *Histoire des insectes*, evokes the comment: 'This is how one should always indicate the sources of knowledge in order to render to each one his due.' D'Alembert, 'a very able writer,' is also praised for mentioning his sources[54]. Berthier concludes his article with a word of justification of his procedure: 'En rapprochant ainsi tant de fois et avec tant de soin le texte des divers dictionnaires, nous croyons satisfaire à une de nos plus importantes fonctions qui est d'apprécier la manière de certains auteurs, et de faire connaître les procédés qu'ils ont tenus dans leurs ouvrages. Il ne nous est pas agréable d'aller ainsi à la recherche des sources et des origines; mais l'*Encyclopédie* nous

---

[52] Armand Brette, *La France au milieu du XVIII* siècle (Paris 1898), p.144.

[53] *ibid.*, p.146.

[54] *J. de T.* (Dec.1751), p.2608.

dédommagera par un bon nombre d'articles travaillés sur des plans originaux et primitifs'.[55]

The *Journal de Trévoux* continues its review of volume i the following month in the same manner, explaining that it is particularly necessary to indicate one's sources because in the *Encyclopédie* each author is indicated by an initial, and the reader will attribute all the material to that writer if the origin is not disclosed. It is also noted that there are 'in several places in the *Encyclopédie*, certain theological explanations which we have difficulty in conceiving.' While the Jesuit editor continues to expose borrowings in the publications, he indicates his approval of many articles which are original. For example, after praising several of Rousseau's contributions, he turns to d'Alembert's article on 'Affectation' of which he states: 'This whole article is full of good judgment and is very well written.'[56] Similarly, the same author's articles 'Affecté,' 'Aiguille aimantée,' 'Air,' 'Algèbre,' as well as those dealing with 'Agathe,' 'Agriculture,' 'Aides,' 'Aimant,' and others are described as considerable articles 'which do honour to the *Encyclopédie*.' Returning to his disclosures of plagiarisms, Berthier reports that the article 'Agir' is one of the most praised contributions in the *Encyclopédie*. In fact, the 'Discours préliminaire' points it out as an illustration of the precision and clarity of the abbé Yvon's metaphysics, but, he adds: 'This article extending almost to three columns in-folio is completely and word for word from father Buffier's *Traité des premières vérités*,' and he quotes lengthily from both works to prove his point. The article 'Amitié' is also presented as coming from Buffier's *Traité de la société civile*.[57]

The *Journal*'s review for the February issue had already been written when volume ii of the *Encyclopédie* appeared. In this review Berthier continues his unrelenting exposition of plagiarisms, but he becomes aroused by a statement contained in the article on the love of the sciences and of letters, to the effect that most men

[55] *J. de T.* (Dec.1751), p.2621. [57] *J. de T.* (Jan.1752), pp.171ff.
[56] *J. de T.* (Jan.1752), p.167.

honour letters as they do religion, that is 'as something they can neither know, nor practice, nor love.' Condemning this as irreligious, 'not to mention its manifest falseness and the indecency which it presents to the reader's eyes,' the editor refutes it and asserts that the article deserves 'the greatest attention on the part of the authors and the editors of the *Encyclopédie* in order that henceforth nothing similar be inserted in it.'[58] In spite of his enmity towards Diderot, Berthier does not let this blind him to the *philosophe*'s extensive contribution to the mechanical arts and trades. With considerable critical acumen the Jesuit editor remarks, albeit somewhat reluctantly: 'En général nous reconnaissons qu'on trouve dans ce dictionnaire beaucoup de choses neuves et recherchées concernant les arts et les métiers; c'est peut-être la partie où il nous paraît se distinguer le plus et le mieux des autres dictionnaires, quoique celui du commerce, par Savary, ne laisse pas de présenter aussi quelques articles dans le même genre . . . . Mais il faut avouer que c'est peu de chose en comparaison des notices nombreuses que celle-ci donne sur les arts mécaniques'.[59]

The storm engendered by the Prades affair against the *Encyclopédie* was rekindled and intensified by the appearance shortly thereafter of volume ii. Its article 'Certitude,' written by de Prades, and echoing the sentiments expressed in his thesis two months earlier, seemed to confirm the accusation that the encyclopedists were responsible for the thesis and were banded together in a plot to overthrow existing authority. In spite of Berthier's warnings and Boyer's precautions, Diderot had managed, with the help of Malesherbes, boldly to reaffirm his ideals. This defiance was swiftly met with a condemnation of the *Encyclopédie* by the archbishop of Paris on 31 January 1752, followed by the suppression of the publication a week later by the Conseil d'état.

The role of Berthier in this first suppression of the *Encyclopédie* should not be underestimated. His was the first voice raised in

[58] *J. de T.* (Feb.1752), pp.312–14.
[59] *J. de T.* (Feb.1752), p.321. In the same issue, the 'nouvelles littéraires' announces volume ii of the *Encyclopédie*.

protest against the work. Albert Cazes states of the Jesuit editor: 'C'est lui qui dès la publication du *prospectus* et du premier volume de l'*Encyclopédie*, a poussé le cri d'alarme et signalé l'impiété essentielle de l'ouvrage: toutes les critiques postérieures dirigées contre l'entreprise encyclopédique sont contenues en germe dans les articles que fit paraître le *Journal de Trévoux*, de janvier 1751 à mars 1752'.[60] The *Journal*'s reviews of the *Encyclopédie* no doubt convinced many of its readers that a condemnation of the enterprise was justified. For example, on 5 February 1752, d'Argenson had noted in his journal that 'the *Journal de Trévoux* for this month thunders against the new volume of that *Dictionnaire encyclopédique* which has just appeared in which it criticizes several things opposed to our supernatural religion,' and he had added approvingly, 'There is in fact at the head of that work a m. Diderot who is very intelligent but who affects too much irreligion.'[61]

With the appearance of volume ii of the *Encyclopédie* it must have seemed evident to Berthier that, the official censorship having failed, the only thing to do was to have the work suppressed completely. In view of the Jesuit editor's friendship with Christophe de Beaumont, the archbishop of Paris[62], it is probable that he was instrumental in procuring the latter's swift condemnation of the *Encyclopédie* on 31 January 1752, six days after volume ii was issued to the public. In describing the importance of Berthier in the suppression of the publication, Albert Cazes mentions as a factor the 'tone of judicious wisdom and the moderation' with which the editor wrote his critiques, and continues: 'De plus, l'austérité et la dignité de sa vie . . ., son influence sur m. de Beaumont, archevêque de Paris, dont il avait la confiance; l'estime en laquelle il était tenu par le dauphin . . .; tous ces détails nous font mieux comprendre l'autorité qui s'attachait aux écrits du

---

[60] Albert Cazes, 'Un adversaire de Diderot,' *Mélanges offerts à m. G. Lanson* (Paris 1922), p.236.

[61] Brette, *La France au milieu du XVIIIe siècle*, p.153.

[62] see Montjoye, *Eloge*, pp.71ff.

p. Berthier et le ressentiment que les "philosophes" n'ont cessé de lui témoigner'.[63]

In the midst of the flurry over the suppression of the *Encyclopédie*, the *Journal de Trévoux* for March continued its review of volume i as if nothing had happened, mentioning volume ii only in a note explaining that this review had been composed before its appearance. Although there is an occasional word of praise such as the statement that 'on the philosophy of the Arabs, erudition and judgment are shown,' and 'this detail deserves to be read,'[64] the bulk of the review is devoted to pointing out the irreligious implications of certain articles. Thus, at the suggestion in the article 'Aristotélisme' that Franciscans do not think, and have depraved minds, 'because they are all cast in the same mould,' Berthier exclaims: 'All this is too much, we find in this detail neither respect nor precision, nor gravity: the truth especially is injured in almost every sentence.'[65] On top of this, a veiled attack has been made on the Jesuits in the article 'Assidéens.' Berthier also accuses the article 'Athée' of putting the arguments for atheism on the same level as those for belief in God, thus justifying the position of atheists. This is denounced by Berthier, who asserts that he cannot accept this placing of the proofs of the existence of God in the category of a problem. It is his duty, then, to 'reject, proscribe and condemn' such a way of thinking[66]. Nor is religion discovered to be the only target of the encyclopedists —the authority of the state is questioned! When the *Encyclopédie* exposes a theory of the social contract in which the governing authority obtains its power through the consent of the governed, the *Journal* retorts: 'These principles (let us dare to say it with

[63] *Mélanges*, p.249. Chaudon attributes the condemnation of the *Encyclopédie* to the writings of Berthier when he says of the work: 'Le journaliste de Trévoux ne vit dans ce magasin des sciences, que larcins, que plagiats, que maximes hardies, contraires à la religion et à l'état. Ces accusations allarmèrent le gouvernement; les travaux des éditeurs furent suspendus; et l'ouvrage supprimé par un arrêt du Conseil du 7 février 1752' (*Dictionnaire*, i.144).

[64] *J. de T.* (March 1752), p.430.
[65] *J. de T.* (March 1752), p.443.
[66] *J. de T.* (March 1752), pp.452-3. 424-469

zeal) seem to us to be very much opposed to the supreme authority, to the constitution of the French empire, and to the public
tranquility.'[67] As a conclusion, the editor restates the policy he
has been following when reviewing the *Encyclopédie*. Noting first
that there are some good sections in the work 'of which we believe
we have given an account without partiality, without affectation,
without exposing ourselves to the reproach of anyone,' Berthier
notes that there have been too many plagiarisms, 'a practice which
could in the long run obscure the glory of the enterprise and cast
shadows on the merit of the authors.'[68] Then, warning his readers
that 'in several instances religion has not been respected,' and
asking them to be extremely circumspect on that point, the Jesuit
editor reiterates the chief purpose of the *Journal de Trévoux*
saying: 'Le premier et le plus grand de nos soins sera de veiller
aussi sur cette partie; d'exercer même une critique grave et soutenue contre tout ce qui donnerait atteinte aux vérités révélées et
à la doctrine des mœurs. Heureux, si par l'étendue de ce zèle,
nous pouvons remplir tout notre devoir, et répondre à tous les
désirs des gens de bien!'[69]

After the suppression of the *Encyclopédie*, the idea was conceived of having the publication continued by a group under the
employ of the king's minister. The result would have been 'an
anodyne, expurgated, and pious encyclopedia,' which would have
compensated for the errors of its previous volumes by its exemplary life under the new editors[70]. Thanks to Malesherbes, however, Diderot's manuscripts were saved from the hands of the
authorities, and the director of publications sequestered them in

[67] *J. de T.* (March 1752), p.464.
[68] *J. de T.* (March 1752), p.468.
[69] *J. de T.* (March 1752), p.469.
[70] Lanfrey, *L'Eglise et les philosophes au 18ème siècle* (Paris 1879),
p.183. Gordon and Torrey state that
'father Berthier had in 1752 even tried
to take over the *Encyclopédie* for the
benefit of the Society' (p.22). Lester

G. Crocker reflects a similar view in
The Embattled philosopher (East Lansing 1954), p.246. While there is no
doubt that Berthier would have wanted the *Encyclopédie* taken away from
Diderot, it was probably less to acquire
it 'for the benefit of the Society' than
to deny its chief editor this outlet for
his 'dangerous' ideas.

his own home until the storm subsided[71]. Diderot continued to work at the preparation of volume iii and d'Alembert, who had been urged to take back his position on the publication after abandoning it when first suppressed in 1752, wrote the 'avertisse-ment' to that volume, in which he attacks the critics of the enter-prise and reasserts its aims and principles. The preface is almost entirely devoted to a refutation of Berthier's critiques, and is written in a calm tone of restrained irony. The writer quotes Berthier's review of the original prospectus and notes that after such liberal praise, he cannot understand why the critic should later attack the same enterprise. As to quoting sources, continues d'Alembert, a good article will be enjoyed whether the original writer is known or not. Besides, he asserts, the *Dictionnaire de Trévoux* borrowed from Furetière and therefore has no right to criticize[72]. Concluding his remarks on plagiarisms, d'Alembert declares that each author is responsible for the article he submits to the *Encyclopédie*, and the two editors, who do not write the material but simply 'put it in order and publish' it, cannot be held responsible for mistakes or borrowings. Turning to Berthier's review of the second prospectus wherein the Jesuit editor had expressed surprise that such a huge enterprise could already have been initiated and be ready for publication, the encyclopedist remarks: 'On a paru aussi trouver fort étrange qu'une société considérable de gens de lettres et d'artistes pût même commencer un pareil ouvrage. Ce reproche est d'autant plus singulier, qu'il a été fait par un écrivain qui entreprend de juger seul ou presque seul de tout ce qui paraît en matière d'arts et de sciences; qui du moins par un rapport fidèle et un examen profond doit mettre le public en état de juger, et qui par conséquent doit être parfaitement instruit d'une infinité de matières. Pourquoi la nature n'aurait-elle pas répandu sur plusieurs ce qu'elle a pu réunir dans un seul?'[73]

[71] Gordon and Torrey, p.16.
[72] 'Avertissement des éditeurs,' *En-cyclopédie* (Paris 1753), iii, p.viii. It is this casual linking of the *Dictionnaire* *de Trévoux* with the *Journal*'s criticisms which caused Berthier to deny any connection between the two.
[73] 'Avertissement', p.x.

Following a general attack on 'inferior censors' who, 'devoured by base jealousy,' vilify their state in life by discrediting useful undertakings, d'Alembert turns to 'those vague accusations of irreligion,' and declares them to be groundless. Referring more specifically to the *Journal*, he announces that 'we cannot dispense ourselves from unmasking to the republic of letters the weak and dangerous men of whom it must especially beware, and the type of adversary against whom it must unite.' Recalling the Jesuits' professed rejection of conversion by coercion, d'Alembert continues: 'Ennemis apparents de la persécution qu'ils aimeraient fort s'ils étaient les maîtres de l'exercer, las enfin d'outrager en pure perte toutes les puissances spirituelles et temporelles, ils prennent aujourd'hui le triste parti de décrier sans raison et sans mesure ce qui fait aux yeux des étrangers la gloire de notre nation, les écrivains les plus célèbres, les ouvrages estimables; ils les attaquent, non par intérêt pour la religion dont ils violentent le premier précepte . . . mais en effet pour retarder de quelques jours par le nom de leurs adversaires l'oubli où ils sont prêts à tomber'.[74] In conclusion, d'Alembert, as if to emphasize the fact that the Jesuits' efforts to prevent the continuation of the *Encyclopédie* have failed, remarks: 'Sheltered from the only truly dangerous and telling blows which malignity can hurl against us, what will it try henceforth against two men of letters who long ago became accustomed through reflection to fearing neither injustice nor poverty.'[75]

The *Journal de Trévoux* in announcing the publication of volume iii of the *Encyclopédie*, after noting that its editor had not yet prepared a review of the new volume, turned to the 'avertissement' and exclaimed: 'What darts they hurl against our *Mémoires*, now in the open, now under the veil of allegory or apologue, sometimes in a private attack, other times including us in general hostilities!'[76] In answer to these attacks, he first points out that 'we did not seek a war with the *Encyclopédie*; we do not wish to

[74] 'Avertissement', p.xii.
[75] 'Avertissement', p.xiii.

[76] *J. de T.* (Nov.1753), p.2660.

190

do anything to perpetuate it, and it is much more agreeable for us to sit in the temple of peace to contemplate from there the success of that great work.' Berthier then reviews his articles on the *Encyclopédie*, from the May 1745 review of the original prospectus to the most recent article, in order to show that he had not been against the enterprise at the beginning; and he attempts to excuse his review of the second prospectus by declaring that although many readers thought they had noticed a tone of irony in the article, no irony was meant. In fact, he adds, when he learned of the unfavourable impression he had caused, he had offered to give his readers a preview of some of the *Encyclopédie*'s contributions to make up for the erroneous interpretation given his words, but its editors had refused him permission. Volume i was well publicized, he pursues, and a special effort was made to be fair. After quoting from his past reviews to illustrate his impartiality, the Jesuit editor then enumerates the causes which led him to criticize the *Encyclopédie*: 'We noticed in the body of the *Dictionnaire* several reprehensible propositions in questions of religion,' he begins, 'and some borrowings from other books made with too little care.' In reviewing the publication, he affirms, he felt it his duty to point out those places where religion had been offended, and to protest the unlimited transcriptions from other works without quotation marks. These plagiarisms, 'and we mention this for the exoneration of the editors, were made without confiding to those two men of letters, the secret of a practice so little favourable to the glory of the enterprise.'[77] The exposition of such borrowings is part of the functions of journalists, he insists, and if later he became an opponent of the encyclopedists, it was because he did not forget the primary purpose of the *Journal de Trévoux*: 'Quand la religion est attaquée, cette fonction de journalistes se convertit, sans effort, en celle d'adversaires et combattants: si c'est là ce qu'on reprend en nous comment pourrait-on nous rendre sensibles à ces reproches? Il est vrai, comme l'obser-

[77] *J. de T.* (Nov.1753), p.2659.

vent les éditeurs, que les "accusations vagues" d'impiété sont quelque chose de très odieux; sans compter le danger auquel on expose la religion en grossissant, par caprice ou par malignité, le nombre de ses ennemis. Mais on doit aussi reconnaître que, dans un siècle comme le nôtre, il est tout-à-fait nécessaire de se défier, d'examiner, d'exiger des sûretés, de souhaiter des éclaircissements, de rejeter des expressions équivoques; et l'obligation de tout ceci croît en raison des circonstances, des personnes, de la qualité des ouvrages et des matières qu'on y traite'.[78]

As if to show that his accusations were not 'vague,' Berthier proceeds to review the objectionable passages he had mentioned, including the inference that most men can neither know, practice, nor love religion; and the placing of the arguments for atheism on the same level with those for the existence of God. As to borrowings, the readers are reminded that not all the remarks in the *Journal* were negative: d'Alembert was praised for quoting his sources as were other contributors to the *Encyclopédie*. The exposure of plagiarisms is actually useful to the enterprise, it is pointed out, because whereas the editors had been unaware of them and individual authors had been abusing the good faith of Diderot and d'Alembert, these two men of letters will be more alert in their review of the material submitted for publication and the *Encyclopédie* will thus become even 'more estimable.' After answering a number of points in the 'avertissement,' Berthier concludes his remarks by turning to d'Alembert's closing words concerning the 'imminent oblivion' of the *Encyclopédie*'s adversaries, and declaring: 'Le *Journal de Trévoux* n'est point un livre nouveau; il existe depuis plus de 52 ans: par conséquent le public sait bien s'il mérite son estime, ou s'il ne la mérite pas. Au cas qu'il en soit digne, quelques traits polémiques de l'*Encyclopédie* ne détruiront pas cette bonne renommée. Si ce journal n'est pas

---

[78] *J. de T.* (Nov.1753), pp.2665–66. In a footnote after the words 'accusations vagues,' Berthier reminds the encyclopedists that when all of Paris was attributing the de Prades thesis to Diderot, the *Journal de Trévoux* refrained from linking it with that author because of the absence of proof.

estimé, ce que l'*Encyclopédie* pourra dire et répéter à son désavantage, n'aggravera pas beaucoup le poids de son infortune. Mais
de l'une ou de l'autre hypothèse, il résultera toujours pour nous
l'obligation étroite de ranimer nos forces; de redoubler de zèle et
d'attention; de chercher dans les livres plutôt le bien que le mal
qu'on peut en dire; de réserver les grands coups de la critique
pour les ouvrages contraires à la religion et aux bonnes mœurs;
de croire après bien des travaux, que nous ne sommes qu'"inutiles," et que nous mériterons toujours mieux qu'aucun auteur ou
éditeur de quelque livre que ce soit d'être parfaitement "oublié".'[79]
Having thus made his position clear, Berthier reverted to the
weapon of silence which he had used in the early part of Diderot's
career, and thenceforth he rarely mentioned the *philosophe* or the
Encyclopédie.

Whether the Jesuit editor knew Diderot to have had a part in
writing a brochure entitled *L'Histoire et le secret de la peinture en
cire* is not known, but in any event it is announced in the *Journal
de Trévoux* as coming from an anonymous author who is a 'man
of intelligence' and who 'writes in an equally adroit and imposing
tone.'[80] The contents of the brochure are not revealed, but Berthier wonders whether the author should not have allowed
Bachelier, from whom the secret process for painting in wax was
obtained, more time to enjoy the advantages of the secret which
is the product of his reflexions, in view of his youth and his good
faith. The advisability of thus disclosing the secret to foreign
countries is also questioned, inasmuch as the discovery could be
developed into an industry which might enrich the state, at least
until the process were finally discovered by foreign competitors.
In any case, the article concludes, the author of the brochure will
be applauded. 'He must be a connoisseur in painting and in chemistry; and he does not lack the talents imparted by literature.'[81]

The review several months later of a publication entitled *Analyse et réfutation de divers écrits modernes contre la religion*, affords

[79] *J. de T.* (Nov.1753), p.2673.   [81] *J. de T.* (May 1755), pp.1329ff.
[80] *J. de T.* (May 1755), p.1329.

Berthier an opportunity to compare Diderot's style in the *Pensées philosophiques* with that of Voltaire in his *Lettres philosophiques*, to the advantage of the encyclopedist. Recognizing the superiority of Diderot as a thinker and philosopher, the editor notes that 'in the *Pensées* there is much more fire and energy than in the *Lettres*: with all the latter melted down together, one could barely express one line of the others.' Although both writers deal at times with the same ideas, 'in the *Pensées* they receive a better temper, they are launched with much more vigour than in the *Lettres*.' Going on to the respective styles of the two works, Berthier remarks: 'Le style des *Lettres* éblouit par ses agréments ingénieux, celui des *Pensées* étonne par ses tours singuliers; là c'est un critique amusant qui égaie sa bile par des observations sacrilèges; ici c'est un enthousiaste éloquent qui exhale en blasphèmes raisonnés une colère réfléchie. L'un avec complaisance développe et étend ses idées pour les insinuer plus aisément; l'autre avec violence serre et entasse ses pensées pour les graver plus profondément'.[82]

Four years later, Berthier again mentions the encyclopedists when reviewing Boulier's *Pièces philosophiques et littéraires*. Noting the author's praise of d'Alembert's 'Discours préliminaire', the editor concurs, declaring: 'This is how one should always recognize the good even in the midst of evil, and do justice to talents without slackening in the essential interests of truth.'[83] Turning to Boulier's discussion of Diderot, the Jesuit editor interjects that the usual snare of this *philosophe* is to 'place on the same line essential truths and the most pernicious errors,' and he explains: 'La piété et la superstition sont pour lui des termes synonymes. Il ne connaît point de milieu entre le déiste et le superstitieux. Le vrai athée et le vrai Chrétien sont à ses yeux des phénomènes qu'il faut apprécier de la même façon'.[84] Berthier then turns to the *Lettre sur les aveugles*—the only mention made of this work by the *Journal*—and notes that 'in this system,

[82] *J. de T.* (Dec.1755), p.2956.
[83] *J. de T.* (Oct.1759), ii.2565.
[84] *J. de T.* (Oct.1759), ii.2568.

humanity and natural knowledge are founded only on "optical appearances". The license to imagine and to pretend is pushed to the strangest absurdities.'[85]

Apart from these few references, the *Journal de Trévoux* refrained from mentioning directly either Diderot or his writings after its article in November 1753. In this policy of silence, Berthier may be said to have attacked Diderot and his enterprise negatively, by denying them any further publicity in the *Journal de Trévoux*. This decision was probably reached when it became apparent that despite the early suppression the enterprise was continuing to publish new volumes, and that the list of subscribers was growing from year to year. It may be, too, that having sounded the alarm when the publication had first appeared, Berthier was satisfied to allow those who had heard the cry to continue the struggle which he had begun against the *Encyclopédie*. When the attempted assassination of Louis xv in 1757, and the publication of Helvétius's *De l'esprit* the following year aroused a new storm against the encyclopedists and led to the revocation of the *Encyclopédie*'s 'privilège' in 1759, the *Journal de Trévoux*, although its editor may have had a part in the condemnation[86], refused to break his silence, and he ignored the event. This was undoubtedly one of the bleakest periods in the career of the encyclopedist, for not only had d'Alembert abandoned the enterprise, but Voltaire too had temporarily given it up as a lost cause[87]. It is thanks to Diderot's boundless courage and tenacity that the *Encyclopédie* weathered the storm, and the fact that Berthier early recognized its editor's strength indicates his perspicacity in realizing from the beginning that here would

---

[85] *J. de T.* (Oct.1759), ii.2570.

[86] Gordon and Torrey list Berthier as one of the leaders in the opposition to the *Encyclopédie* between 1757 and 1762 (p.19).

[87] see the chapter on Voltaire, above, for his letter to Bertrand concerning the *Encyclopédie*. In the same mood the *philosophe* wrote to Formey: 'Vous avez donc travaillé aussi à l'*Encyclopédie!* Eh bien, vous n'y travaillerez plus; la cabale des dévots l'a fait supprimer, et peu s'en est fallu qu'elle n'ait été brûlée comme les œuvres de Calvin. Laissons aller le monde comme il va' (M.xl.81).

be his most formidable and most dangerous adversary. The suppression of the Jesuits in 1762 was a profound relief to the harassed *philosophe*. In announcing this event to Sophie Voland, Diderot declared: 'At last I am delivered of a great number of powerful enemies.'[88]

Diderot certainly had every reason for satisfaction that this voice of the Jesuits had fallen silent, for he could not have failed to notice that Berthier's critical spirit was often among most discerning. While he had been one of the encyclopedist's most formidable opponents, still their quarrel had not blinded the Jesuit editor to the *philosophe*'s genius. It was Berthier who had called his readers' attention to the value of a project which had been so close to Diderot's heart—the *Encyclopédie*'s great contribution to a clearer understanding of the mechanical arts and trades. And again it was Berthier who had the courage and perhaps the perspicacity to compare to Diderot's advantage the *Pensées philosophiques* with the *Lettres philosophiques* of the already famous Voltaire. It may well have been with this in mind that Diderot, even while attacking Berthier in the *Encyclopédie* article 'Jésuite,' paid tribute to the editor's intellectual honesty—albeit reluctantly —when he noted that the journalist of Trévoux was 'a good man, so they say.'[89]

[88] Diderot, *Œuvres*, xix.98.
[89] *ibid.*, xv.284.

The Journal de Trévoux and the enlightenment

The present study of the *Journal de Trévoux* has already shown us that the new ideas popularized by the *philosophes* were not limited to the *philosophes* themselves but had spread to many groups including such churchmen as Berthier. We shall now attempt to show more clearly to what extent the Jesuit editor accepted the main tenets of the enlightenment and, when he differed with its leaders, the reasons for those differences. The following definition of the enlightenment as presented by professors Fellows and Torrey will serve as a yardstick permitting us to study Berthier's views more methodically: ' "Enlightenment" is a term applied to a definite revolution in the history of thought and especially to its manifestations in eighteenth-century France. It signifies not only the popularization and dissemination in literary form of scientific knowledge but also an all-pervasive philosophic and critical spirit. The leaders of the movement were called "philosophers," although few of them established definite systems of philosophy. The main tenets of the group were a sincere belief in the idea of progress, the application of the experimental method in science, the free and unfettered use of the God-given faculty of reason in all affairs, human and divine, and the ardent faith that reason, controlled by experience, was, with all its limitations, the final judge and the best guide available for the conduct of life'.[1]

The belief in the idea of progress, so characteristic of eighteenth-century thought, is often reflected in the pages of the *Journal de Trévoux*. In discussing an attack on philosophy as useless to society made by the abbé Pluche in *Le Spectacle de la nature*, Berthier condemns the author's depreciation of the contributions

[1] *The Age of enlightenment* (New York 1942), p.1.

to the progress of society of Descartes, Newton, Gassendi, Leibnitz and others, and replies: 'Ne sont-ce pas ces philosophes qui ont perfectionné l'astronomie, la géographie, la navigation, et la plupart des arts? Ne leur avons-nous pas l'obligation de nous avoir guéris d'une foule de préjugés au sujet des comètes, des éclipses, des aurores boréales: de nous avoir démontré le naturalisme de tant de phénomènes qui effrayaient nos pères, de nous avoir dévoilé les sources secrètes de nos goûts, de nos sentiments et de nos pensées, de nous apprendre tous les jours des choses que nous ne savions pas, et de nous en désapprendre, que nous croyions savoir: et ce qui est encore plus estimable, de perfectionner, d'éclairer, et d'étendre notre intelligence?'[2] Philosophers, pursues the editor, are the most peaceful members of society and seek only to be of utility to mankind. 'It is ignorance, heresy and enthusiasm which have upset the world. Philosophy has worked only to enlighten and pacify it.'[3]

We have already seen that Berthier viewed the progress of philosophy since the time of Aristotle, and since Descartes, as perfectly natural since knowledge is cumulative, and men are constantly advancing by using the discoveries made by these pioneers of thought as stepping-stones toward greater achievements. This idea of progress extended into the arts as well. In keeping with his view of progress, Berthier decried the imposition of rigid classical rules in the arts, and pleaded for an end to servile imitation, with more freedom for the creative artist. On the occasion of his review of de Mermet's *De la corruption du goût*, the Jesuit editor had cited the progress in the construction of musical instruments as well as the increase in musical knowledge as reasons for breaking with traditional forms of music, declaring: 'In profane or indifferent arts, why limit minds and talents to servile

[2] *J. de T.* (Dec.1746), p.2780.
[3] *ibid.*, pp.2284–85. Cf. Voltaire's letter to Rousseau in 1755 wherein he reflects a similar view: 'Avouez que le badinage de Marot n'a pas produit le Saint-Barthélémey, et que la tragédie du *Cid* ne causa pas les guerres de la fronde. Les grands crimes n'ont été commis que par de célèbres ignorants' (M.xxxviii.449).

imitation or to a cold and insipid copying?'[4] Similarly, when Denesle in his *Les Préjugés du public*, defends imitation of the masters by insisting that this is inevitable when one has read widely, Berthier counters that the author need not fear that he is imitating others, 'il n'y a qu'à suivre son génie, penser et écrire naturellement, pour éviter l'écueil, dont il s'agit; la nature est plus abondante et plus variée qu'on ne pense; elle se diversifie autant dans la tournure des esprits, que dans les traits du visage: c'est l'imitation de la nature, et non pas celle des modèles, qui a formé les grands maîtres, et nous ne croyons pas, comme notre auteur, qu'une tête, une attitude, une passion, qui aurait été copiée trait pour trait sur le Guide, ou sur le Titien, si elle était bien saisie, si elle entrait naturellement dans le sujet, rendrait le copiste auteur'.[5] Imitation of the ancients presents a further problem to the artist, continues the article, for if a literary technique such as the duplication of the galloping of a horse through sounds is highly effective for Virgil's Latin, it does not follow that it would be equally valid for the French language. Denesle is unjustified in demanding that we admire Bartas's imitation of the song of a lark on the grounds that Virgil does the same thing. What seemed beautiful to the Greeks and Romans might well shock French ears[6].

While encouraging change in artistic forms, the Jesuit editor refused to assume the disdainful attitude of many of his contemporaries in regard to pre-classical French verse. When Denesle reflects this attitude by thanking God that such forms as the rondeau, the ballad and the sonnet are no longer used, and calling them 'puerile forms of writing' which reflect 'gothic simplicity,' Berthier defends them declaring: 'Nous convenons que la mode de tout cela est un peu passée, mais nous ne croyons pas pourtant que c'est par mépris que nous l'avons changée. On lira toujours avec plaisir un rondeau, un sonnet, un triolet, où il y aura du sel. Ce n'est peut-être que la difficulté d'y réussir, qui y a fait renoncer. Nous convenons avec lui que les rimes féminines sont fort

[4] *J. de T.* (Dec.1746), p.2639.   [6] *J. de T.* (Aug.1747), p.1633.
[5] *J. de T.* (Aug.1747), p.1626.

désagréables pour le chant; mais pourquoi vouloir bannir abso-
lument la rime et la mesure de la comédie? Sont-elles si mal dans
le Misanthrope et dans le Tartuffe?'[7]

This general attitude toward the arts reflects not only a faith in
progress but also another tenet of the enlightenment, that is, 'the
free and unfettered use of the God-given faculty of reason.' The
evils of confining the mind with too many rules and precepts are
pointed out by the Jesuit editor in connection with a review of
Buffon's *Histoire naturelle*. Praising the scientist's reliance on observation rather than on preconceived notions, Berthier points
out the weakness of other systems by noting: 'Il n'y a pas de doute
que l'histoire naturelle, ainsi que tant d'autres sciences dont on
parle tous les jours, ne pût être présenté sous des dehors didac-
tiques et dans un appareil de préceptes, de méthodes, d'observations géantes: or cette manière est le fléau des esprits, la ruine de
l'éducation et des belles connaissances. Comme dans les sociétés
la multitude des lois indispose les cœurs, ainsi dans l'empire des
sciences et des arts le poids excessif des règles accable le génie et
étouffe les talents'.[8] Buffon's insistence on learning through one's
own observation rather than through dogmatic precepts is called
an 'excellent theory which deserves to be transported from natural
history to all other sections of the arts and sciences.' Pedagogues
should try to 'interest more fully our natural curiosity.'[9] Dogmatic systems and rigid, inflexible rules in the arts and sciences,
therefore, will constantly be decried by Berthier. Controversy
and differences of opinion in these matters were viewed as a
wholesome stimulus to finding truth. Thus, when Rameau, in his
Observations sur notre instinct pour la musique states that if it had
not been for the recent controversies over music he might not
have discovered the truth about harmony, the Jesuit journalist
points this out as proof that despite the hostilities in the heat of
the battle, 'the debates over the sciences and the arts are useful to
the progress of human knowledge.'[10]

[7] *J. de T.* (Aug.1747), p.1637.
[8] *J. de T.* (Sept.1749), p.1854.
[9] *J. de T.* (Sept.1749), p.1856.
[10] *J. de T.* (Aug.1754), p.2004.

The addition of the word 'divine' to the belief in the 'free and unfettered use of the God-given faculty of reason in all affairs, human and divine,' would not have caused Berthier to reject this tenet, primarily because he was convinced that his religion was based on reasons so compelling that they would convince any impartial judge. Thus in 1747 he wrote: 'Nous vivons dans un siècle où le merveilleux, dès qu'il se présente, devient un objet de critique. Cela est louable à bien des égards. On prévient par là l'erreur, la superstition, le fanatisme, effets honteux d'une admiration précipitée. Mais en ceci, comme dans tout le reste, la critique doit être judicieuse, pour saisir le point précis de la controverse; impartiale, pour chercher le vrai indépendamment des divers intérêts qui se rencontrent; attentive, pour découvrir tous les moyens d'attaque et de défense, et par ce moyen se mettre en état de décider la question avec le plus d'équité qu'il est possible'.[11]

When attacking Locke for declaring that anything opposed to reason should not be an article of faith, the abbé Pluche in his Le Spectacle de la nature had insisted that reason must submit to faith even when the truth proposed was clearly unreasonable. Berthier had decried this position, exclaiming that this would mean that two contradictory propositions could at the same time be true. 'What would we come to if such a philosophy were ever established?' Locke's statement is 'a truth which is very luminous, important, and authorized by the most zealous defenders of religion.'[12] There can be no contradiction between scientific truth and religious truth, maintained the editor. While the truths reveal-

---

[11] Berthier, Histoire de l'église gallicane, xvi.449–520. Writing this in connection with the history of Joan of Arc, Berthier continues by saying: 'Appliquons ces règles à l'histoire de la pucelle d'Orléans qui fait le sujet de ce discours.' He then proceeds to show that Rapin-Thoyras, in attributing Joan of Arc's exploits to deception and political manoeuvering, does not proceed as a true historian since the only contemporary source he cites is Monstrelet, while he overlooks completely the writings of Jean Chartier, Alain Chartier, the herald of Charles VIII, Gui Pape, Gerson, Jean Nider, Saint Anthony, the archbishop of Florence, pope Pius II, Martin Franc and others whom Berthier quotes to uphold his own statements.

[12] J. de T. (Sept.1746), p.1761.

ed by God are beyond human comprehension, men must investigate the authenticity of such a revelation if their faith is to be reasonable. Thus, in considering the historical facts which are the grounds for belief, 'one is not only permitted but very particularly urged to exercise one's reason so that the submission to faith will not be charged with imprudence or enthusiasm.' The reasons for belief in the Christian religion 'are invincible, whereas its mysteries rise above all the powers of the human intellect.'[13]

We have already seen that in investigating these grounds for belief, Berthier insisted that an historical approach was necessary. The question to ask was not 'Can a man rise from the dead?' but 'Did a man rise from the dead?' 'The precision of geometricians or metaphysical evidence are not the methods of a religion which rests on facts, which cannot be proved except by facts.'[14] For this reason, Diderot's statement that he would not believe that a dead man can rise even if he saw it with his own eyes, seemed to Berthier to be an unreasonable attitude. If it actually happened, the fact that it was incomprehensible to human understanding would not make it any less a fact: 'La raison n'est faite que pour se soumettre au joug de la révélation divine, quand elle en a reconnu l'authenticité: l'étendue de ses droits se borne à la vérification du sceau que porte la révélation: sa divinité constatée, l'incompréhensibilité des mystères ne saurait justifier la résistance de l'incrédulité: alors le devoir de la raison est de les croire, sans en concevoir la profondeur'.[15]

If the grounds for belief in Christianity were so compelling, why were there unbelievers? The reasons suggested by Berthier were varied. Chief among them was intellectual pride. Christianity, proclaiming as it does the equality of all men before God, is repugnant to men who consider themselves superior to the masses. As believers, they are obliged to work out their salvation exactly in the same way as do ignorant men; even their faith is a gift which they have not earned. While they are permitted to investigate the

[13] *J. de T.* (Jan.1762), i.153.   [15] *J. de T.* (Sept.1757), p.2204.
[14] *J. de T.* (Jan.1750), p.141.

evidence for belief in revelation, they are not allowed to question the truths thus revealed once they are convinced of their divinity. Finally, Christianity preaches humility and attacks the unbeliever's pride: 'Voilà l'écueil des faux-savants et la source de leur incrédulité: il semble qu'ils ne sauraient pardonner à la providence d'avoir mis la foi et le salut à la même portée pour eux et pour le peuple: cette divine économie qui caractérise une bonté universelle, scandalise, en quelque sorte, leur présomption particulière; ils aiment mieux se perdre dans l'abîme de leurs propres ténèbres, que de se sauver à la faveur des lumières communes'.[16]

A second reason frequently put forth by the Jesuit editor for the incredulity of some people was that Christianity would require them to suppress their baser passions and deny them the sensual pleasures they seek. The attraction of Bayle, for example, is 'neither the solidity of his doubts nor the weight of his arguments,' but his libertinism. He invites them 'to profess an independence in which they will be unrestricted except for an external compliance with a few civil manners.'[17] This is one reason for the growth of materialism. 'Materialism owes its partisans to the interests of the passions and of libertinism. They would like to perish completely at death because they wish to live an epicurean life.'[18] Thus, according to Berthier, the refusal of some people to accept Christianity was not so much due to its dogmas but because its morality would prevent them from gratifying their passions: 'Après tout, ce qui

[16] J. de T. (June 1757), p.1483–84.
[17] J. de T. (Sept.1757), p.2206.
[18] J. de T. (Sept.1757), ii.2505. See also the chapter on Voltaire for a similar statement. The denial of hell was one of the building blocks to incredulity for Berthier. On another occasion, the Jesuit editor states: 'I am strongly tempted to believe that there are very few persons really persuaded of the existence of hell. If this truth were believed would not mankind pursue a different line of conduct? If we were properly convinced of an eternity of punishment, would not a prudent and well-regulated self love cry out against the life which is led, I will not say in the great world and in licentious companies, but even in professions that are apparently holy? From this incredulity, or, if you will, from this weak faith on the truth of hell, springs, in a great measure the growth of irreligion' (An Exposition of the lamentation of the prophet Jeremiah [New York 1850], p.68, tr. by William Walsh).

les révolte le plus, ce n'est pas l'incompréhensibilité des mystères, les phénomènes qui leur sont les plus familiers dans la nature ne surpassent guères moins leur intelligence; la sainteté des devoirs que la foi impose, les rebute beaucoup plus que l'incompréhensibilité des dogmes'.[19]

A third explanation for the spread of incredulity has been indicated in our chapter on Voltaire, namely, some readers are dazzled by the genius and wit of irreligious writers and accept their witticisms in lieu of reasons. There is 'an infinity of minds for whom a flash of wit is a demonstration against religion,' notes the editor[20]. One can admire genius without sharing the views of the writer who possesses it, he contends. When de Bastide complains in *Les Choses comme on doit les voir* that Bayle's attackers do not appreciate his genius, Berthier replies that the author 'does not distinguish sufficiently between talent and its abuse; he accuses those who do not adore his errors of failing to appreciate his genius,' and he adds: 'Bayle et ces autres écrivains auront toujours assez d'admirateurs de leur esprit, et trop de partisans de leurs travers. Qu'on dépouille leurs idées singulières des charmes que leur prête la beauté de leur génie, elles rentreront humblement dans la catégorie des absurdités surannées'.[21]

Of all the reasons offered by Berthier for the spread of incredulity, the second, that its partisans wish to destroy the moral restraints of Christianity in order to indulge their passions, was viewed with the greatest alarm. Convinced that 'the passions are movements full of disorder and revolt; consequently, they are defects, enemies, and evil inclinations,'[22] Berthier foresaw dire consequences for the nation if a philosophy giving free rein to

[19] *J. de T.* (June 1757), p.1484.
[20] *J. de T.* (Jan.1747), p.52.
[21] *J. de T.* (April 1757), i.857–58. If Berthier was accused of not recognizing a writer's genius because he disagreed with his ideas, he was also accused of tolerating the ideas of the 'incrédules' because he admired their genius. The Jansenists declared of the 'impies': 'Les Jésuites les flattent, jusqu'à trouver "tout grand" dans leurs écrits. Qui les empêchera donc de renverser l'évangile?' (*Nouvelles ecclésiastiques* [3 July 1754], p.108).
[22] *J. de T.* (Jan.1762), i.151.

man's baser inclinations were allowed to spread. Christianity was a safeguard for the peaceful existence of the state. If it were discarded for a deterministic, relativistic view of morality, society would fall into an 'abyss.' In his attack on Helvétius's *De l'Esprit*, the Jesuit editor brands the *philosophe*'s denial of free-will and insistence that no man is bad but merely selfish as an 'encouragement to crime and to licentiousness if not an induration in the most abominable practices.' In this system, 'since it does not admit any law binding the conscience, the only guilty person will be the one who does not succeed.'[23] Thus, for Berthier, irreligion was linked closely with sedition against the state because he believed it destroyed the moral basis essential to any society. Not only do the writings of unbelievers destroy religion, but also 'customs, zeal for the public welfare, and the links that attach the people to their sovereign.'[24] Such writings, far from preventing the political and economic excesses of the nation, were viewed as removing all sense of moral duty from the ruling authority. In so doing, unbelievers were jeopardizing their own rights. By denying any absolute moral principles prescribed by God for all men, they were placing in the hands of human legislators the right to prescribe what is 'just' or 'unjust' according to their own whims: 'Il est vrai que les philosophes incrédules, pour pallier la fureur qui les anime contre toute religion, transportent aux souverains et aux législateurs les droits dont ils dépouillent la divinité. Ils attribuent à la législation le pouvoir d'imprimer à nos actions, quelle qu'en soit la nature, le sceau du juste et de l'injuste, et de le briser au gré de leur caprice et de leur intérêt, des temps et des circonstances. Ainsi les droits qu'ils refusent à l'autorité divine, ils

---

[23] *J. de T.* (Nov.1758), p.2842. While such philosophers as Diderot and Voltaire did not go so far as Helvétius, and rejected his complete determinism, they as well as most *philosophes* had favoured the view of the basic goodness of men's natural passions and the legitimacy of indulging such passions in opposition to the traditional concept of man as a creature whose passions would lead him to sin as a consequence of original sin, and who therefore must suppress his baser inclinations.

[24] *J. de T.* (Oct.1758), ii.2659.

les accordent à l'autorité humaine. Mais, en les acceptant elle en serait bientôt la dupe et la victime. Ses droits, même les plus légitimes, ne sont en sûreté que sous la garde de Dieu, qui les confère, les confirme, les protège et les venge'.[25]

Thus, such irreligious doctrines had dangerous political consequences. Since most of these 'impious' writers attack the governing authorities as 'despotic' and seek to undermine the existing government, 'would it not be surprising that the defenders of this horrible system should receive from kings or ministers, we do not say any protection or consideration, but even any indulgence or tolerance whatsoever?'[26] We have seen that for Berthier civil strife was the worst calamity that could befall a nation. If there were abuses in the monarchy, they should be remedied by the proper education of the heirs to the throne in their moral duties toward their subjects. Irreligious writers, by preaching a disregard for traditional values and for the ruling authority, were spreading a theory of sedition and revolt and it became the duty of the government to protect itself and its subjects from the inevitable destruction and bloodshed which such civil strife would entail. While Berthier maintained that no authority had any jurisdiction over the private opinions of men, he felt that the public dissemination of dangerous doctrines could and should be forbidden if they endangered the existence of the state. In such a case the government could not be accused of despotism for enacting laws against endangering the life of the state any more than a law against poison can be viewed as an encroachment on men's liberties[27]. Thus, to the editor, the justification for censorship rested more on political rather than on religious grounds.

The views of Berthier regarding 'the application of the experimental method in science' have already been studied in some detail. His praise of Trembley, Needham and Newton, for example, was based on an admiration for their reliance on experimentation and facts rather than on dogmatic 'systems.' This same approach

[25] *J. de T.* (July 1759), ii.1806.
[26] *J. de T.* (Dec.1754), p.2981.
[27] *J. de T.* (Sept.1747), pp.1782-83.

by Buffon in the *Histoire naturelle* evoked a series of favourable reviews in the *Journal de Trévoux*. The first of these begins by concurring in the scientist's plea for less emphasis on theories and more observation of the facts. Summing up the preliminary discourse to volume i of the *Histoire naturelle*, Berthier calls its conclusion 'the most exquisite part of the learned author's whole doctrine,' explaining: 'Car s'élevant au-dessus des modernes qui n'ont souvent fait que des méthodes de mots et des nomenclatures abstraites; portant aussi ses vues au-delà des anciens qui n'étaient pas assez versés dans la physique expérimentale, il nous apprend à chercher et à trouver la vérité dans l'étude des choses naturelles. Or cette vérité consiste dans la découverte des causes ou plutôt des effets plus généraux qui tiennent lieu de causes; et l'on s'assure de cette découverte par des observations réitérées, comparées, capables de constater les faits et de servir aux conséquences qu'on en veut tirer'.[28]

The following month the *Journal de Trévoux* considers Buffon's theory on the origin and history of the earth and begins by pointing out that while de Maillet's theory was a product of his imagination, the same is not true of Buffon's conclusions. 'M. de Buffon proceeds as an historian, he depends on facts and observations.'[29] What is more, the scientist respects religion and attempts to reconcile with Genesis his theory that the planets were originally parts of the sun broken off as a result of a collision with a comet. While it is observed that the theory does not follow the biblical account of creation in certain details, such as the order in which various elements were created, Berthier suggests a possible interpretation of the theory to answer the objections of its attackers. If anyone wonders why a man who is such a declared enemy of arbitrary 'systems' can indulge in such speculation, concludes the editor, Buffon answers the question himself when he makes a distinction between a hypothesis 'in which only possibilities are considered, and a theory founded on facts.'[30]

[28] *J. de T.* (Sept.1749), p.1870.
[29] *J. de T.* (Oct.1749), ii.2227.
[30] *J. de T.* (Oct.1749), iii.2244. Buffon's study of the earth's structure

The appearance in the *Journal de Trévoux* of this favourable review caused the editor of the Jansenist *Nouvelles ecclésiastiques* to denounce the publication as favouring incredulity because it was incapable of recognizing the 'venom' of this 'pernicious' *Histoire naturelle*. Admitting that the *Journal*'s editors point out a few of Buffon's errors, the Jansenist editor accused the Jesuit publication of 'immediately hastening to erase them.'[31] Questioning the sincerity of Buffon's religious orthodoxy, the periodical accuses the scientist of materialism because he had stated that 'one can descend by almost imperceptible degrees, from the most perfect creature to the crudest matter.'[32] The naturalist's theory of the origin of the earth is also censured as being opposed to the biblical account of creation. While Berthier had interpreted the 'days' of creation to mean simply 'periods,' the editor of the *Nouvelles ecclésiastiques* adopts a literal interpretation of the word and shows that the events depicted by Buffon could not have occurred in the space of one week[33].

Berthier's conviction that Buffon's orthodoxy was sincere seemed borne out by the scientist's defense of the spirituality of the soul in volume ii of his *Histoire naturelle*. Presenting the naturalist's arguments showing the superiority of the soul over matter and declaring that the differences between matter and the immaterial soul are too great to be confused with each other, the Jesuit editor exclaims: 'This is how a wise and enlightened philosophy speaks and judges.' He then turns to the author's style and remarks: 'Une chose qu'on ne peut se lasser d'admirer dans cet ouvrage, c'est la manière dont il est écrit. Quelque matière qui tombe sous la plume de m. de B. elle y est peinte avec ses couleurs

received an equally enthusiastic response from the *Journal de Trévoux* in its Nov.1749 issue, pp.2362–77.

[31] *Nouvelles ecclésiastiques* (6 Feb. 1750), p.21.

[32] *ibid., loc. cit.* Berthier had questioned this passage in his article but had defended Buffon's position by pointing out that the scientist's declaration was qualified with the warning that this applied only to the material side of man and not to his soul (*J. de T.* [Sept.1749], pp.1871–72.)

[33] *Nouvelles ecclésiastiques* (13 Feb. 1750), p.26.

et ses nuances propres, et toujours avec force, avec élégance et avec netteté. On ne lira peut-être cet ouvrage que pour apprendre des choses qu'on ne savait pas, ou pour en désapprendre qu'on croyait savoir: on pourrait le lire pour apprendre à écrire, à présenter et à développer ses idées avec des expressions propres, énergiques, naturelles, et éloignées de cette précision énigmatique, de ce style précieux, affecté, ou gigantique et boursouflé qui déshonore tant de productions puériles'.[34]

While the *Journal de Trévoux* was generally favourable toward Buffon, its editor did not always accept his conclusions. In exposing passages in the *Histoire naturelle* which were of questionable orthodoxy, Berthier was careful, however, not to provoke the author, and he generally attenuated his criticisms with words of praise. It was as if, knowing Buffon to be sincere in his religious convictions, the Jesuit editor considered it unnecessary to attack him strongly, believing that the mere pointing out of objectionable passages would be sufficient to cause the scientist to reexamine his statements. With the appearance of volume iv of the *Histoire*, Berthier must have felt that his course of action had been a judicious one, because Buffon answered his attackers with a letter at the head of the volume stating that he had no intention of contradicting scripture and he was only presenting his hypothesis as 'a purely philosophic supposition.' As if to underline his point of view, the Jesuit editor remarks of this letter: 'In so precise and so sincere a declaration, m. de Buffon gives testimony of his orthodoxy to the doctors, and to the philosophers, an example of an amended submission to the faith he professes.'[35] A lengthy

[34] *J. de T.* (March 1750), pp.595–96. Volume iii of the *Histoire naturelle*, written by Daubenton, is reviewed in the June 1750 issue, pp.1288–1303.

[35] *J. de T.* (Dec.1753), i.2316–17. Berthier was doubtless less impressed by this declaration of Buffon than by the scientist's general attitude toward religion in the bulk of his writings. When Helvétius made a substantially similar declaration in presenting *De l'esprit*, the Jesuit editor was quick to remark: 'L'auteur croit prévenir toutes les difficultés qu'on peut lui faire sur la religion, en disant qu'il parle comme "philosophe," non comme "théologien"; il répète cela de temps en temps, il paraît rendre hommage à la beauté du Christianisme: mais ce langage est une sorte de précaution dont usent

exposition of Buffon's description of the nervous system is then made without editorial comment, except to note that this applies only to the instrument at the service of the soul and not to the soul itself, which is spiritual. In this connection Berthier disagrees with the naturalist's view that animals are wholly material as well as with his identification of ideas with sensations. Either we must restrict an animal 'to the Cartesian automaton, or animate it with a non-material principle, or finally attribute to matter faculties which reason and religion absolutely refuse to give it.'[36] Animals do not derive the activities they have in common with their species from 'education, imitation, practice, and experience,' he continues, but each animal has an instinct which causes it to act 'without invention, without design, without intelligence and without liberty.' It is not the bees which should be admired for building combs but God who has given them the instinct. The editor concludes with the remark: 'Nous prions m. de Buffon d'agréer, ou du moins de nous permettre ces observations: elles nous empêchent de goûter et d'adopter tous les principes de son système, avec autant de sécurité et de confiance, que nous estimons et que nous admirons la beauté de son génie'.[37]

If Berthier seemed convinced of the honesty of Buffon's position in regard to the church, the Jansenists continued to suspect this scientist whom they considered to be 'newly converted' to orthodoxy to avoid difficulties with the authorities. The above *Journal de Trévoux* article was the object of a bitter attack in the *Nouvelles ecclésiastiques*, whose editor, remaining firm in his view that Buffon was preaching a materialistic morality, declared: 'Les journalistes de Trévoux n'ont rien dit contre cette exécrable morale, parce que sur bien des points la morale de la société rentre dans celle des sectateurs de la religion prétendue naturelle: mais les journalistes ont fait observer que m. de Buffon met les sensations et les passions dans la matière .... Cependant leur critique

souvent les incrédules. Il n'est pas difficile de lever le voile et de saisir la pensée de l'auteur' (*J. de T.* [Sept. 1758], p.2289).

[36] *J. de T.* (Dec.1753), i.2838.
[37] *J. de T.* (Dec.1753), pp.2845–46.

est mêlée de tant de flatteries, qu'on ne sait si l'on ne doit pas être encore plus indigné du personnage qu'ils font, que de celui de l'académicien'.[38] The Jansenist editor then quotes Berthier's closing paragraph cited above as an illustration of his fear of attacking incredulity openly, exclaiming: 'Is this how to show all the horror one should have for impiety and be diligent in inspiring that horror in others?'[39]

Buffon's excesses were usually considered by the Jesuit editor as the effects of an over-active imagination rather than as deliberate impiety. In such a case, a false accusation of incredulity would not only be unjust, but could also create a resentment in the author which might drive him to a break with the church. The same attitude can be seen in his treatment of Condillac's *Traité des sensations*. After displaying the philosopher's method for studying man's senses by endowing a statue with one sense at a time, Berthier pauses to note: 'Ce système sur les sensations passe, auprès quelques critiques, pour exhaler une odeur de matérialisme: soupçon odieux, et qu'on ne doit pas hasarder sans les plus grandes preuves. Nous croyons, pour nous, que la spiritualité de l'âme fait une des branches essentielles de ce traité, et que, sans ce dogme, tout le système n'aurait aucune consistance. D'ailleurs l'auteur s'explique si disertement sur la divinité, sur la création, et sur la révélation, qu'à tous ces égards, son orthodoxie paraît hors de toute atteinte'.[40]

For Berthier, no dogmatic position could be held in questions of science, and therefore no one should be condemned for suggesting new and radical scientific theories so long as their authors did not seek to utilize these theories to attack revealed religion —the only certainty held by man. If revelation gave man certainty as to what God had created, no such infallible source was available to explain how he did it. Man was free to examine God's creation and speculate on how it was accomplished. Thus Berthier

[38] *Nouvelles ecclésiastiques* (3 July 1754), p.105.

[39] *ibid.*, p.106.

[40] *J. de T.* (March 1755), pp.659–60.

delves into the question of the formation of the earth and planets along with Buffon, and he speculates on the origin of ideas with Condillac but, since these studies are purely human, no one can say for certain that a given conclusion is accurate beyond a doubt. Indeed, the more generalizations we make the more we risk going astray. Thus, when the errors of Aristotle and Pliny in the study of natural history are discussed by Daubenton, Berthier points to them as a lesson, stating: 'Ils n'étaient pas infaillibles; le sommes-nous? Si nos observateurs l'emportent sur ces grands hommes, c'est plutôt du côté des instruments que du côté du génie. Les anciens ne se sont guères trompés qu'en généralisant trop leurs notions. Si nous avons découvert les erreurs qui s'étaient glissées dans quelques-uns de leurs résultats; connaissons-nous tout le faible de nos systèmes; pouvons-nous même répondre de toutes nos expériences?'[41] It will behooves us therefore, to propound scientific theories dogmatically. The true scientist is humble and cautious in his inquiry.

This is particularly true in so uncertain a matter as the origin of ideas and knowledge. When the *Journal de Trévoux* considers Condillac's *Essai sur l'origine des connaissances humaines*, the editor reviews the efforts of Descartes, Malebranche, Leibnitz and Locke to explain this question and notes that their lack of success in adequately explaining how ideas are formed should deter us from jumping to hasty conclusions, adding that perhaps the creator did not intend that man should know all things. 'The author of nature has hidden from us the how and why of most things, satisfied to instruct us as to their existence.' Therefore, continues Berthier: 'Assurons ce que nous savons, et taisons-nous sur ce que nous ignorons. Des conclusions timides siéent si fort à notre raison: et l'aveu de notre ignorance, sur certaines matières, fait plus d'honneur au philosophe que le ton dogmatique et décisif de la présomption'.[42]

Those writers who misuse scientific theories to attack revealed

[41] *J. de T.* (Jan.1754), p.137.   [42] *J. de T.* (May 1747), pp.806-7.

religion are considered 'dogmatizers' by Berthier. They are guilty of presumption since they put forth dogmatically what was only conceived as a possibility. Unbelievers are accused of so misusing the speculations of Locke: 'Locke ne tenait point formellement au matérialisme . . . mais il donnait des atteintes évidentes aux dogmes essentiels de la spiritualité et de l'immortalité de l'âme; c'est à ce titre qu'il reçoit tant d'éloges des matérialistes et des incrédules. C'est pour ainsi dire, le premier pas et comme l'ABC de l'impiété: on commence par louer beaucoup m. Locke, puis le reste de la doctrine des prétendus esprits-forts se développe: telle est la marche de l'incrédulité actuelle'.[43]

Condillac, while espousing many of Locke's ideas, is favourably reviewed by the *Journal de Trévoux* because he does not utilize science as a weapon against the church, but rather upholds revelation. Berthier commends him, for example, when he defends the spirituality of the soul and rejects Locke's idea that matter can think. The editor takes issue with some of the writer's ideas, 'not to criticize him but to prevent the abuse that could be made of his principles.' Thus when in the *Traité des sensations* the soul of the statue is said to be in a state of unconsciousness before the statue is endowed with senses, the Jesuit editor asserts that the soul has a consciousness of its own existence, and it does not identify itself with the senses, as suggested in the *Traité*, but recognizes a sense impression as something distinct from its own individuality. Condillac confuses sensations with ideas. 'Independently of the senses and of sensations, there are moral principles and maxims which direct the soul in the exercise of its faculties and in the use of its senses.'[44]

Those writers who depart from the experimental method and utilize the theories of scientists to further their own irreligious doctrines are attacked by Berthier. While Buffon and Condillac are approved for respecting the Christian revelation, Helvétius is denounced for attempting to undermine religious truths. In *De*

---

[43] *J. de T.* (March 1759), p.600. [44] *J. de T.* (March 1755), p.665.

l'esprit, following the lead of Hobbes, he attacks natural law and the spirituality of the soul, reducing all faculties to sensations. Preaching an indifference toward religion, he exalts the passions and removes all responsibility for men's actions[45]. While the *Journal*'s reviews of *De l'esprit* were presented as incomplete expositions of the author's false doctrines to serve as a warning to readers against this 'pernicious' book, pending a more complete refutation by more erudite writers, they evoked two letters in defense of Helvétius's work. The first, an anonymous *Lettre aux Journalistes de Trévoux*, attacks natural law and insists that 'good' laws are conceived differently by different nations; to which Berthier replies that no human legislation should contradict natural law since it is the basis of all law.

The second communication, a *Lettre au père Berthier sur le matérialisme*, by the abbé Coyer, is in a lighter vein and suggests that materialism is non-existent, being merely a metaphor. Thus, we speak of 'the soul of a violin,' or we call a crafty man a 'fox,' etc. The Jesuit editor rebukes the author for coming to the defense of materialism and accuses him of disrespect toward the scriptures[46]. It would seem that a rumour had been circulated in a 'public leaflet' to the effect that Berthier had approved *De l'esprit* before its publication and had even congratulated its author on the merits of the work. The Jesuit journalist answers the query of one of his readers concerning the rumour by declaring emphatically: 'Le p. Berthier affirme très-positivement qu'il n'a ni approuvé, ni même connu le livre *De l'esprit*, avant qu'il ait vu le jour. Il ajoute qu'il n'a jamais écrit de lettres à l'auteur de *l'Esprit* et qu'il ne lui a jamais parlé. Sur tous ces points, le même P. B. défie quiconque de produire aucune preuve contraire à la présente déclaration'.[47]

The acceptance by Berthier of the tenet expressing faith in reason as a guide to man has already been treated in this chapter: to demand the free and unfettered use of reason in all matters is to

---

[45] *J. de T.* (Sept.1758), pp.2297–99; (Oct.1758), ii.2649–72; (Nov.1758), pp.2825–56.

[46] *J. de T.* (Feb.1759), pp.535–59.
[47] *J. de T.* (Feb.1759), p.574.

indicate one's faith in the ability of reason to distinguish truth in those affairs. Not only civilized men but primitives and men of all ages are endowed with this faculty, which permits them to discover universal truths. When an anonymous critic of Rousseau's *Discours sur les sciences et les arts* places primitive men on the level with animals to show how the arts and sciences have elevated him, Berthier objects, stating: 'Les hommes ont partout les lumières naturelles, les loix de la conscience, la connaissance du juste et de l'injuste . . . . C'est une pensée très-peu solide, pour ne rien dire de plus, que celle qui égale, en quelque sorte, les sauvages aux animaux. Faudrait-il encore aujourd'hui des décisions ecclésiastiques pour apprendre aux Européens que les peuples de l'Amérique sont des hommes?'[48] Maupertuis is similarly reproached when in his *Essai de philosophie morale* he excuses the Stoics for their view on suicide because they did not know any better. There was in ancient times, counters the Jesuit editor, 'as for all men, a strict obligation to make use of the natural light of reason which uncovers the existence of the sovereign being and his main attributes.'[49] We have seen in our chapter on Voltaire how Berthier praised that author for his defense of natural religion, discernible through the use of reason. When an unnamed critic of the *Poème sur la loi naturelle* attacked the idea of natural law, declaring he doubted 'that man was made for reason,' the journalist had exclaimed that there was 'nothing more false or more impious,' than the statement that 'instinct' rather than 'reason' should be man's guide[50].

If the Jesuit editor espoused natural religion it was because he was convinced that revealed religion was its crowning point and

---

[48] *J. de T.* (July 1755), ii.1738–39.
[49] *J. de T.* (Jan.1750), p.136.
[50] *J. de T.* (Aug.1757), pp.2095–96. The Jansenists rejected the concept of a natural religion discoverable through the use of reason, calling it a 'système impie que l'on affecte de répandre dans des livres de toute espèce, et que déjà des personnes de tout état et en très

grand nombre ont le malheur d'avoir embrassé' (*Nouvelles ecclésiastiques*, 9 Oct.1749, p.161). See also the passage quoted above in which the editor accuses the Jesuits of favouring the doctrine of the unbelievers because they shared their belief in natural religion.

gave to it the final seal of truth which could only come from God. Were it not for the Christian revelation, complete certainty in religion would be no more attainable than in science, since it would be limited by human fallibility. As has been noted, the acceptability of this revelation for Berthier was to be arrived at through reason. To him, a man who used unbiased judgment would be convinced of the truth of Christianity. Christian principles, since they represented truth, were the only safeguard for humanity. Modern unbelievers, Berthier contended, by attacking religious truths, 'have struck at the foundation of mores, laws and religion. They have spoken only of humanity but they have become exclusively attentive to their own interest which is so often hard, inhuman, despotic and unjust.'[51] Man is naturally inclined toward selfishness and therefore he 'needs more lofty motives for loving his fellow men.'[52] If the certainty of religious truths were removed from him, the result would be chaotic: 'Que nos incrédules réussissent à proscrire la foi chrétienne de notre hémisphère, bientôt nous retomberons dans un chaos d'opinions monstrueuses, dont la confusion et la licence, redoutables à l'autorité de tous les gouvernements, nous réduiront à envier aux plus stupides Indiens la créance aveugle, qu'ils ont aux songes de leurs Brachmanes et aux rêveries de leurs Talapoins: alors nous serons d'autant plus à plaindre que l'art de raisonner, dont nous nous glorifions, deviendra la source et l'apologie des excès les plus énormes. Cette seule réflexion bien pénétrée devrait faire conspirer toutes les puissances contre le progrès de l'incrédulité'.[53]

Berthier's belief in progress, then, is tempered by the qualification that such progress is only possible if guided by Christian principles, otherwise the future of man looked dim indeed. Scientific progress alone will not better men's life without the preservation of moral values to guide him, he felt. When an anonymous writer states that the science of ethics is useless to the morals of a nation, Berthier declares: 'Oui, la "science" profane et philoso-

[51] *J. de T.* (Feb.1760), p.473.
[52] *J. de T.* (Jan.1752), i.149.
[53] *J. de T.* (Sept.1757), pp.2207–2208.

phique des "mœurs," non celle qui est dans l'évangile de Jésus
Christ. Cette dernière opère tout, quand elle se rend maîtresse
des cœurs: c'est même avec elle, et avec elle seule que l'étude des
autres sciences perd sa contagion et sa malignité. Qu'on se retourne
tant qu'on voudra, les Sciences perdront les hommes, tant que les
hommes ne seront pas Chrétiens'.[54]

In reviewing the position of Guillaume François Berthier within
the framework of the eighteenth-century intellectual revolution,
we have seen that the Jesuit editor was a product of the age in
which he lived. His writings reflect the aspirations of the enlightenment, stressing as they do the idea of progress, the insistence on
the experimental method in science, the use of reason in investigating all questions, human and divine, and the acceptance of
reason as a valid guide for man in his quest for truth. If his concept of truth was not always that arrived at by the *philosophes*,
his defense of his view is itself proof of his acceptance of the main
tenets of the enlightenment, for he never doubted that it reflected
the only position compatible with reason. It is no wonder that
d'Alembert, one of his most formidable opponents, could testify
to the strength of the Jesuits' stand when, upon their suppression,
he wrote to Voltaire telling him that he need not fear the Jansenists
because their doctrine was too 'absurd' to succeed, and adding:
'La doctrine des ci-devant jésuites était bien plus faite pour réussir; et rien n'aurait pu les détruire s'ils n'avaient pas été persécuteurs et insolents'.[55]

[54] *J. de T.* (July 1755), ii.1755–1756.
[55] M.lxi.349.

Conclusion

Voltaire's highly amusing and caustic satire, *La mort du jésuite Berthier*, has given a dubious immortality to the editor of the Jesuit *Journal de Trévoux*. Voltaire frequently felt it necessary to utilize the talents of his satirical pen in blasting with scathing wit some lesser contemporary who opposed his ideals and those of the encyclopedists. There is reason to believe, however, that in father Berthier Voltaire found a far more formidable antagonist than an Elie Fréron or a Le Franc de Pompignan proved to be. Why is this so? what kind of a man was Berthier? and, in particular, what were precisely his attitudes toward the great currents of the age of enlightenment in which he took such an active interest? These are some of the questions which this study has examined and, whenever possible, has attempted to answer. But unlike many previous studies of Berthier and of the *Journal de Trévoux*, this study has sought to avoid presenting the Jesuit editor from a partisan viewpoint. Both the Voltairean picture of Berthier as representing ignorant, superstitious bigotry savagely opposed to the enlightenment, and Montjoye's portrayal of a shining defender of the faith against the 'satanic' and godless 'incrédules' have been avoided. An attempt has been made to present an objective appraisal of the man, with his strength and weaknesses, in relation to the age in which he lived.

Berthier, as an eighteenth-century man, shared many of the views of his contemporaries the *philosophes*. Like them, he was revolted by the abuses of the monarchy, and the pitiful condition of the people obliged to pay for the excesses of courtly life through poverty and unjust taxation. As did Voltaire, Berthier looked for the solution of the problem to an enlightened monarch who through proper education would become a benevolent ruler with the good of his people as his prime objective.

In other fields the *Encyclopédie* and the *Journal de Trévoux* frequently found themselves to be championing the same cause, as, for example, in the case of the quarrel over French versus Italian music, or in the fostering of the idea of progress in the arts and sciences. Both publications reflected Voltaire's sentiment that while Descartes is to be admired for his pioneering, Newtonian physics, arrived at by the experimental method, supplanted earlier concepts relying on metaphysical speculation.

Nor should we wonder at the difference between this view of Berthier and that of some of his predecessors. The editors of the *Journal de Trévoux* cannot be viewed—and this has been a shortcoming of previous studies of the publication—as a static, unchanging body sharing the same conservative views. Such an approach loses sight of the fact that the *Journal* was in the hands of different individuals at different times. Thus, an editor in 1701, being the product of the late seventeenth century, would undoubtedly have a different outlook from an editor in 1760 who had assimilated new ideas which earlier might have been controversial but by his time were generally accepted. Had Berthier belonged to a previous generation or to a different religious coterie, his views would probably not have been the same. As it is, he illustrates the progress of the enlightenment in an important group of men of his time. It is this dynamism in the *Journal de Trévoux* which accounts in part for the influence and prestige it enjoyed in its day, for, although refusing to abandon traditional religious values, it remained in tune with the temper of the age of enlightenment.

While some churchmen such as Huet and Pluche looked upon science almost as a dangerous adversary, and the Jansenist *Nouvelles ecclésiastiques* frequently attacked new scientific ideas as subversive to faith, Berthier condemned such a view, and maintained that there could not possibly be any contradiction between scientific and religious truths. On the contrary, such new scientific discoveries only served to make us appreciate and wonder the

more at the workings of the creator. When a new scientific truth
seemed to contradict revealed truths, Berthier sought to reconcile
the apparent conflict by reevaluating the traditional interpretation
of revelation in the light of the new discovery. Buffon's theory
of the origin and development of the earth and its creatures is a
case in point. Berthier maintained that the Bible was not intended
to be a treatise on physics. God had revealed to us what he had
done, but not how he did it, and man was therefore free to speculate on how the creation was accomplished. By reevaluating the
interpretation of the 'days' of creation according to Genesis, the
Jesuit saw no difficulty in accepting the new theory. In so doing,
both Berthier and Buffon—who as a professed believer had also
resolved the problem of reconciling both accounts of creation to
his own satisfaction—could be considered as early developers of
modern Christian apologetics. By elaborating on Buffon's suggestions and correcting such details as might seem unorthodox,
Berthier did much to formulate and disseminate among his
readers an enlightened viewpoint which believers could accept
without danger to their faith and in keeping with the realities of
new scientific advances.

In fostering a spirit of inquiry and a freedom of investigation,
Berthier did not exclude religion. He had argued for fewer re-
strictions in the arts and sciences, calling for less reliance on 'dogmatic' literary and scientific theories. Thus, we find him calling
for more unhindered self-expression in music and literature, and,
in the sciences, a greater reliance on the scientific method based
on experimentation and observation. In religious questions, he
rejected the view held by some churchmen that men must believe
blindly, and he underlined the need and the responsibility of all
men to investigate the claims of religion before accepting it. The
Jesuit editor was convinced that the historical evidence for the
Christian revelation was so conclusive that an impartial judge
would not fail to recognize its truth. The mysteries revealed by
God were beyond the power of men to comprehend, he declared,
but their credibility could be ascertained through reason. Thus

free inquiry in religious questions would be all to the good in spreading Christianity.

While Berthier's views were generally close to those of the *philosophes*, there could be no such harmony in their attitude toward religious principles. The Jesuit editor recognized the right of every individual to his own opinion, and considered it both futile and wrong to try to force anyone to espouse Christianity. He was convinced, however, that such views when disseminated publicly in print were detrimental to the common good. By preaching a disrespect for authority and an indulgence of the passions, the *philosophes* were paving the way for civil strife, and were endangering the nation. It became the duty of the government to protect itself and its people from their destructive doctrines because, besides the fact that theirs was a Christian nation, progress without Christianity to guide it would be ruinous to the virtues necessary for any society. The cleavage between the Jesuit editor and the *philosophes*, then, occurred not so much because of the latter's rejection of Christianity but because of the doctrines they sought to substitute for it. The real danger to society, for Berthier, lay in the substitution of relativistic standards of morality and conduct for standards based on universal principles set down by God. Thus, while he praised Voltaire for upholding a God-given natural law in the *Poème sur la loi naturelle*, he attacked Montesquieu for making morality depend on geographic or climatic factors, and Helvétius was denounced for denying that men are responsible for their actions, for rejecting fixed concepts of right and wrong, thus destroying the moral basis necessary for a peaceful society.

In attacking the *philosophes*, Berthier confined himself to refuting the doctrines he considered objectionable without engaging in personalities. As a general policy he strove to be moderate and even conciliatory when there seemed to be a possibility that the writer in question was not obdurate in his anti-Christian leanings but was sincerely seeking the truth. Voltaire was highly praised even when his views were not orthodox until it became apparent that he was irrevocably committed to a campaign against the Christian religion. Similarly, Rousseau was sympathetically treated because even in his most unorthodox deviations he seemed motivated by a true regard for Christian virtues. Diderot's position, on the other hand, appeared unequivocal from the start and was consequently the most promptly and strongly opposed. While the original prospectus for the *Encyclopédie* had been favourably reviewed by the *Journal de Trévoux*, the attitude of its Jesuit editor changed as soon as the name of Diderot became dominant in the enterprise. Thereafter, an attempt was made first to cause the public to lose interest in the venture, and, when Berthier was convinced that his fears had been justified, to have the *Encyclopédie* censored more vigorously or suppressed entirely. These measures having failed, the publication was resisted negatively by denying it any further mention in the *Journal de Trévoux*.

Throughout his struggle against the *philosophes*, Berthier showed himself to be moderate and judicious in his critiques. While attacking their doctrines when they seemed to oppose his religion, the Jesuit editor was not blind to the genius and the contributions of his adversaries in secular fields. Voltaire's literary talent was constantly praised even when it was felt that he had put it to bad use. Diderot's forceful style and his extensive contribution to a fuller knowledge of the arts and crafts were justly recognized. In truth, Berthier could easily recognize the value of the scientific and literary pursuits of his opponents because he was himself deeply imbued with the spirit of his age. But he was also a man of sincere and profound religious faith for whom there could be no neutrality when his religion was attacked.

If this study dealt solely with the views of one individual in the eighteenth-century, its value would be limited. Actually, Berthier, as an official spokesman for the Jesuits of France, represented a large and significant body of opinion. The true importance of a study of the *Journal de Trévoux* lies in determining as far as possible the official position of a very strong and influential group in the face of the revolution in ideas championed by the *philosophes*.

But to present the views of one editor as representative of the official Jesuit stand is misleading unless we specify the period in question and the influence of that editor on his colleagues. The period in which the eighteenth-century struggle of ideas is most significant coincides with the period during which Berthier was in charge of the *Journal de Trévoux*. The attacks made against the publication by the *philosophes* are almost invariably attacks against its editor-in-chief, Berthier. Furthermore, Berthier comes nearer to representing an official Jesuit position than any other editor. We have seen that in the periods preceding his editorship, there was division and diversity of opinion in the *Journal de Trévoux*, so much so that such editors as fathers Castel and Hardouin, who had singularly personal views, frequently caused embarrassment for their colleagues, who were obliged to apologize for their excesses. Berthier, on the other hand, had full charge of the publication and brooked no interference. His influence is attested by Castel, who calls him the 'idol' of the Jesuits, and who had warned Montesquieu that he would never be absolved by the society for *L'Esprit des lois* unless he were approved by Berthier's *Journal de Trévoux*. Similarly, the strong Jesuit stand against the *Encyclopédie* is attributable to Berthier, who first sounded the alarm against it, and whose influence with the archbishop of Paris as well as with the dauphin, was instrumental in having the publication suppressed. On the dissolution of the Jesuits in 1762 it was again Berthier who was called upon by his superiors to write an official defense of the society. Thus the views of Berthier are not only interesting as an isolated example of the influence of the enlightenment on one man, but they also represent a position disseminated in a widely-read journal as the official position of a powerful and influential religious group of its day. They are representative, therefore, of a large group of eighteenth-century believers who had assimilated the aims and tenets of the enlightenment to the point that they found the ultra-conservative views of such religious groups as the Jansenists no longer tenable, but who refused with equal vigour to follow the leaders of the enlightenment in abandoning their traditional religious beliefs.

In 1759 Voltaire had written in his *Relation de la mort du jésuite Berthier*: 'Thus passed from this life to the next, brother Berthier, on October 12, at 5:30 P.M.' This announcement was rather premature, and, as happened frequently when the *philosophe* wished to ridicule an opponent into oblivion, the satirical proclamation of Berthier's death was to have the reverse effect: for, ironically enough, it is perhaps thanks to Voltaire that Guillaume François Berthier has acquired a permanent place in the history of the age of enlightenment.

List of sources

I

Manuscripts

BIBLIOTHEQUE NATIONALE, PARIS

Berthier, Guillaume François, *Discours sur la fermeté à l'usage de Monseigneur le dauphin*. Nouv.acq.franç.6280.

Letter (dated 1 Feb. 1754) from Berthier to Pierre Jean Grosley explaining the critiques he will make of Grosley's contribution. Nouv.acq.franç.803, p.85.

Letter (dated 1756) from Grosley to Berthier expressing satisfaction over Berthier's review of his *Discussion sur Venise*. Nouv. acq.franç.803, p.88.

Letter (dated June 1741) from Jean Stiltingh to Eugène Souciet submitting material to the *Journal de Trévoux*. Fr.24427.

Letter (dated at Cologne, 21 April 1731) from Rodrigue to Souciet attesting to the reputation of the *J. de T*. Fr.24457.

Letter (dated 22 April 1730) from dom Charles Beaunier to Souciet stating that he is preparing a 'table' of the *J. de T*. Nouv. acq.franç.674, f.2.

Letter (dated 1720) from Thoubeau to Bouhier explaining how contributions to the *J. de T*. should be prepared. Fr.24420.

BIBLIOTHEQUE SAINTE-GENEVIEVE, PARIS

Déclaration du P. Tournemine sur des écrits supposés. MS.1473, f.57.

Barre, le P., génovifain, *Réflexions à propos des Journalistes de Trévoux*. MS.1023.

Letters from abbé Breyer to Raveneau concerning the *J. de T.*, *Lettres de l'abbé Remi Breyer*, MS.2570.

Letters (dated 22 Feb., and 15 May 1724) from Le Courayer to the *J. de T.* MS.1965-1967, vol.i, f.13.

BIBLIOTHEQUE MAZARINE, PARIS

Pièces diverses en vers et en prose sur le P. le Tellier, les Jésuites, etc. MS.2458 (2861), p.42.

Letter from Le Tellier to Chauvelin concerning cardinal de Noailles. *Lettre du P. Tellier (le) à M. de Chauvelin.* MS.2459 (2273), p.263.

BIBLIOTHEQUE VICTOR COUSIN, SORBONNE, PARIS

Mélanges XVIIIe siècle, 'J. Goullier au très rév. Père Bertier.' MS.27, f.38.

BIBLIOTHEQUE CALVET, AVIGNON

Letter (dated at Paris, 1 Feb. 1758) from Berthier to the marquis de Cambis-Velleron, refusing the latter's contribution as too controversial for publication. *Lettres du P. Berthier au Marquis de Cambis-Velleron*, MS.3467, f.297.

Letter (dated 4 Feb.1758) from Berthier to same, returning his contribution. MS.3468, f.298.

Letter (dated 19 May 1758) from Berthier to Cambis-Velleron accepting for publication his discussion on laws. MS.3468, f.300.

Letter (dated July 1759) from Berthier to the same explaining delay in answering, and discussing irreligion in France. MS.3468, f.302.

BIBLIOTHEQUE MUNICIPALE, ROUEN

Letter (dated Paris, 7 June 1749) from Berthier to the editor of the *Journal des Savants* concerning his critiques of a history of Germany. *Aut. Duputel* 7.

BRITISH MUSEUM, LONDON

Letter (dated Paris, 28 July 1737) from Charlevoix, an editor of the *J. de T.*, to sir H. Sloane thanking him for a book he donated to the Jesuit library in Paris. *Letters to Sir H. Sloane*, Sloane 4055, f.139.

Letter (no date) from Charlevoix asking Sloane for information on Japan to be used in a history he intends to publish. Sloane 4058, f.114.

Letter (no date) from Sloane to Charlevoix discussing differences between American and European plants. Sloane 4068, f.254.

Letter (dated London, 20 Sept. 1736) from Sloane thanking Charlevoix for his *Histoire du Japon* and stating that he is sending a copy of his own *History of Jamaica* to the Jesuit library in Paris. Sloane 4068, f.301.

Letter (dated 30 April, no year) from Tournemine, editor of the *J. de T.*, to De Monaud congratulating him on the second edition of his work. *Tournemine, Jesuit to [F.A.P.] de Monaud*, Egerton 27.

UNIVERSITY OF LEYDEN LIBRARY

Letter (no date) from Hardouin to Papebrock concerning the latter's critique on the lineage of Herodotus. Pap.15, *Hardouinus (Joh.) ad Papebrock (Dan.)*, No. 4.

Letter (no date) from Tournemine to Marchand thanking him for his contribution to the *J. de T.* and describing type of material wanted for publication. March. 2, *Tournemine ad R. Marchand* 2.

Letter (no date) from Hardouin to the Dutch publisher Huguetan requesting secrecy in publishing an unidentified work Pap.15, *Hardouinus (Joh.) ad Huguetan*, No.30.

KONINKLIJKE BIBLIOTHEEK, THE HAGUE

Letter (no date) from Tournemine to Rhenferd congratulating him on his recently published theological dissertation. *Tournemine, R. J.*, No.7²D.14b.

BIBLIOTECA NACIONAL, MADRID

Letter (copy) Routh to Mgr. Gualterio, describing confession and last hours of Montesquieu. No.9601 = Ee–75 Routh. Soc. Jes.: Noticias de la muerte de Monteschieu.

II

Printed works

Alembert, Jean Le Rond d'. *Œuvres*. Paris 1805.

Allard, Emmy, *Die Angriffe gegen Descartes und Malebranche im Journal de Trévoux*. Halle 1914.

Alzog, Johann, *Manual of universal church history*, trans. by F. J. Pabisch. Cincinnati 1903, 3 vol.

Bachaumont, Louis Petit de, *Mémoires secrets*. Londres 1777–1789, 36 vol.

Backer, Augustin and Aloys de, *Bibliographie des écrivains de la Compagnie de Jesus*. Paris 1890.

Beaune, Henri, *Voltaire au collège*. Paris 1867.

Belin, J. P., *Le mouvement philosophique de 1748 à 1789*. Paris 1913.

Bersot, Ernest, *Etudes sur le XVIIIᵉ siècle*. Paris 1855.

Berthier, Guillaume François, *Histoire de l'église gallicane* [begun by Longueval, Fontenay and Brumoy, vols. xiii–xviii by Berthier]. Paris 1747–1749, 6 vol.

— *Recueil de lettres sur la doctrine et l'institut des Jésuites*. [c.1762.]

— *Observations sur le Contrat social de J.-J. Rousseau*. Paris 1789.

— *Réflexions spirituelles*, ed. Du Pinet. Toulouse 1811, 5 vol.

— *Les Pseaumes traduits en françois, avec des notes et des réflexions*. [Edited by de Querbeuf]. Paris 1785, 8 vol.

— *Les Psaumes traduits en françois, avec des réflexions*, ed. Henrion. Paris 1829, 5 vol.

Berthier, Guillaume François, *Les Psaumes traduits en français, avec des réflexions.* [Edited by de Baudry.] Lyon 1831, 8 vol.

— *La Présence de Dieu*, ed. R. Boileau. Montreal 1952.

— *An Exposition of the lamentation of the prophet Jeremias*, trans. by William Walsh. New York 1850.

Bertrand, M., *Un rêve de savant au XVIIIe siècle: le père Castel.* Paris 1868.

Brette, Armand, *La France au milieu du XVIIIe siècle (1747–1757)* d'après le journal du marquis d'Argenson. Paris 1898.

Brumoy, Pierre, *Lettres du père Brumoy*, ed. J. M. Prat. Paris 1857.

Cazes, Albert, 'Un adversaire de Diderot,' *Mélanges offerts par ses amis et ses élèves à m. Gustave Lanson.* Paris 1922.

Charma, A., and G. Mancel, *Le Père André, Jésuite. Documents inédits pour servir à l'histoire philosophique, religieuse et littéraire du XVIIIe siècle.* Caen 1844–1856, 2 vol.

Chaudon, Louis Mayeul, *Dictionnaire anti-philosophique, pour servir de commentaire et de correctif au Dictionnaire philosophique.* Avignon 1771.

— *Anti-dictionnaire philosophique.* Paris 1775.

— *Dictionnaire universel, historique, critique et bibliographique.* Paris 1810–1812, 20 vol.

Crocker, Lester G., *The Embattled philosopher.* East Lansing, Mich. 1954.

Desfontaines, Pierre François Guyot, ed., *Observations sur les écrits modernes.* Paris 1735–1743, 33 vol.

Desnoiresterres, Gustave, *Voltaire et la société au XVIIIe siècle.* Paris 1867–1876, 8 vol.

Destruction des Jésuites en France, anecdote politique et intéressante trouvée dans les papiers d'un homme bien instruit des intrigues du temps; publiée à Londres en 1766. Paris 1827.

Dictionnaire de théologie catholique. Paris 1950 &c.

Dictionnaire universel français et latin, vulgairement appelé Dictionnaire de Trévoux. Nancy 1734; Paris 1771.

Diderot, Denis, *Œuvres complètes*, ed. Assézat and Tourneux. Paris 1875–1877, 20 vol.

Diderot, Denis, *Correspondance*, ed. Georges Roth. Paris 1955 &c.

Dumas, Gustave, *Histoire du Journal de Trévoux*. Paris 1936.

— 'Voltaire's Jesuit chaplain,' *Thought* (Fordham University, March 1940).

Encyclopédie ou Dictionnaire raisonné des sciences, des arts et des métiers. Paris 1751–1780, 35 vol.

Faux, Jean M., 'La Fondation et les premiers rédacteurs des Mémoires de Trévoux (1701-1739) d'après quelques documents inédits, *Archivum historicum Societatis Iesu* (Rome Jan.-Jun. 1954), xxiii.131-151.

Feller, F. X. de, *Dictionnaire historique, ou histoire abrégée*. Paris 1818, 12 vol.

— *Mélanges de politique de morale et de littérature*. Louvain 1822–1824.

— Fellows, Otis E., and Norman L. Torrey, *The Age of Enlightenment*. New York 1942.

Fréron, Eli, ed. *L'Année littéraire*. Amsterdam 1754–1776.

Gordon, Douglas H., and Norman L. Torrey, *The Censoring of Diderot's Encyclopédie*. New York 1947.

Goujet, Claude Pierre, *Mémoires historiques et littéraires*. La Haye 1767.

Green, Frederick C., *Eighteenth-century France*. New York 1931.

Guettée, René François, *Histoire de l'Eglise de France*. Paris 1847–1856, 12 vol.

Hamy, Alfred, *Chronologie biographique de la Compagnie de Jésus*. Paris 1900, 4 vol.

— *Galerie illustrée de la Compagnie de Jésus*. Paris 1893, 8 vol.

Hatin, Eugène, *Bibliographie historique et critique de la presse périodique française*. Paris 1866.

— *Histoire politique et littéraire de la presse en France*. Paris 1859.

Havinga, Jan Christiaan Adolph, *Les Nouvelles ecclésiastiques dans leur lutte contre l'esprit philosophique*. Amersfoort 1925.

Jobez, Alphonse, *La France sous Louis XV*. Paris 1867, 4 vol.

La Harpe, Jean François, *Le Pseautier en français*. Paris 1797.

Lanfrey, Pierre, *L'Eglise et les philosophes au XVIIIe siècle*. Paris 1879.

Masson, Pierre Maurice, *La religion de J.-J. Rousseau*. Paris 1916 3 vol.

Mémoires pour l'histoire des sciences et des beaux-arts. Trévoux [Lyon; Paris] 1701–1767, 265 vol.

Mémorial catholique. Paris 1824–1830.

Montesquieu, Charles Louis de Secondat, baron de, *Correspondance*. Paris 1914, 2 vol.

Montjoye, Felix Louis Christophe, *Eloge historique du père G.-F. Berthier, garde de la Bibliothèque du roi, adjoint à l'éducation de ll. mm. Louis XVI et Louis XVIII*. Paris 1817.

Mourret, Fernand, *A History of the Catholic church*, trans. by N. Thompson. St. Louis 1930–1945, 6 vol.

Naves, Raymond, *Voltaire et l'Encyclopédie*. Paris 1938.

Nouvelles ecclésiastiques, ou mémoires pour servir à l'histoire de la constitution Unigenitus. Paris 1728–1803, 76 vol.

Oliver, A. Richard, *The Encyclopedists as critics of music*. New York 1947.

'Omaggio voltairiano alla Compagnia di Gesù,' *L'Osservatore Romano* (June 1950), no.136.

Palmer, Robert R., *Catholics and unbelievers in eighteenth-century France*. Princeton 1939.

Pastor, Ludwig, *The History of the popes from the close of the middle ages*, trans. by Frederick I. Antrobus. London 1923 &c.

Pellisson, Maurice, *Les hommes de lettres au XVIIIe siècle*. Paris 1911.

Pierron, Alexis, *Voltaire et ses maîtres*. Paris 1866.

Pomeau, René, 'La confession et la mort de Voltaire d'après des documents inédits,' *Revue d'histoire littéraire de la France* (Paris juillet–septembre 1955), lv.299–318.

Pommier, Jean, *Diderot avant Vincennes*. Paris 1939.

— 'Autour de la "lettre sur les sourds et muets",' *Revue d'histoire littéraire de la France* (Paris juillet–septembre 1951), li.261–272.

Prévost, Antoine François, ed. *Le Pour et le contre*. Paris 1733–1740, 20 vol.

Ranke, Leopold von, *The History of the popes during the last four centuries*, trans. by E. Foster. London 1908, 3 vol.

Rousseau, Jean Jacques, *Confessions*. Paris: Garnier.

— *Correspondance générale*, ed. Théophile Dufour. Paris 1924–1934, 20 vol.

— *La Profession de foi du vicaire savoyard*, ed. P. M. Masson. Paris 1914.

— *Rêveries d'un promeneur solitaire*, ed. Marcel Raymond. Lille 1948.

Schier, Donald, *Louis B. Castel, anti-Newtonian scientist*. Cedar Rapids 1941.

Sommervogel, P. C., *Essai historique sur les Mémoires de Trévoux*. Paris 1864.

— *Table méthodique des Mémoires de Trévoux*. Paris 1864.

Tocqueville, Alexis de, *Histoire philosophique du règne de Louis XV*. Paris 1847.

Torrey, Norman L., 'L'Encyclopédie de Diderot: "une grande aventure" dans le domaine de l'édition,' *Revue d'histoire littéraire de la France* (Paris juillet–septembre 1951), lv.306–307.

— *The Spirit of Voltaire*. New York 1938.

— 'Voltaire's reaction to Diderot', *PMLA* (Menasha, Wis. December 1935), pp.1107–1143.

Venturi, Franco, *Jeunesse de Diderot, 1713–1753*. Paris 1939.

Voltaire, *Œuvres complètes*. [Edited by Louis Moland.] Paris 1877–1885, 52 vol. [cited as M.].

— *Voltaire's correspondence*, ed. Theodore Besterman. Institut et Musée Voltaire: Genève 1953 &c. vols. i–xx (1704–1752), *in progress* [cited as Best.].

— *Briefwechsel Friedrichs des Grossen mit Voltaire*, ed. Koser and Droysen. Leipzig 1908–1911, 3 vol.

Warcy, Paillet de, *Histoire de la vie et des ouvrages de Voltaire*. Paris 1824, 2 vol.

INDEX

ADAM, le p., 134

AESCHYLUS, 97

AGUESSEAU, HENRI FRANÇOIS D', 30

AIGUILLON, ANNE CHARLOTTE DE CRUSSOL-FLORENSAC, duchesse D', 74, 76

ALEMBERT, JEAN LE ROND D', 72, 107–109, 112–118, 129, 133–136, 146, 169, 170, 174, 180, 181, 183, 184, 189–190, 192, 194, 195, 217

ANDRE, YVES MARIE, 28

ANTHONY, saint, 201

ANTOINE, GABRIEL, 56

ARGENSON, MARC RENE DE VOYER DE PAULMY, marquis D', 182, 186

ARGENTAL, CHARLES AUGUSTIN FERIOL, comte D', 133

ARISTOTLE, 26, 27, 53, 54, 96, 198, 212

AUBERT, abbé, 33

AZOR, 56

BACHELIER, 193

BACON, FRANCIS, 170–173, 175–177, 179, 181

BAIUS, MICHAEL, 126

BARBOT, 69

BARRAS, DE, 167

BARRIERE, PIERRE, 95

BARTAS, 199

BASTIDE, DE, 204

BATON, CHARLES, 148

BATTEUX, abbé, 179

BAYLE, PIERRE, 119, 203, 204

BEAUMONT, CHRISTOPHE DE, 185, 186

BEAURANS, 149

BELL, J. J., 65

BENEDICT XIV, 91

BENOIT, le p., 22

BERRY, duc DE, 60

BERTHIER, GUILLAUME FRANÇOIS, 9, 18, 21; *J. de T.* his work, 22; policy of moderation, 23–24, 37–38, 221–222; quarrel with Castel, 25–26; opinions of contemporaries, 27–29, 31, 32, 38–39, 61, 158; displeasure with role of editor, 30–31; family background and education, 36; personality, 38–40; defense of monarchy, 40–42; attacks abuses of the court, 42–44; abuses remediable by proper education of dauphin, 44–47; defense of religious intolerance without coersion, 48, 78, 81, 112, 123, 124, 127–128; denies conflict between science and faith, 48-49, 102, 201, 219–220; defense of scientific method, 50–51, 206–207; praises Descartes but favours Newtonian physics, 51–54; activities after suppression of Jesuits, 54–55, 58–62; defends Jesuits after their suppression, 55–57; upholds natural religion as base for revealed religion, 106, 109, 123; defends Italian against French music, pleads for abandonment of Lully, 143–146; upholds reason against passions as man's guide, 150–151, 160–161, 204, 215; attacks the theatre, 155–157; rejects impartiality in questions of religion, its defense is *J. de T.*'s chief rôle, 24, 40, 101, 121, 191–193; defends idea of progress, 197–198; pleads for freedom of inquiry in arts and sciences, 198–200; encourages free inquiry in religion, 201–202, 220–221; suggests reasons for incredulity, 202–206; relativistic morality of unbelievers is dangerous, 204–205, 221; irreligion